# IN MEMORY OF

IRENE FLAUGHER, MY BIRTH MOTHER

MAUREEN REAGAN, MY SISTER

AND OF COURSE MY DAD,

RONALD WILSON REAGAN

# IN DEDICATION TO

JANE WYMAN, MY MOTHER

COLLEEN, MY WIFE

CAMERON, MY SON

AND ASHLEY, MY DAUGHTER

# TWICE
# ADOPTED

# TWICE
# ADOPTED

# MICHAEL
# REAGAN

### WITH JIM DENNEY

BROADMAN
&HOLMAN
PUBLISHERS

NASHVILLE, TENNESSEE

0-8054-3144-6

Published by Broadman & Holman Publishers
Nashville, Tennessee

Dewey Decimal Classifaction: B
Subject Heading: REAGAN, MICHAEL

Unless otherwise noted, Scripture quotations are from the
Holy Bible, New International Version, copyright © 1973,
1978, 1984 by International Bible Society. Other Scripture
versions are as follows: NASB, the New American Standard
Bible, © the Lockman Foundation, 1960, 1962, 1963,
1968, 1971, 1972, 1973, 1975, 1977; used by permission,
and KJV, King James Version.

1 2 3 4 5 6 7  09 08 07 06 05 04

# Contents

# FOREWORD

## By Sean Hannity

Michael Reagan is a great American, a great conservative, and the son of one of our greatest presidents. But none of that has anything to do with this book, because *Twice Adopted* is not a book about politics. It's a book about love, hope, and redemption.

I am honored that Mike asked me to write a foreword for this book. But more than that, I am honored that Michael Reagan is my friend. The most important thing you should know about him is not his political affiliation, but his character.

Mike is a courageous, compassionate, and generous human being. He is honest to a fault. In this book, Mike turns his life inside-out and dumps it on the table for the whole world to see. He has held nothing back.

In *Twice Adopted*, Mike reveals the pain, fears, and tortured memories of a survivor of childhood sexual abuse. He also shares the story of his salvation and redemption from those painful memories and his self-destructive behavior.

Here Mike points the way to the healing grace of a loving and merciful God. He also points us to the practical action we can take to help make the world a safer place for families—and especially for kids.

If you are a child of adoption, a survivor of abuse, a parent of minor children, a casualty of divorce (either your own or your parents' divorce), or if you struggle with shameful secrets or anger toward God—then you must read this book.

Mike's story will make you angry. It will bring tears to your eyes. It will challenge, inform, and motivate you. And one more thing . . .

It will change your life!

Sean Hannity is a nationally syndicated radio talk show host and cohost of *Hannity and Colmes* on the Fox News Channel.

# FOREWORD

## By Dr. Jack Hayford

In *Twice Adopted,* Mike opens up every corner of his life and tells us his story—a story of pain and abuse, but also a story of healing and redemption. The grace of God flows like a life-giving stream through every chapter of this book.

I have heard Mike tell his story on a number of occasions. I can never listen to him talk about his childhood pain without choking back tears. It is a story that breaks your heart, yet at the same time lifts your spirit to God.

There is no pretense with Mike. He is truly one of the most honest, transparent men I have ever known. The Michael Reagan you see on TV, hear on the radio, and read in this book is the same Michael Reagan I have known personally for over fourteen years.

He and his wife, Colleen, have long been a treasured part of our church family. I have prayed with Mike countless times. I wept with him when Scott Bauer—my beloved son-in-law, Mike's close friend, and the senior pastor of our church—suddenly passed away in October 2003.

Mike's story brings to mind the ancient words Job wrote about his relationship with God: "When he is at work in the north, I do not see him; when he turns to the south, I catch no glimpse of him. But he knows the way that I take; when he has tested me, I will come forth as gold" (Job 23:9–10 NIV).

For many years, Mike couldn't see God and he actually thought God hated him. But the Lord knew every step of the pathway that Mike Reagan took. After being tried and tested, Mike Reagan has come forth as gold—the genuine material!

This is his story. May God richly bless and touch your heart as you read these words.


Dr. Jack Hayford is the Senior Pastor at The Church on the Way in Van Nuys, California.

# PREFACE

On Saturday, June 5, 2004, my father, Ronald Reagan, passed from this life and into the presence of his Lord. There are many verses of Scripture that would characterize his life, but probably the most fitting is 2 Timothy 4:7: "I have fought the good fight, I have finished the race, I have kept the faith."

We had known for a while that, for Dad, the "good fight" was nearly over. He had not opened his eyes for days. But in the closing moments of his earthly life, he opened his eyes and the last sight he saw on earth was the face of his wife, Nancy. The next thing he saw was the face of God. As my sister Patti said, "If a death can be lovely, his was."

The week that followed was the most amazing week of my life. There was the impromptu memorial in front of the funeral home in Santa Monica, where thousands of people left flags, flowers, balloons, cards, and handwritten messages of love.

There were the public viewings at the Reagan Library in California and the Capitol Rotunda in Washington, D.C., where thousands of people came to say good-bye. Perhaps the most moving sight as my father lay in state at the Rotunda was the moment when Marine Corporal James Wright, who had lost both hands in Iraq, saluted my father's flag-draped casket.

At the memorial service in the National Cathedral, I was touched when former president George H. W. Bush choked back tears while recalling my father's kindness and courage. I was warmed within as Lady Margaret Thatcher remembered the assassination attempt in 1981. "Ronnie believed that he had been given back his life for a purpose," she said, "and surely it is hard to deny that Ronald Reagan's life was providential when we look at what he achieved in the eight years that followed."

But as grateful as I was for the tributes from such leaders as President George W. Bush and former Canadian prime minister Brian Mulroney, the most awe-inspiring, heart-warming tribute of all came from you, the American people. Our family experienced it many times, as when we rode behind the hearse from Andrews Air Force Base to the Capitol, or from Point Mugu to the Reagan Library.

Looking out the window, we saw an ocean of people, seemingly without end. Some people waved, some held flags, some wept openly. We saw the firemen's ladders arched over the freeway, draped with Old Glory, the firemen saluting my dad as his hearse passed by. I was amazed to see that not only was traffic stopped in our lanes, but the opposite lanes as well. On both sides of the freeway, people stood on their cars, waved signs, and expressed their love for my father.

Throughout that entire week, there was not one moment, not one detail that wasn't absolutely right and fitting. I'll always be grateful to the members of the military who carried the casket, played the music, and fired the salutes.

Every man and woman involved demonstrated both care and professionalism.

This amazing outpouring of love gave us in the Reagan family so much comfort and strength. Thank you, America, for your prayers and support which truly got us through that week, and which continue to sustain us even now.

Finally, before you turn the page and begin reading the story of how I was not only adopted into the Reagan family, but *twice* adopted, I'd like to share once more the words I spoke at the sunset memorial service at the Reagan Library, Friday, June 11, 2004, just before my father was laid to rest:

> Good evening. I'm Mike Reagan. You knew my father as governor, as president, but I knew him as Dad. I want to tell you a little bit about my dad—a little bit about Cameron and Ashley's grandfather, because not a whole lot is ever spoken about that side of Ronald Reagan.
>
> Ronald Reagan adopted me into his family in 1945. I was the chosen one. I was the lucky one. And in all of his years, he never mentioned that I was adopted, either behind my back or in front of me. I was his son, Michael Edward Reagan.
>
> When his family grew to be two families, he didn't walk away from the one to go to the other. He became a father to both families. To Patti and then Ronnie, but always to my sister Maureen and myself.
>
> We looked forward to those Saturday mornings when he would pick us up. We'd sit on the curb on Beverly Glen as his car would turn the corner from Sunset Boulevard, and we would get in and ride to his ranch and play games—and he would always make sure it ended up a tie. We

would swim and we would ride horses or we'd just watch him cut firewood. We were in awe of our father.

As years went by and I became older and found the woman I would marry, Colleen, Dad sent me a letter about marriage and how important it was to be faithful to the woman you love—with a P.S.: "You'll never get in trouble if you say 'I love you' at least once a day." And I'm sure he told Nancy every day "I love you," just as I tell Colleen.

He also sent letters to his grandchildren. He wasn't able to be the grandfather that many of you are able to be because of the job that he had. So he would write letters. He sent one letter to Cameron and said: "Cameron, some guy got ten thousand dollars for my signature. Maybe this letter will help you pay for your college education." He signed it, "Grandpa," then added, "P.S. Your grandpa is the fortieth president of the United States, Ronald Reagan."

Those are the kinds of things my father did.

At the early onset of Alzheimer's disease, my father and I would tell each other we loved each other and we would give each other a hug. As the years went by and he could no longer verbalize my name, he recognized me as the man who hugged him. So when I would walk into the house, he would be there in his chair opening up his arms for that hug hello and the hug good-bye. It was a blessing truly brought on by God.

We had wonderful blessings of that nature— wonderful, wonderful blessings that my father gave to me each and every day of my life. I was so proud to have the Reagan name and to be Ronald Reagan's son. What a great honor.

He gave me a lot of gifts as a child. He gave
me a horse. He gave me a car. He gave me a lot
of things. But there's a gift he gave me that
I think is wonderful for every father to give
every son.

Last Saturday, when my father opened his eyes
for the last time, and visualized Nancy, he gave
her such a wonderful, wonderful gift. When he
closed his eyes, that's when I realized the gift that
he gave to me, the gift that he was going to be
with his Lord and Savior, Jesus Christ.

Back in 1988, on a flight from Washington,
D.C., to Point Mugu, he told me about his love
of God, his love of Christ as his Savior. I didn't
know then what it all meant. But I certainly
know now.

I can't think of a better gift for a father to give
a son. And I hope to honor my father by giving
my son Cameron and my daughter Ashley that
very same gift he gave to me.

It's the gift of knowing where he is this very
moment, this very day—that he is in heaven. And
I can only promise my father this:

Dad, when I go, I will go to heaven too. And
you and I and my sister, Maureen, who went
before us, will dance with the heavenly host of
angels before the presence of God. We will do it
melanoma—and Alzheimer's-free.

Thank you for letting me share my father,
Ronald Wilson Reagan.

# PROLOGUE

Have you ever felt that God was angry with you?

Did you ever do something so shameful that you lived in fear that someone would find out? That your secret would be exposed?

Did you ever feel that something you did was so horrible and vile that God could never forgive you?

Have you ever been convinced that you were going to hell and there was nothing you could do about it?

Have you ever felt angry toward God—a raging anger over something terrible that happened in your life? Something that hurt you and violated you? Something for which you blamed God?

Did you ever hate God?

Did you ever believe that God hated you?

That is how I felt for more than thirty years of my life.

I was born out of wedlock and adopted by two people. One would become an Academy Award-winning actress, the other would become president of the United States of America. From the time I was three, I was raised by a single mother.

My adoptive parents told me I was "chosen," but the kids at school told me I was a "bastard."

At the age of seven, I read one verse in the Bible, and I thought it was telling me I was going to hell. I wouldn't open a Bible again until I was in my thirties.

While in the third grade, I was sexually molested by an after-school day-camp counselor. He said it was our secret. Then he took pornographic photos of me which he had me develop. The scariest words I ever heard were when he bent close to my ear and said, "Wouldn't your mother like to have a copy of that picture?"

By the time I was eight years old, I hated myself, and I believed that God hated me. As I grew from childhood to adolescence to adulthood, I sabotaged every relationship I truly cared about because of the shame, fear, and self-hatred that the molester instilled in me.

This is my story of redemption.

This is the story of how I was twice adopted.

# 1

# ONCE ADOPTED

$M$y sister Maureen bought me for ninety-seven cents.

Maureen was just three years old when she went with Mom and Dad to Schwab's Pharmacy—that's right, the famous Schwab's at Sunset and Crescent Heights, where Lana Turner was discovered. While Mom and Dad were in the aisles shopping, little Maureen went up to the counter, opened her purse, and plunked ninety-seven cents on the counter.

The pharmacist said, "What do you want, little girl?"

"I want a brother," she said.

Well, back in 1944, there wasn't much a pharmacist could do about such things. Mom and Dad—Jane Wyman and Ronald Reagan—saw this discussion going on between the pharmacist and their daughter. They hurried over and told Maureen to put her money away.

The incident was embarrassing, but it made Mom and Dad think: *Maybe Maureen really did need a little brother to play with*. So they started thinking about bringing another child into the family. After Maureen's birth, the doctors had told Mom that she shouldn't get pregnant again. So they decided to adopt.

I was born in Los Angeles on March 18, 1945, to a woman named Irene Flaugher. Although I wouldn't know it until more than forty years later, Irene Flaugher loved me very much. She loved me enough, in fact, to give me up to another family.

Three days after I was born, I was adopted by Ronald Reagan and Jane Wyman. When they brought me home from the hospital, Maureen was disappointed. All of her friends had older brothers, so she expected me to be older than herself.

A nurse accompanied Mom and Dad from the hospital, and when Maureen saw the nurse, she dashed upstairs to her room, grabbed her piggy bank off her dresser, and tried to pry the cork out of the bottom. When she couldn't pull the cork out, she threw her bank to the floor and broke it. She grabbed ninety-seven cents out of her broken piggy bank, ran downstairs, and pressed the money into the hand of the startled nurse who was on her way out the door. The nurse wanted to give the money back, but Mom and Dad told her to keep it.

Maureen *paid* for me to come into the Reagan family—that's how I got in!

## MY TWO MOTHERS

My adoptive parents named me Michael Edward Reagan. When I was born, however, my birth mother gave me another name: John L. Flaugher. Irene Flaugher was an unmarried young woman from Ohio. She had an affair with a married man, an army corporal named John Bourgholtzer. Shortly after Irene discovered she was pregnant, the army sent John to Arizona, and Irene followed him there. One night John took Irene to a bar off the base for some drinks and to discuss what to do about her pregnancy.

They arrived back at the base, and John was stopped at the gate by a staff sergeant who said, "You're out of uniform, soldier." Well, John was out of uniform; he didn't have his fatigue cap on. All he had to do was take his cap out of his belt and put it on his head, but he felt the sergeant was picking on him. So John Bourgholtzer decked the staff sergeant.

After a brief struggle, John was arrested. Before the MPs led him away to the hoosegow, John reached into his pocket and pulled out a roll of bills, about $600. He peeled off $400 and gave it to Irene Flaugher. "Here," he said. "Go to California and have the baby." Immediately afterward, Corporal Bourgholtzer was demoted to private and shipped off to France to fight in the war.

Irene Flaugher went to California to have the baby. Understand, she could have had me aborted. Though abortion was illegal in those days, it was not uncommon. She could have had the procedure, then gotten on with her life after a few days' recuperation. She gave birth at the Queen of Angels Hospital in Los Angeles and named me John after my birth father.

Irene wanted to make sure I would have a good home, so she insisted on meeting the adoptive parents. She found it easier to give me up when she learned that her baby would be raised in the home of a wealthy Hollywood couple, Ronald Reagan and Jane Wyman. Before the adoption was finalized, my two mothers, Irene and Jane, met in the hospital room and talked for about an hour. The adoption process was completed three days after I was born.

Irene passed away the day after Christmas 1985, two years before I began searching for my birth mother. She never got to hear me say, "Thank you, Irene, for giving me life." Though I never got to meet her and thank her, I honor her.

So I have two mothers: One gave birth to me and loved me enough to give me life and give me away. The other loved me enough to take me into her home and raise me as her own flesh and blood. And as you will see in this book, I am truly Jane's son.

For most of my life, I really couldn't grasp the depths of my birth mother's love. I didn't understand how any mother could love her baby yet give that baby away. What I now see as love I used to see as rejection. It took me decades of pain and anger to understand the loving sacrifice Irene Flaugher made for my sake. Today I have nothing but praise and gratitude for my birth mother.

Every year I celebrate two Mother's Days. On January 22, the anniversary of the *Roe v. Wade* decision that legalized abortion on demand, I honor Irene Flaugher because she chose to give me life rather than have an abortion. And on the traditional Mother's Day, the second Sunday in May, I honor Jane Wyman. She is the mother who brought me home from Queen of Angels Hospital, the mother who raised me and taught me some of the most important lessons of my life.

I thank God every day for my two mothers.

## "WHERE DID YOU HEAR THAT WORD?"

I learned about my adoption from my sister Maureen.

Maureen was eight years old, and she was home for Christmas break from Chadwick School, the boarding school she attended in Palos Verdes, California. Maureen's birthday was January 4, so Christmas and her birthday got combined into one long season of gifts. I was not quite five years old at the time, and I had seen my mother wrapping Maureen's gifts.

I liked being close to my big sister. Mom had nicknamed her Mermie, and the family called her Merm. She was my best friend, and I looked up to her. I figured that one way to get in really good with her was to share secrets with her. So I came into Maureen's room while she was in front of her full-length mirror, brushing her long blonde hair. "Merm," I said, "I know what you're getting for your birthday."

"Don't tell me," she said. "I don't want to know."

In my four-year-old wisdom, I knew that Maureen couldn't be serious. After all, what kid wouldn't be dying to know a secret like that? So I said, "You'll really like it!"

"Michael, I mean it," Maureen said. "Don't tell me! I'm warning you! If you tell me a secret, I'm going to tell you a secret!"

Well, that was the wrong thing to say! If Maureen had a secret she was keeping from me, I *had* to know what it was! So I said, "You're getting a blue dress for your birthday."

In her most snotty voice, Maureen said, "And *you* were *adopted*."

I guess she thought that her secret was an even trade for mine!

I didn't understand what my sister had just told me, so I ran downstairs to find my mother. Maureen hurried along behind me. She knew she had made a serious tactical blunder.

We found Mom in the den. I said, "Mom, what does *adopted* mean?"

You may have watched Jane Wyman as Angela Channing on *Falcon Crest,* which ran on CBS from 1981 to 1990. Remember the withering look she used to give to Lance (Lorenzo Lamas) on the show? Her eyes would get big and round, and her nostrils would flare. Let me tell you, that wasn't acting! That was my mother. Whenever I saw that look—and I've seen it a number of times over the years—I knew that either Maureen or I had done something wrong. When I said the word *adopted,* that's exactly the look she gave me.

"*Where* did you hear that word?" she asked.

"From Merm," I said. "She said I was adopted. What does that mean?"

Mom didn't answer my question. Instead she excused me from the room, and she and Maureen had a long talk behind closed doors. I don't know what words were exchanged between my mom and my sister, but later that night my mother and I had a talk of our own.

Mom took me into the living room, sat me down, and looked me in the eye. "Michael," she said, "when you were born, you had parents who weren't able to take care of you, so they found a couple who could give you a nice home and be your mommy and daddy. That couple was your father and me. We chose you to be our little boy because you were just what we wanted. You are a chosen child, and that makes you special, and we love you very much. Now do you understand what *adopted* means?"

I nodded and said I understood, but I really didn't grasp it. The only thing I really picked up on was the fact that I was *chosen*. I could tell that being chosen was a good thing.

But I also picked up on the fact that Mom wasn't my *real* mother, whatever that meant. At some time in the past, I'd had another mother, and now she was a mysterious and hidden part of my past. There was something about all of this that wasn't good because it was never spoken of. It was a secret I wasn't supposed to know—a secret Maureen had been forbidden to tell me. I could see that Mom was uneasy about something, and her discomfort with the subject of my adoption made me anxious.

I told her I understood even though I didn't because I was afraid to ask any more questions. The fact is, I knew so little about how babies are born that I didn't even know what questions to ask. So I let the matter drop.

### "YOU'RE JUST A BASTARD"

Mom and Dad divorced when I was three. When I was five and a half, Mom sent me to Chadwick School, the boarding school where Maureen attended. When I was home, I lived in a one-parent household.

One day, when I was in the second grade at Chadwick, I got into an argument with a kid at school. It was one of those "my dad is better than your dad" debates. We took a few turns one-upping each other, and finally I said, "I'm better than you because I'm special! I was chosen!"

The other kid said, "What do you mean, you were 'chosen'?"

"I was adopted," I replied. I said it proudly, as if being adopted was the best thing that could happen to a kid.

Well, he didn't know what to say to that because he didn't know what *adopted* meant. But he went home and asked his mom and dad, and they explained it to him. A day or two later, he saw me on the playground again, and he pointed and laughed.

"What's so funny?" I asked.

"You told me you were 'special' because you were adopted!" he said. "But my mom and dad told me what *adopted* means. You're not special; you're just a *bastard!*"

I wasn't about to admit that I didn't know what a bastard was, but I didn't have to. This kid was happy to define the term for me. "Your real mother wasn't married, and she didn't want you, so she gave you away! That's why you got adopted—bastard!"

There were other kids standing around, and they thought

that it was pretty funny that I had pretended to be "special" and "chosen," when I was really just a kid whose mother didn't want him. I felt stupid and ashamed because I hadn't even known the truth about myself, and suddenly I felt that there was something wrong with me.

I wondered: *Who was my birth mother? Why did she give me away? Why didn't she want me? And what about Mom? Did she know I was a bastard? If she found out, would she still love me? Would it break her heart? Would she send me away, like my birth mother had?* So many questions—and I had no one to ask.

I couldn't ask Mom. Since I was at boarding school most of the time, I didn't want to spoil our brief time together with unpleasant questions. I didn't even know what questions to ask. Besides, I couldn't ask a question without divulging information. I couldn't say, "Why did my birth mother give me away? Was it because I'm a bastard?" From my childlike perspective, Mom couldn't have known I was illegitimate, or she never would have adopted me, and I sure didn't want her to find out! If my birth mother sent me away because I was illegitimate, then Mom might send me away, too. So I never asked my mother any questions.

When that kid at school hung the "bastard" label on me, my self-image changed. That label affected my security as a member of the Reagan family. I had seen maids, cooks, and nannies come and go, and I wondered if my own status in the family wasn't just as shaky. From that day forward I felt I needed to earn my way into the Reagan family.

I never again bragged at school about being "chosen." And I never again felt "special." But I did feel marked.

## HATING MYSELF, HATING GOD

The next time I went home for the weekend, I went to the library of my mother's home. There were hundreds of books in that room, but one huge leather-bound book dominated the rest: my mother's big Bible. I had often seen Mom reading that Bible. I thought, *Maybe the Bible has an answer for me.*

I was seven years old and had never read the Bible on my own. I didn't even know where to begin. I knew some books had an index in the back. So I flipped to the back of the Bible and found the concordance. I looked for the word *bastard*—and I found it. *Good,* I thought. *I'll find out what the Bible says about a bastard.*

The concordance pointed me to Deuteronomy 23:2. There, in the King James Version, I read these words: "A bastard shall not enter into the congregation of the LORD; even to his tenth generation shall he not enter into the congregation of the LORD."

My heart froze inside me. I snapped the book shut. In my limited seven-year-old understanding, I thought that those words meant, "A bastard can never go to heaven. A bastard is damned to hell, and so are his kids and grandkids and great-great-great-great grandkids, to the tenth generation."

That was in 1952. I didn't open a Bible again until 1978.

Today, of course, I realize that the book of Deuteronomy is a book of laws governing the community of ancient Israel. The words I read had nothing at all to do with heaven or hell, but how could a seven-year-old understand such things while reading the Bible for the very first time? When I read those words, I thought my eternal fate was sealed.

Then the thought hit me: *My gosh! That must be why my birth mother got rid of me! Nobody wants a child who's going to hell! And what about Mom? She's so religious! What if she finds out I can never go to heaven?*

I lived in fear—not only fear that I would spend eternity in hell but also fear that my mother would find out I was illegitimate. I had no one to talk to, so I started to live within myself. I didn't want anyone to learn the truth about me. At the age of seven, I began the process of hating myself and hating God.

## THE LOST PIECE OF THE PUZZLE

I went through my early years feeling I had the mark of the beast upon me. My birth mother had given me away, my adoptive mother had sent me away to boarding school, and God had rejected me. Everybody kept sending me away. Why? For something I had no control over: my illegitimate birth.

I grew up with a big hole inside of me. Most adoptees grow up sensing that same hole inside of them. That hole is our missing sense of identity, of belonging, of knowing our own unique place in the world. It starts small, but it grows year by year and experience by experience into a gnawing emptiness that we seek to fill any way we can. Many people spend their whole lives searching for something to fill that hole.

According to David M. Brodzinsky, author of *The Psychology of Adoption,* we adoptees face enormous emotional challenges. We worry about being abandoned. We struggle with issues of identity and intimacy. Adoptees seek mental and emotional therapy at rates above the general population. Up to 5 percent of adoptees are referred to outpatient mental health facilities; up to 15 percent end up in residential care facilities. Brodzinsky also notes that adopted children have higher rates of learning disorders, attention deficit disorder, delinquent behavior, and drug abuse than the general population. I believe that every one of these issues in the life of adoptees can be directly traced to that void inside, the sense of incompleteness that children of adoption usually experience.

I realize now that, when I began searching for my birth mother, I was really searching for love and affirmation. I had to know that the woman who gave me life didn't reject me—she loved me. You might think that being loved by your adoptive parents should be enough. But if you have that gnawing hole in your soul, you know it's never enough.

That hole isn't something that is felt only by children of adoption. I've learned that it's common to the entire human race. We adoptees are more keenly aware of that void in our lives, and we mistakenly think that we feel that void because we don't know who our birth parents are. In reality, it's a

God-shaped hole. Every human being born on this planet has that God-shaped hole in the soul. Sadly, most of us spend our lives trying to fill it with something other than God.

Our lives truly are like jigsaw puzzles, and we all have pieces missing. If you're an adoptee, you try to fill this hole with your birth parents. If you're an alcoholic, you try to fill it with booze. Some people try to fill it with drugs, sex, pornography, money, possessions, power, or fame. But the hole in our souls has a specific shape, a God shape. It's just like working a jigsaw puzzle: you have to find the one piece that fits or the picture makes no sense.

We are all searching for our Creator-Parent. Everyone searches, not just adoptees. We are looking for our identity, an assurance that the One who brought us into the world still loves us and accepts us, that he doesn't reject us. Adoptees make the mistake of thinking that the One we are looking for is a human being—a birth parent. In reality the One we are looking for is God himself.

## EVERY CHILD IS A WANTED CHILD

My sister Maureen is with God now. She went into his presence on August 8, 2001. The world remembers her as an author, a political analyst, and a tireless campaigner for a cure for Alzheimer's disease. But I'll always remember her as the sister who broke into her own piggy bank to bring me into the Reagan family.

Maureen had great diplomacy skills. Somehow she managed to pull off that delicate feat of remaining close to our mother Jane Wyman while also, in the end, becoming close to our stepmother, Nancy Reagan.

She also had a heart full of love. Near the end of Dad's presidency, Maureen and her husband, Dennis Revell, represented the White House on a goodwill tour of Africa. They visited the Daughters of Charity orphanage in Uganda where they met a three-year-old girl who absolutely won their hearts. They started giving financial support to the orphanage, and they began the process of adopting this child, whose name was Rita Mirembe. From the time Rita was three until she was eight, Maureen and Dennis were blocked from adopting her, due to Ugandan law. Finally, they brought Rita to the US on a student visa, though they still couldn't legally adopt her.

By February 2000, when the Ugandan government finally relaxed the restrictions on overseas adoption, Maureen was battling melanoma. Because of her medical issues, she couldn't meet the requirements of Ugandan law. Ultimately, a private bill was introduced in Congress to grant Rita permanent residency. It was signed into law by President Bush shortly before Maureen died, clearing the way to make Rita's adoption permanent. So Maureen was responsible for bringing two children into the family—Michael Edward Reagan and Rita Mirembe Revell.

Perhaps because she was the sister of an adopted child, Maureen knew what a gift of love adoption is. She couldn't adopt every child in the world, but she could adopt one, and she made a profound and lasting difference in the life of a child from the other side of the world. She gave a gift of love.

Tragically that loving gift is all too rarely given in our society today. According to the D.C.-based National Committee for Adoption, fewer than fifty-eight thousand children are adopted each year in the USA—about fifty-one thousand American children and fewer than seven thousand children from other countries. No statistics are kept on how many couples are waiting to adopt, but authorities in the field estimate that they may number up to two million. At the same time so many couples are waiting, 1.3 million unborn babies are aborted every year. Only 4 percent of women with unwanted pregnancies choose adoption. According to those statistics, if every one of those unwanted pregnancies were miraculously to end in adoption instead of abortion, all of those so-called "unwanted" babies would instantly find loving homes.

Planned Parenthood promotes abortion with a catchy little slogan: "Every child a wanted child." Catchy but misleading. The fact is, every child is *already* a wanted child. Loving parents are waiting to receive and love every single child aborted in America. What Planned Parenthood's catchy slogan really means is that if a birth mother doesn't want the child, the child should be destroyed. Then, supposedly, the only children who remain alive will be "wanted" children.

The most common fetal abnormality is Down syndrome, which causes mild to moderate mental retardation, shortened physical height, and a distinct facial profile. Though Down syndrome is not a severe disability, fully 92 percent of all unborn babies detected as having Down syndrome are killed by abortion. In fact, the National Institutes of Health reports that 95 percent of all pregnancies in which prenatal tests detect a genetic abnormality are ended by abortion.

Some abortion advocates would have us believe that killing is actually compassion for so-called "defective" children. The reality is that killing these children is not compassionate. It's selfish. It's a misguided attempt to cleanse our population of human beings who are seen as a "burden" on their parents and society. When we start to look at people as "defective" (and therefore disposable), we have started down a road that has already been traveled by the eugenics experiments in Nazi Germany.

Go to any adoption agency, and they will tell you they have a waiting list of eager, loving parents who will love not just the physically perfect kids but even kids with Down syndrome and other physical and mental deformities. Every child is wanted by someone—every child without exception. You cannot care for a child by killing her.

Just as adoption is a gift of love, abortion is the denial of love.

For most people abortion is merely a political issue, a matter of right versus left. For me, however, abortion isn't political; it's personal. My own existence once depended entirely on a woman's choice. It was not just a matter of "reproductive rights." It was a life-or-death decision.

Abortion on demand promotes an attitude in our society that children are expendable and should be discarded if they get in our way. This unloving attitude endangers even the children who are born. It tempts abusive parents to think, *Why didn't I abort that child when I had the chance?* It cheapens the lives of children and subjects them to increased danger of abuse, sexual exploitation, and child murder—all of which have risen dramatically since *Roe v. Wade* legalized abortion on demand.

I'm not saying that life is easy for adopted kids. My own story was painful. But even if my life had been twice as tough, even ten times as tough as it was, I would rather go through all the pain than to have missed out on my entire life and end up as an abortion statistic.

Over the years I've conducted my own little nonscientific survey. Every time I encounter an adoptee, either in my personal life or on my radio show, I ask a question: "Are you glad you were adopted, or do you wish you had been aborted?" Some of the adoptees I've asked have gone through some incredibly painful and tragic experiences. Yet the result of my survey is unanimous: Every single adoptee I've asked has said, "I'm glad I was adopted and not aborted. Even a painful life is better than no life at all."

Abortion doesn't just kill children. Abortion kills love. The "right" to abortion on demand is nothing less than a society-wide failure to love and cherish children. We have placed our sex drive and our selfishness above love for children. We are telling generations to come that life has no value and that human beings have no moral responsibility. We are teaching our young people that human beings are nothing but animals who copulate without conscience. Then we flush the consequence of our actions out of the womb and down a drain. We are teaching a generation that it's OK for a child to die so that we can live as we please.

## HOW TO CHANGE THE WORLD

As Christians, we look at *Roe v. Wade,* and we see all the destruction that abortion on demand has produced in human lives and in our society. And we say, "This is intolerable! God is going to judge this nation for the way we are slaughtering our own children on the altar of our own selfishness. We have to overturn *Roe v. Wade!*" And I agree. *Roe v. Wade* should be overturned, and we should all pray, work, and sacrifice to that end.

But even if *Roe v. Wade* were overturned today, thousands of abortions would still be performed tomorrow. Why? Because overturning *Roe v. Wade* would not end abortion. It would simply return the decision-making power to the states, many (if not most) of which would continue to keep abortion on demand legal. And even if abortion were suddenly out-lawed, abortionists would still perform them illegally, and women and girls with crisis pregnancies would still seek them.

If we truly want to deal with the slaughter of innocents in our society, we cannot simply look to the government to change the abortion laws. We have to find a new way to deal with crisis pregnancies—a way that is loving and redemptive, not merely legislative and institutional. We have to acknowledge that some of the girls and women who go to abortion clinics are our own daughters. We have taught them that abortion is a horrible sin, yet they are going to the clinics anyway. Why? Because we have chased them there.

Many kids in Christian homes are hearing, "You'd better not come home and tell me you're pregnant! If you get pregnant, you can just get out of my house!" I have talked to parents with this kind of attitude, and I have talked to the children of such parents, and I can tell you for a fact that some Christian parents have sent their kids into the arms of Planned Parenthood with their unchristlike attitudes.

Obviously, we need to teach Christian morality in our homes. We need to teach that sex belongs within the safe and sacred enclosure of marriage. But at the same time, we need to tell our children, "We are a Christian family, and these are Christian standards; but if you ever mess up, we want you to come to us, talk to us, and let us help you. There is nothing you can ever do that would make us stop loving you. We may be disappointed, but we would never reject you, condemn you, or turn you out of our house."

We should either help our children find a loving Christian home for the child, or we should adopt the child ourselves. If we, who claim to be followers of Christ, will respond to a crisis pregnancy in a Christlike way, if we will love our daughters as Christ loved the church, then we will begin the process of making abortions unnecessary.

You and I may not be able to change the law. We may not be able to change society. But we can change ourselves. We can change our attitudes. We can choose to become more like Christ. And we can have a healing and redemptive influence on our children and our children's children. When we face the challenge of a child who has morally failed, we can ask ourselves, "What would Jesus do with this child?" And Jesus has already shown us the answer to that question.

In John 8, a group of judgmental religious men brought a woman to Jesus. They threw her down at his feet and said, "This woman was caught in the act of adultery. In the Law, Moses commanded us to stone such women to death. What do you say?" Jesus answered, "Let the one among you who is without sin be the first to throw a stone at her." His answer silenced every one of the woman's accusers, and they all left.

Then Jesus said to the woman, "Where are they? Doesn't anyone condemn you?"

She said, "No one, sir."

"Then I don't condemn you either," Jesus told her. "Go, and from now on, do not sin."

Jesus didn't condemn her, but neither did he condone her sin. He found that redemptive balance we all need to find whenever we deal with sin and moral failure. Jesus was uncompromisingly moral and uncompromisingly loving. He accepted and forgave this woman with a statement of unconditional love.

That is how we, as Christian parents, should give moral guidance and loving acceptance to our children. Jesus is our model of redemptive love.

It is also important that, as Christian moms and dads, we do everything within our power (and God's power) to build stable, committed, intact homes. Writing in *College Student*

*Journal,* December 2001, researchers Franklin B. Krohn and Zoe Bogan of State University of New York compared daughters from single-parent homes with daughters from intact homes. They found that daughters from single-parent homes are 111 percent more likely to have children during their teens, 164 percent more likely to be single parents, and 92 percent more likely to divorce. When girls grow up without a sense of a father's love and without the security and self-worth that comes from a stable two-parent home, they often set out in search of love—a search that frequently ends in teen pregnancy and abortion.[1]

Ultimately, however, the solution to the abortion crisis isn't a political change but a personal change. The solution begins within each of us and within our own families. We can't expect to change the world until we change our own hearts and begin living out the redemptive love of Jesus Christ.

## WHY I WROTE THIS BOOK

In recent months I have been talking to people and reading stories in the newspaper that remind me of my own experiences. I've been discussing issues on the radio that are personal and painful to me—issues such as adoption, abortion, fatherlessness, child molestation, and child pornography. I've been talking on the air about horror stories in the news—stories of priests molesting children; stories of mothers who murder their children in order to be with a man; stories of angry, fatherless boys who pick up a gun and take out their rage on innocent people.

I've gone on the radio and talked about a 1965 document entitled "The Negro Family: The Case for National Action," now more commonly known as "The Moynihan Report." Its author, Daniel Patrick Moynihan, was a member of the Lyndon Johnson White House; he later became a four-term Democratic senator from New York. In his report Moynihan warned that nearly 25 percent of African-American babies were born out of wedlock by the mid-1960s and that the illegitimacy rate was rising year by year. He predicted that this trend would bring enormous devastation and misery to the black community. His findings were dismissed, his warnings ignored; but history has proven Moynihan right.

Today nearly a third of American children of *all* races—black, white, and brown—are born out of wedlock, and that rate rises at 1 percent per year. In the African-American community, the out-of-wedlock birthrate is now—are you ready for this?—69 percent! And the illegitimate birthrate among whites is now approaching 25 percent—equaling the trend in the black community that so alarmed Moynihan in 1965.

He warned us that increasing illegitimacy and fatherlessness in the black community would destroy the black community, resulting in worsening poverty, crime, drug abuse, rage, despair, and other social calamities. It has happened just as he predicted. And now the rest of our society is headed in the same direction. All of the devastation that we currently see in the African-American community is spreading out into the rest of American society as our values and our families break down.

As I have watched the deconstruction of America, I have sensed God's gentle but insistent tug at my sleeve. He has been quietly telling me, "Michael, there's a reason behind every-thing you've gone through. There is a reason you were born to an unwed mother, given up for adoption, sent away from home to a boarding school, and molested and photographed by a sexual predator, a child pornographer. There is a reason you have gone through feelings of worthlessness, emptiness, shame, and rage. Michael, I can take the things that have hurt you, and I can use them to heal other people."

I have written this book because I want God to use my past and the painful things I've gone through to bring help and healing to other people. This is a book about love and redemption.

All the things that are wrong with America today—abortion, child abuse, child pornography, fatherless homes, addiction, crime, suicide, hopelessness, and despair—come down to a failure of love. The solution to every problem that afflicts us is love—God's love, authentically lived out and demonstrated to the world in the lives of those who claim to be his people. We must demonstrate his love to the least, the last, and the lost in our society. We must demonstrate love through genuine forgiveness to those who have failed and have fallen. We have to show the world that lives that seem broken beyond repair can be redeemed and made whole.

That's what we're going to talk about in the rest of this book—how to solve the problems and heal the hurts of our families, our neighborhoods, and our world, one broken life at a time. I know that the solutions I talk about in this book work because I am living proof. If they didn't work, I literally would not be alive today to talk about them.

We're going to talk about how to solve the problems of our society—divorce, child abuse, child pornography, gangs and youth crime, fatherless families, our failing educational system, and churches that protect perpetrators instead of children. And we're also going to talk about how to solve the deepest problems of our own families and our individual lives. Most important of all, we're going to talk about what it really means to love one another and to be loved by God.

Over the years I have learned that almost every experience in life happens for a reason. There's a reason you are reading this book right now. I believe God has brought you and me together through the pages of this book. Perhaps something I say will strike a responsive chord within you. Or perhaps, after you have read this book, you will have some idea or insight to share with me through a letter or a call to my radio show. I hope so. I'd like to hear what you have to say.

Let's talk.

# 2

# A BROKEN WORLD

*B*efore I started preschool, I spent a lot of time with a nanny and two Scottish terriers, Scotch and Soda. I didn't see much of Maureen because she was at boarding school, and I didn't see much of my parents because they worked six days a week. Dad was elected president of the Screen Actors Guild in 1947, so he was busy with union activities as well as making movies. And Mom was at the height of her acting career.

About two years after I was adopted, Mom got pregnant. It was an unplanned pregnancy; the doctors had told Mom not to get pregnant again after Maureen's birth. Though the pregnancy was unplanned, it was not unwanted. Once my mother knew she was pregnant, she wanted that baby very much.

In June 1947, Mom gave birth to a daughter and named her Christina. The infant girl was born prematurely and died three days later. I don't remember my mother's pregnancy, nor do I remember Christina's funeral. I do know that Dad couldn't be with Mom during the terrible time of Christina's birth and death. He was in another hospital at the time, recovering from a severe bout of pneumonia.

So Mom had to deal with this tragedy alone. It was probably the most painful experience of her life, and I don't think she ever truly recovered from it. Though she would rarely talk about the baby or her own grief, Christina has always been in her memory.

One day in mid-1948, Dad came home, and Mom told him the marriage was over. He was stunned. Dad couldn't imagine being a divorced man, separated from his family. But he saw that Mom was determined to divorce him, and nothing he could say would change her mind. Dad blamed himself and his busy schedule with the Screen Actors Guild for the failure of his marriage. He once said, "Perhaps I should have saved my own home and let someone else save the world."

In June 1948, exactly a year after Christina died, Mom filed for divorce on grounds of "mental cruelty," a commonly used catchall phrase without a precise legal definition. It's impossible to imagine Dad being cruel to anyone, but in those days you had to fill in the "grounds for divorce" blank, and those two words filled the space. Mom's public explanation for the divorce was that she and Dad no longer had anything in common. In his gentlemanly fashion, Dad chose not to contest the divorce, and Mom got custody of the two children.

I am told that Dad took Maureen and me out to his car and tried to explain the divorce to us. I was only three at the time, and I don't have any memory of that conversation. I only remember one thing about the divorce: I had a sudden and disturbing awareness that Dad didn't come home anymore. For reasons I could never fathom, he was simply gone. He had moved into an apartment in Hollywood, and from then on I could only see him every other Saturday.

On those alternating Saturdays when I could be with my dad, I would go outside at ten o'clock, walk to the street, and sit down on the curb in front of my mother's two-story colonial mansion at 333 South Beverly Glen. There I would watch and wait, eager to spot his car.

Before long I would see Dad's red station wagon make the turn from Sunset Boulevard down Beverly Glen. I would yell to Maureen, "Come on, Merm! He's here!" Or sometimes I would take a friend with me for the weekend. I was always excited when Dad arrived to pick us up because those days with my father were so important to me and so rare.

To an adult two weeks is just two weeks. But to a child, having to wait two weeks to see your father is like waiting forever. Once Dad pulled up at the curb, I didn't want to waste a moment of our time together.

Maureen and I would pile into the car, and Dad would drive us to his ranch in Northridge, where he raised thoroughbred horses. The ranch was about an hour's drive from Beverly Hills and could only be reached by a narrow two-lane road. The Northridge ranch was primitive. The only structure was a one-room shack where Dad and his foreman, Nino Peppetone, stayed when they were working with the horses.

At the ranch Maureen and I played with the chickens and goats, and we watched Dad and Nino put the thoroughbreds through their paces. Dad always brought a picnic lunch along, and we'd sit on the grass and eat and talk and watch the clouds drift by over the mountains.

On Sunday mornings Dad would often pick up Maureen and me at Mom's house and take us to his mother Nelle's house in Los Angeles, and she would take us to Sunday school and church. Nelle Wilson Reagan was a wonderful Scots-English woman with reddish-brown hair, a ready smile, and a quick and lively wit. Nelle was also a strong Christian who had sometimes preached in churches, in addition to writing poetry and plays. She drove us to Sunday school in her old Studebaker, then took us back to her house for Sunday brunch.

Later Dad would pick us up at Nelle's and take us home to Beverly Hills. Then Mom would drive us back to Chadwick. The Sunday night trip back to boarding school was the longest drive of the weekend.

## JUST LIKE *OZZIE AND HARRIET*

The year 1949 was a terrible year for Dad. He had already lost his wife and his children. That year he also broke his leg in an amateur baseball game. That put him in the hospital for a while and left him on crutches for weeks. He had stopped making movies for a time and was going through the worst dry spell of his career. He carried a gun because of threats against his life in connection with his union activities.

In those days Dad was a committed anticommunist, the head of a union, and a liberal Democrat. (A liberal Democrat in the late 1940s was more like a moderate Republican today.)

On the one hand, Dad was concerned about communist infiltration of the Hollywood film community; on the other hand, he was concerned because many nonpolitical, noncommunist actors—including Barbara Stanwyck, Lana Turner, Bette Davis, and Robert Taylor—were being falsely smeared.

Director Mervyn LeRoy asked Dad to see if he could clear the name of Nancy Davis, a blacklisted actress who was then under contract to MGM. Dad did some checking and determined that she had been mistaken for another actress by the same name. After his divorce from Mom became final, Dad and Nancy Davis began dating. After dating Nancy for about a year, he introduced her to Maureen and me.

By this time Dad had bought a new ranch in Malibu—four hundred acres of meadows, shade trees, and rolling hills surrounded by a white fence that Dad had built with his own hands. There were separate houses for the family and the foreman, plus a swimming pool. Dad called the place Yearling Row. Dad, Nancy, Maureen, and I would all go to the Malibu ranch together.

Maureen and I eagerly looked forward to our Saturdays at Yearling Row. There Dad taught Maureen and me to ride, and you couldn't ask for a more knowledgeable and patient teacher. I also enjoyed watching Dad do his chores. I've never known a man who could get more pleasure out of painting a fence post or splitting firewood. I was in awe of my dad, and I wanted to be just like him when I grew up.

As we drove to the ranch, I sat in Nancy's lap, and she rubbed my back. Receiving that attention from Nancy was something of a guilty pleasure for me. I instinctively sensed that in being close to Nancy, I was somehow being disloyal to Mom.

When Maureen and I were alone together, we talked about Dad and Nancy. We both thought it would be great if they got married because then we'd have two moms. I was also hoping that if Dad and Nancy got married, I could move in with them and have a normal home, just like *Ozzie and Harriet* on TV.

Then I wouldn't have to go to boarding school anymore.

## LIKE PING-PONG BALLS

On weekends when Mom was working, and Maureen and I couldn't go home, Dad and Nancy would drive up to Chadwick and visit us. I still look back on those visits with nostalgia. When they drove away, I felt the loneliness crash over me like an ocean wave.

Though I felt my loyalty should be to my mother, I felt like I was really part of a family when I was with Dad and Nancy, and I found myself blaming my mother for the divorce. Though Mom never said a derogatory word about Nancy (or anyone else), I felt divided in my loyalties. I couldn't help feeling that if I had too good a time with Dad and Nancy, I was being disloyal to Mom, though she never said anything to make me feel that way.

Like most children of divorce, I quickly learned how to play Dad and Mom against each other. For example, if I didn't like Mom's rules, I would say, "But when I'm at the ranch with Dad, he lets me do this, or I get to do that." I learned how to manipulate like a pro. I continually pitted Mom and Dad against each other in a game of "Who's gonna give me more?"

Dad and Nancy got married on March 4, 1952, at the Little Brown Church in the Valley, an old-fashioned pinewood chapel in Studio City. Maureen and I found out about their marriage after the fact, when they called us at Chadwick with the news.

Maureen and I didn't know it then, but that should have been our first clue that our relationship with Dad was about to take another turn for the worse. Divorce had reduced his role in our lives to that of a twice-a-month visitor. Remarriage would take him even further away from us.

The change was not immediately apparent. We still took our weekend drives up to the ranch. After Nancy became pregnant, she would let me put my hand on her stomach and feel the baby kicking. To me, the fact that she actually had a baby moving inside her was the most amazing thing in the world. Soon I could no longer sit in her lap in the car anymore because she no longer had a lap!

Once I was physically relegated to the backseat of the car, I began to realize that I had been symbolically moved to the backseat as well. This, I have since discovered, is a common occurrence in divorce and remarriage: A divorced dad does all he can to stay connected to his kids after the divorce. But when he remarries and has children with his new wife, emotional forces frequently cause those first kids to be shunted aside. Suddenly the divorced and remarried dad has a new family and new responsibilities, and it's a lot harder for him to keep up the relationship with the kids from his first marriage.

I was still struggling with feelings of rejection because my birth mother had sent me out of her life and because Mom had sent me away to boarding school. When Nancy came into our lives, I had started to feel part of a real family once more, and I had thought everything would just get better and better after Dad and Nancy got married. I was wrong. The affection and attention Nancy had once lavished on me began to dwindle away.

In the beginning Nancy had treated Maureen and me as if we were her own kids. But after Patti was born, Maureen and I didn't fit comfortably into the new family arrangement. Sure, we still had our every-other-weekend visits, but it became clear that we would never have more than that.

We had lost a lot of our relationship with Dad in the divorce. We lost still more when he remarried.

## My "new father"

Around that same time Mom introduced Maureen and me to Fred Karger, a Hollywood composer and music director who had scored a lot of musicals, including *Tars and Spars* (with Sid Caesar) and *Ladies of the Chorus* (with Marilyn Monroe). He also conducted a dance band that played in the Starlight Room at the Beverly Hilton Hotel. (Fred would later write music for films ranging from *Gidget* and *Gidget Goes Hawaiian* to *From Here to Eternity*; he also taught James Darren to sing.)

On Halloween night 1952, Fred brought his daughter

Terry over to our house to go trick-or-treating with Maureen and me. I was all set to rush out the door in my cowboy costume when Mom said, "Wait, I want you children to come into the den. There's something I want to tell you."

So we all went into the den. Mom turned to Maureen and me and said, "Children, Fred is going to be your new father." Then she turned to Fred's daughter and told her, "And Terry, I'm going to be your new mother." This, of course, was Mom's way of telling us that she and Fred were going to get married. But that's not the way I took it.

When Mom said that Fred was going to be my "new father," I actually wondered, *What about Dad? Does this mean Dad won't be my father anymore?* To an adult that's a silly question. But from my seven-year-old perspective, it was a perfectly reasonable question. In my world adults gave their babies away, sent kids away to boarding school, and took fathers away from children through divorce. After all I had been through, it wouldn't have surprised me at all if Mom had simply removed Dad from my life and replaced him with Fred.

I could see that Mom thought she was giving us some absolutely wonderful news—though to me it was the most awful news imaginable. My heart was in my throat. I didn't want a new father. I wanted my dad. But I didn't want Mom to be upset with me, so I forced myself to smile even though I felt like crying.

Terry, Maureen, and I went trick-or-treating after Mom's announcement. I collected loads of candy, but I didn't feel much like eating candy that night.

The next day, November 1, was a Saturday. Maureen and I went to Yearling Row with Dad, and when we came home Saturday night, Mom was gone. I asked Carrie, the household cook, where Mom was, but she would only grin and say, "She'll be back." Carrie was a warmhearted black woman who was like a substitute mother to me. I frequently turned to her for advice, and I could always count on Carrie to tell me the truth—only this time she had apparently been sworn to secrecy.

On Sunday morning Carrie called Maureen and me downstairs. When we had both arrived in the entryway, Carrie told us to put out our hands, and she filled them with rice.

"What's the rice for?" I asked.

Carrie pointed at the front door. "Your mother and Fred are going to come through that door," she said. "When they do, you throw this rice at them."

So Mom and Fred entered. Maureen and Carrie and I showered them with rice. Mom and Fred were married. They had eloped to Santa Barbara.

I didn't particularly care for my new father. He wasn't mean or unpleasant, but he wasn't very outgoing, and he always seemed uncomfortable around Maureen and me. We didn't talk much, and he never took me to the park or to ball games. Another odd thing about Fred was that he seemed to have a lot of trouble with toothaches.

The first morning after they were married, Fred came downstairs before breakfast, took me aside, and said, "Where does your Mom keep the toothache medicine?"

I said, "Did you look in the medicine cabinet in the bathroom?"

"No, no," he said, "not *medicine*-medicine. Don't you know what toothache medicine is?"

I shook my head.

"Booze, Michael," he said. "You know, liquor."

"Oh," I said, wondering why he didn't say so in the first place. I knew that mom had a wet bar in the den, so I led him there. From then on, Fred would frequently ask me to get him the toothache medicine, and I would always bring it to him. I wanted to keep Fred happy because I knew that if he was happy, chances were Mom would be happy too—and that would make life happier for me.

I was relieved that Dad continued to come by every other Saturday to take Maureen and me to the ranch. Fortunately, my "new father" hadn't replaced Dad after all.

Still my life had become incredibly complex. I found myself navigating the treacherous relational waters between Fred and Mom, Mom and Nancy, Dad and Mom, and so forth.

The one person who seemed to understand my confusion and anxiety was Dad. He sensed that I was feeling entangled in all of these conflicting loyalties caused by my parents' divorce and remarriages. So he did a surprising thing: he invited Fred out to the Malibu ranch. Looking back, I realize what a wise and thoughtful act that was on Dad's part. He knew there was no way he would get Mom and Nancy together, but he wanted me to see that both of my fathers could get along.

We spent the day hiking, riding horses, and touring the ranch. I thought it was great that Dad and Fred got along so well. At the end of the day, as Fred and I were driving home, Fred told me, "Let's not tell your mother how much fun we had today, OK? It would only make her upset."

I had hoped I would be invited to live with Dad and Nancy after they got married, so we could be a real family. No such luck. Now Mom, Fred, Maureen, Terry, and I were a family— sort of. But it wasn't like I had pictured. Mom was still busy with her movie career. Fred was busy composing and band leading, and he never had time for us. Maureen and I still spent most of our lives on top of that hill at Chadwick School.

One incident from Fred Karger's marriage to Mom stands out in my memory. He planned a big Hollywood birthday party for Mom and invited a lot of celebrities. My sister and I went birthday shopping for her, and Maureen talked me out of the present I wanted to buy: a serving tray illustrated with a photo of Marilyn Monroe lying nude on red satin. I'm not sure if I thought Mom would love it or if I wanted it for me. In any case, Maureen's tastes prevailed. We bought a sugar bowl instead.

On the night of the party, Mom put me in charge of answering the door. I was dressed up in my new suit, and I welcomed the guests with a carefully rehearsed greeting. Once, when the doorbell rang, I opened it and there was Marilyn Monroe! She looked exactly as she did on that serving platter—only with all her clothes on, of course. I was so shocked that I forgot my rehearsed greeting, and I almost slammed the door in her face. I later learned that she and Fred were friends from working together on *Ladies of the Chorus.*

At the ripe old age of seven, I had to deal with a lot of chaos and confusion that the adults in my life had created. I had a birth mother I didn't know. I had a mom and a dad who didn't live together. I had a "new father" who was essentially a live-in stranger. And I had a stepmom, Nancy, who had been warm and affectionate at first but who now seemed to have little time for me.

The irony of it all was that I was a kid with five parents, yet I felt like I had no parents at all.

## How Divorce Hurts Kids

Want to hear my definition of *divorce?* Divorce is where two adults take everything that matters to a child—the child's home, family, security, and sense of being loved and protected—and they smash it all up, leave it in ruins on the floor, then walk out and leave the child to clean up the mess.

You've probably never heard that definition of divorce before. Why? Because we adults always look at things like divorce and remarriage through adult eyes—through the eyes of our own grownup selfishness. We never stop and try to look at these issues through the eyes of the child.

We're so busy arguing and bickering, so busy insisting on our needs and our rights, so busy breaking crockery and marriage vows, that we don't stop and think about the scared little child over in the corner whose entire world is being torn apart.

Maybe if we would think a little more about that child and a little less about ourselves, we wouldn't be so quick to pull the divorce trigger and shoot our wedding vows through the heart.

I have been blessed (or cursed) with a long and vivid memory of what it felt like to be a child of divorce. I remember the fear and insecurity I felt when Dad didn't live in our house anymore. I remember how scared I was when I heard the news that I was going to have a "new father." I remember all the questions that went through my mind but I didn't dare ask because I didn't want the grown-ups to get upset. I remember how a child thinks and feels when his whole world is falling to pieces around him.

How does divorce affect a child? Here are a few of the effects you should know about:

1. *Kids get scared.* They worry, first, about themselves: "What's going to happen to me? My parents stopped loving each other—will they stop loving me? If I argue with my parents, will they divorce me like they divorced each other? What's the future going to be like?"

Kids also worry about the parent who is leaving the house: "Why is my parent leaving? Doesn't he (or she) love me anymore? Will I see him (or her) again?"

2. *Kids feel guilty.* Children of divorce commonly blame themselves for their parents' divorce. Psychologists tell us that the thought processes of a child tend toward "self-referential thinking." That is, kids are quick to assume that everything that happens around them is either related to them or caused

by them. The younger the child, the more likely she'll interpret situations in a self-referential way. So if Mom and Dad get a divorce, children frequently blame themselves for it and carry that burden in silence.

3. *Kids undergo personality changes.* Some become angry, contentious, and rebellious. Some become quiet and withdrawn. Whether a child becomes openly hostile or silently withdraws into a shell, that reaction is a defense mechanism the child uses to cope with the fear that comes when life spins completely out of control.

The child's anger also may be due to the frustration he feels because of the many changes that have suddenly invaded his life. Suddenly the child has lost access to one parent and wants to know, "Why can't you get along? Why can't you just forgive each other and stay together?" The older the child, the harder it is for the child to let go of the anger.

4. *Kids feel isolated, lonely, and rejected.* Divorce takes up all of the grown-ups' energy and attention, so that they have no time for their kids. As a result, children feel neglected and ignored. The kids try to get their parents' attention, and the parents say, "Go find something to do! Can't you see we're busy?" The children see Dad walk out the door for the last time, and they wonder, *Why is Dad leaving me and rejecting me? What's wrong with me?* And those feelings of loneliness and rejection turn into feelings of self-hate.

5. *Kids feel that their loyalties are divided.* Children of divorce feel torn between their parents. When the parents

date and bring other adults into the picture, those loyalties become even more tangled and confusing. Children are forced to play emotional games with their parents in order to win parental favor. They quickly learn that they can please Mom by dissing Dad and his new girlfriend or wife. Then on the weekends they can earn points with Dad by playing the same game in reverse.

6. *Kids perform poorly in school.* Children age seven and up tend to show decreased academic performance at school. They also tend to have more conflicts with their peers. Children of divorce are more likely than children from intact families to engage in truancy, delinquency, and running away from home.

7. *Kids feel resentment over their parents' remarriage.* Sometimes a stepmom or stepdad will come into the picture and try to assert parental authority. Sometimes stepparents will even attempt to impose punishment on the child. The child looks at this near stranger in his life and says, "You're not my boss! You're not my parent! I don't have to live by your rules! You can't order me around, and I don't have to obey you!" The result is often a tug-of-war between the child and the stepparent that threatens to blow the new marriage apart.

Another problem with divorce and remarriage is *change.* Kids hate change because it makes them feel insecure and uncertain about the future and about their status in the family. When I was a kid, my life was continually changing. And every change that came along made my life worse, not better. Kids need stability. Divorce destabilizes a child's life, and remarriage only compounds the problem.

8. *Kids become damaged in their ability to trust.* The emotional trauma of divorce is so painful that many children pull into a shell of distrust and become guarded and wary in relationships. Feeling abandoned by the parent who has left the home, many kids also begin to fear being abandoned by the remaining parent. As children of divorce grow up, they often transfer their distrust of parents to other relationships, including relationships with the opposite sex and even to their relationship with God, the heavenly Parent.

9. *Kids suffer long-term emotional and relational damage.* Columnist Michael J. McManus reports that

> children of divorce are twice as likely as those from intact parents to drop out of school, three times as apt to get pregnant as teenagers, six times as likely to be in poverty, twelve times more likely to be incarcerated. When the child enters adulthood, "the unexpected legacy of divorce" hits, according to Dr. Judith Wallerstein. Two-thirds are unable to form lasting bonds with someone of the opposite sex. She tracked a hundred children of a hundred divorces for twenty-five years. Only sixty married, of whom twenty-four divorced.[1]

These are some of the most important effects of divorce upon a child, and every one of these effects fit me. How do I know that divorce hurts children? Because I lived it.

## Is "no-fault" at fault?

What can we do to prevent kids from being damaged by divorce? Well, the first and most obvious piece of advice is: Don't get a divorce!

I used to share a radio studio with Dr. Laura Schlessinger, and she often advised her listeners that there are only three valid reasons for divorce—what she called "The Three A's—Adultery, Abuse, and Addiction." In other words, you should remain married no matter what—*unless* your mate is involved in behavior that is dangerous or detrimental to you and your children.

Adultery makes the list because an adulterer has broken the marriage vows, could bring sexually transmitted diseases into the relationship, and is teaching destructive values to the kids. Physical or sexual abuse makes the list for obvious reasons: your life and your children's lives are at risk. Addiction (including alcoholism) cannot be tolerated because of the harm that such risky behavior causes, the distortion these substances cause in personalities and relationships, and the horrendously bad example this behavior causes.

The problem is that we have made divorce too easy in our society. We have greased the skids of marriage so that it has become easy for people to slide away from their responsibilities, their marriage vows, and their duty to provide a stable, secure home for their children. And do you know who's responsible for making divorce too easy? Would you believe—Ronald Reagan?

Until 1969, almost every state in the Union had a fault-based system of divorce laws. (The lone exception was Oklahoma, which introduced no-fault divorce in 1953.) Under the fault-based system, a plaintiff (the aggrieved party in the divorce action) had to charge the defendant with certain actions that constituted grounds for divorce. Those grounds might include mental cruelty, physical abuse, desertion, adultery, imprisonment, alcohol or drug addiction, or insanity. Without showing grounds for divorce, no divorce could be granted.

California's no-fault divorce law was drafted by Assemblyman James A. Hayes and signed into law in 1969 by then-Governor Ronald Reagan. The rest of the nation quickly followed California's lead. By 1974, forty-five states had passed no-fault statutes of their own. By 1985, every state in the union was a no-fault state. According to Judy Parejko, author of *Stolen Vows: The Illusion of No-Fault Divorce and the Rise of the American Divorce Industry,* Assemblyman Hayes "was responsible for doggedly pursuing [the no-fault divorce] bill because he was facing a divorce and he didn't like the rules at the time. Nowadays, his actions would be called a conflict of interest."[2]

And why did Ronald Reagan, the pro-family conservative, sign such a law? I believe that some of his reasons were personal. Notice that Dad signed the no-fault divorce law some twenty years after going through his own divorce. His wife, Jane Wyman, had divorced him on grounds of "mental cruelty." Even though listing grounds for divorce was largely a formality, those two words were probably a bitter pill for him to swallow. He wanted to do something to make the divorce process less acrimonious, less contentious, and less expensive.

Dad later said that he regretted signing the no-fault divorce bill and that he believed it was one of the worst mistakes he ever made in office. That law set in motion one of the most damaging social experiments in the history of our nation. Not only did the divorce rate skyrocket as a direct result of the no-fault experiment, but divorce conflicts and legal costs remain as ruinous as ever. The acrimony in divorce has simply shifted to different issues. Instead of fighting over who gets blamed for what, couples battle primarily over custody, visitation rights, and child support.

According to a nationwide survey conducted by *The Journal of Marriage and the Family,* the divorce rate soared by 250 percent over a twenty-year period from 1960 to 1980. There is only one factor with nationwide implications that could have caused such a dramatic shift in the divorce rate: the national movement to no-fault divorce.

Today roughly half of all marriages end in divorce— 40 percent of first marriages (versus 16 percent in 1960), and 60 percent of remarriages. Three-fifths of all divorces affect the lives of minor children. By making divorce easier to obtain, the no-fault divorce laws have created a lucrative "divorce industry" that impoverishes families (including children) while enriching divorce lawyers.

I believe that one of the more troubling (but less visible) effects of no-fault divorce is that it has contributed to the spread of no-fault morality in our culture. Our no-fault approach to divorce sends a message to people that the "till death do us part" clause in the marriage vow is more of a goal than a commitment. It's OK to bail out on marriage if it becomes too much work or if we find a new partner who gives us the warm fuzzies inside.

Today's attitude toward divorce says, in effect, that permanent commitments are old-fashioned. Today we should look upon marriage as a temporary arrangement. In fact, maybe instead of marriage, we should call it "serial monogamy," or "registered cohabitation," or even—as David Wagner of the Family Research Council puts it—"notarized dating."

And since we are free to obtain no-fault, no-guilt divorces without regard to how divorce affects children, why not take the next logical step and admit that we don't really care whether children are born and raised in wedlock? Could it be that our no-fault notion of divorce is one of the factors underlying an illegitimacy boom that is rising at a rate of 1 percent per year?

Our divorce laws need reform. We need to make it a little less easy to get a divorce in America. We should create more incentive for couples—and especially parents—to work a little harder at their marriage relationships. Parents and the courts need to think a little bit harder about the needs of children.

Today 80 percent of divorces are initiated by one party over the objections of the other. That means that in the vast majority of cases, one partner is willing to try to make the marriage work. It is tragic that our no-fault laws side with the initiating partner and strip the nonconsenting partner of all legal power. Under no-fault laws the initiating partner can even grab half of the family assets on the way out the door, even if guilty of adultery!

We should give the nonconsenting partner more legal power to fight for the marriage and for the needs of the children. We need to apply the brakes to those spouses who are all too willing and eager to destroy their homes and shatter the lives of their children.

According to studies on the economic effects of divorce, the standard of living of a man goes up 42 percent during the first year after a divorce; in that same period the standard of living of a woman and her children drops 73 percent. Perhaps if the economic effects of divorce were more evenly distributed between the parties, there would be more incentive to work on the marriage, and we would see a decline in the divorce rate.

Attorney Allen Parkman, in his book *Good Intentions Gone Awry* (Rowman & Littlefield, 2000) has suggested a slate of reforms that would make our marriage and divorce laws more child friendly:

First, make no-fault divorces available only to childless couples in the early years of marriage. This would enable childless couples to "undo" a marriage "mistake" while requiring couples with children to consider what's best for their kids.

Second, require mutual consent for any divorce involving minor children. This would encourage both parties to work on the marriage for the sake of the children. Only if both partners agreed that the marriage was unsalvageable could the divorce take place.

Third, require a one-year "cooling off" period before the divorce can be finalized. This allows time for rethinking and reconciliation. One state, Maryland, has such a law in place today; and the divorce rate in Maryland is the second lowest among all fifty states.

Fourth, when couples file for divorce, they should be informed by the courts of programs that help couples to reconcile.

Fifth, for the sake of the children and their safety, divorce proceedings should not be impeded when there are urgent grounds for divorce, such as abuse, adultery, addiction, or desertion. In those rare cases where one parent poses a physical danger to the child, then divorce is actually in the best interests of the child and should not be delayed.[3]

The evidence is in on no-fault divorce. We know that it is a social experiment that has failed miserably. It has proven especially tragic for our children. It's time we put an end to this failed experiment that began with good intentions and the stroke of my father's pen and resulted in so much tragedy for American families.

## MAKING THE BEST OF A BAD SITUATION

Even if we put an end to no-fault divorce in America, you and I must still face the divorce issue that lurks in our own hearts. Every day we must face the question: Am I going to do the things today that build my marriage up or the things that tear it down? Will I focus on loving my wife, my husband, my children, as God intended me to, or will I pursue my own selfish wants and insist on my own selfish demands?

Relationships are dynamic not static. Relationships either move forward, toward deeper love and security; or they move backward, toward resentment, bitterness, and divorce. So while there is still time, we must do the things that build a healthier marriage relationship.

But what if your divorce is inevitable or has already taken place? Is there anything you can do to protect your kids from the harmful effects of a divorce? There's no question, divorce hurts kids. I know because I've been there. But I have some suggestions for making the best of a bad situation so that your kids can find healing from the hurt of divorce:

1. *Try to put yourself in the child's place.* Your family is your child's entire world. Divorce splits your child's world right down the middle. So it's important to remember that your children don't see the world through adult eyes. Be aware of their fears, insecurities, sorrow, and grief. Tune in to the feelings they are afraid to express or don't know how to express in words.

2. *Both parents should sit down together with the children and explain the divorce.* Explain calmly and clearly what is going to take place. Take responsibility for the marital breakup; make sure you leave no room for the kids to blame themselves. Assure the children that you will both continue to be part of their lives. Explain what the future will be like: the

kids will live with one parent most of the time but will visit the other parent on a regular basis. Be candid, but help to allay their fears and uncertainties.

3. *Truly listen to your kids.* When you as a parent are going through divorce, there is a tendency to focus only on your issues, your hurts. Especially at a time like this, children need to know that they are being heard and understood by their parents. You may have to draw your kids out and help them express what they are feeling. Be especially sensitive to their moods and ask questions like, "Are you feeling sad? Are you feeling angry? It's OK to tell me that you're angry, even if you're angry at me. I won't get mad at you. I just want to listen to you and help you."

Never tell a child, "You shouldn't feel that way." Instead say, "It's normal to feel that way. Your life is really hard right now, but it's going to get better." Avoid interrupting or trying to talk a child out of his or her feelings. Don't try to make the child's feelings go away; just accept those feelings, make sure the child knows they are normal feelings, listen and empathize, and reassure the child with words like, "I know you miss your dad. I'm sorry this hurts you."

4. *Assure the children of your never-ending love for them.* Divorce shakes a child's security and emotional foundation. Kids need to be reassured that their parents still love them not just once but continually. Tell them you love them, hold them, and demonstrate your love by listening to them, spending time with them, taking them places, being at all their recitals or soccer games, and continuing to be regularly involved in their lives.

5. *Be totally supportive of your children's relationship with the other parent.* As long as the other parent is not dangerous to the child, make sure your child has the best possible relationship with the other parent. Set aside your grown-up resentment and anger, so that you can focus on what is best for your child. Even if the other parent treats you unfairly, you have to do what's right. Don't try to disrupt the visitation schedule. Don't criticize or attack the other parent. Don't use your child as a weapon to get even with the other parent. Never put your child in a situation where he or she must choose loyalty to one parent or the other.

6. *Allow the child to go from one parent's home to the other without conflict or guilt.* Avoid dirty looks, probing questions, arguments, or other forms of conflict about the child's visit in the other home. Don't make the child feel guilty for having a good time at the other parent's home.

7. *As much as possible, agree with the other parent on maintaining consistent rules, discipline, and values in both homes.* If there are differences of opinion, both parents should be willing to bend a bit toward the other's parenting style. The important thing is not which parent wins the popularity contest but the fact that kids need stability. They need rules and expectations they can rely on, whether at Mom's house or Dad's.

8. *Keep your promises.* Divorce takes a heavy toll on a child's ability to trust other people. You can only rebuild your child's ability to trust by demonstrating that you are trustworthy. When you make a promise to your child, don't you dare break it.

9. *Whenever possible, involve your children in major decisions.* Children of divorce are constantly dealing with change and with the chaos that adults inflict on their lives. They feel helpless and powerless to control events. You can help them feel more in control by involving them in the decision-making process. Make sure that issues affecting their lives are explained to them in terms they can understand. Try to introduce changes to their lives slowly, incrementally, and with plenty of warning and discussion so that they are able to adjust and feel that they have some control over their lives.

10. *Live in the same town as the child's other parent.* Don't move to another state in order to take your kids away from your ex. If it means you have to take a pay cut in order to stay close to your kids, then take the pay cut and show your kids that they mean more to you than money. If it means you have to move to the same state your ex just moved to, then do that. Whatever you do, stay involved in your kids' lives, and keep your ex involved as well.

11. *Never fight with your ex in front of the kids.* Children who are exposed to ongoing conflict between their parents tend to have a difficult time with trust and relationships later in life. Children of divorce need to be supportively, lovingly coparented—not bickered over. Never use your children to carry on your grown-up divorce wars. Never criticize the other parent to the child. Above all, never criticize the child with a comment such as, "You're just like your mom!" or "You're just like your dad!" The child will instantly get the

message that, since you divorced that other parent, then you just might divorce the child too.

Sure, you'll get angry from time to time. But for the sake of your kids, get over it. The better you are able to make the emotional adjustment to the divorce and get on with your life, the better your kids will make that same adjustment. If your kids are able to see their divorced parents reaching agreements and treating each other with civility and respect, they will feel more secure, and they will learn mature ways of dealing with conflicts and problems.

12. *Pray.* Prayer is the most important thing you can do in helping your kids heal from the hurt of divorce. And as you pray *for* your kids, don't forget to pray *with* your kids, verbally and consistently. Teach them how to pray by exemplifying a lifestyle of prayer. If the kids don't have a lot of contact with their dad, it's especially important for them to see how they can make a connection with a loving and reliable heavenly Father who never moves away from them and who will always care.

## THROUGH THE EYES OF A CHILD

Looking back at my early life through adult eyes, I realize that Mom and Dad loved me and did the best they could to provide for Maureen and me through an emotionally difficult time. We all have our limitations, and Mom and Dad both did the best they could within their limitations.

My reason for laying out what I went through as a child of divorce is not to complain about my parents but to do something redemptive with my own experience. If I can get one person who is considering divorce to stop and think about what divorce is like through the eyes of the child, then this entire book will have been worth it. I'm asking you to think about how the things you do and say as an adult are perceived by your child.

Does your child feel that you've pushed him or her to the backseat of your life? Have you considered all the changes, losses, and chaos your child has to deal with as a result of the decisions you and your spouse (or ex) have made? Are you placing your child in a no-win situation, forcing that child to divide his or her loyalties in order to survive the chaos you and your mate have created? All I'm asking is that you try to get inside the head and the heart of the child God has entrusted to you. Look at the world through his or her eyes.

Childhood is the time when values are being instilled, when personality is being shaped, when young people are learning the coping skills they will rely on for the rest of their lives. Even the most civil and reasonable divorce process is hard on children. If divorce can be avoided, if the marriage can be put back together, we owe it to our kids to do so.

But if the marriage is broken beyond repair, we can still raise strong, secure children if we will take the time to understand what our kids are going through, if we will focus on their emotional and spiritual needs above all else, and if we will look at the divorce process through their eyes.

# 3

# In the Care of
# Strangers

When I was four, my mother sent me to preschool at The Buckley School in North Hollywood. I have only one real memory of the place, but it's a vivid one. I was in my classroom, and I raised my hand and told my teacher I needed to go to the restroom.

"You should have gone to the restroom before class," she said. "If you can't wait, you'll just have to go in your pants." She probably thought I could wait, but I wasn't bluffing. I really had to go! So I did—all over myself. I spent the rest of the day in wet pants.

I learned two lessons that day. I learned to use the restroom before I went to class, and I learned what shame feels like.

When I was five and a half years old, I was sent off to join my sister at Chadwick School in Palos Verdes Estates. It was a coed boarding school with separate dorms for boys and girls.

I lived in the boys' dormitory at Chadwick for two weeks, then Maureen and I came home every other weekend. On those alternating weekends, we left school on Friday afternoon and returned Sunday evening at seven, when Mom would drive us back to Chadwick.

Some Chadwick students were day students; they only came for the day and went home after school. I envied the day students who got picked up every day, had dinner with their parents every evening, and slept in their own beds at night. When you get punished as a kid, what do your parents say? "Go to your room!" So, for most of us boarders, being sent to boarding school was like being sent to our rooms. We felt as if we were being punished.

I spent my first- and second-grade years boarding at Chadwick, and I constantly missed my mother. Don't get me wrong—Chadwick was a great school, and my days were enjoyable and full of activities. The teachers were friendly, and they actually became a surrogate family to me because I spent more time with them than with my real family.

But boarding school is what it is. The other boarding students and I all lived in a dormitory, and most of us were lonely and cried ourselves to sleep at night. At lights out, you could literally hear kids sobbing in their pillows all around the dorm.

My saving grace at Chadwick was Maureen. Though she was four grades ahead of me, she made a point of coming by and checking on me. She has always been a protector and a mother hen. I couldn't have asked for a better big sister.

I would live for those moments when Mom would pick me up and take me home. My loneliness at Chadwick grew progressively worse after I learned I was adopted and illegitimate. Chadwick, of course, is where I had told a classmate that I was "chosen," and he had informed me that I was a "bastard" and that my "real mother" gave me away because she didn't want me.

And it was during one of my weekend breaks from Chadwick that I read the Bible passage in Deuteronomy that convinced me I was doomed to hell. So one of the thoughts going through my head as I cried myself to sleep was the fact that God didn't love me and there wasn't anything I could do about it.

Discipline at Chadwick was strict. The teachers wouldn't hesitate to redden my knuckles or my posterior with a wooden ruler. Fact is, I sometimes acted up with the deliberate intention of getting punished. I was so starved for attention, any attention, that a whack with a ruler was almost as good as a kiss on the cheek. I just wanted some adult to notice that I existed and that I had feelings. And I was not unusual in that regard; many kids at Chadwick acted up in order to get attention.

People used to tell Maureen and me how lucky we were to be rich kids from Beverly Hills. We went to school with Bing Crosby's kids and Joan Crawford's kids. But if all the rich kids at Chadwick were so lucky, why did all four Crosby boys grow up with alcohol problems? Why did two of the Crosby boys commit suicide as adults? And why did Gary Crosby write a tell-all book that portrayed his father as distant and uncaring? If we were all so lucky, why did Christina Crawford write *Mommie Dearest?*

Their parents were stars, legends, icons, held in high esteem by the public. If the Crosby kids or the Crawford kids tried to tell anyone about how their parents *really* treated them, nobody wanted to believe it. People would see Bing Crosby in the *Road* pictures or as Father O'Malley in *Going My Way,* and they'd think that the lovable, affable, easy-going character on the screen was the real Bing Crosby. The Crosby kids knew that their dad wasn't like that at home, but try and convince a starstruck public!

We kids of famous parents are keepers of the family secrets. To the world, we have no problems. After all, how could anyone have problems with all of that wealth and fame? But we have the reality. We know that there are problems, but we can't get anyone else to believe us. That's why we grow up frustrated and angry.

One reason children of celebrities often have it harder than most people realize is that children have a strong developmental need for attention and affirmation. But actors and other celebrities also demand attention and affirmation; that's why they got into show business! Actors and actresses are always the center of attention wherever they go, and their kids can't get them to give that up.

Christina Crawford and many other Hollywood kids were adopted by narcissistic Hollywood parents primarily as an image enhancement. They were not adopted for love but as props for publicity photos. I, at least, was able to realize at a certain stage in life that my parents truly did love me; other Hollywood kids were not so fortunate, and many of them have been lost to drugs, alcohol, or suicide.

Another reason people always told us Hollywood kids we were lucky was because we were rich and had everything we wanted. True, Mom's house on Beverly Glen was a palace. We had cooks, maids, and nannies. We had a laundry chute that dropped from the second floor all the way to the basement. Maureen and I slid down that chute many times. (We piled up sheets at the bottom to prevent injury.)

If Mom ever caught us sliding down the laundry chute, she sent us to our rooms for an hour; but sliding down the chute was so much fun, it was worth it. Besides, whenever Mom sent me to my room, I would go out the bathroom window, shinny down the tree, and go play with the neighbors for an hour. (At least, that's what I did until the time Mom caught me.)

I really enjoyed living in all of that luxury when I was home. Problem was, I was rarely home to enjoy it. Except for two years, I spent all my school years in boarding school, from first grade through my senior year in high school.

## I'D QUIT MY CAREER AND FLIP HAMBURGERS

When you're five, six, seven years old or so, you don't understand the adult world. You don't understand when your parents explain that they can't keep you at home because of the jobs they have. When you're that age, all you know is that Mom and Dad have sent you away, put a bunch of strangers in charge of you, and will only let you come home on alternating weekends. You feel hurt and angry, and you wonder—

*Why did my mom and dad send me away?*

*Why don't they like me?*

*What's wrong with me?*

Of course, I knew Mom was busy. She'd been busy as far back as I could remember. I just wanted her to be busy with *me*.

The year I was born, she was working on *The Yearling*, for which she later received her first Oscar nomination. Two weeks before my first birthday, her movie *The Lost Weekend* collected a whole shelfful of Oscars, including Best Picture. That was also the year she filmed *Magic Town* with Jimmy Stewart. Two months after Christina died, Mom went to Mendocino County and began filming *Johnny Belinda*—the role that would bring her the Academy Award for Best Actress. Then she made *The Lady Takes a Sailor, A Kiss in the Dark, Stage Fright,* and *The Glass Menagerie*.

In the late '40s and early '50s, Mom was averaging two or three pictures a year. She also found time to record a pair of hit songs with Bing Crosby, "In the Cool, Cool, Cool of the Evening" and "Zing a Little Zong." On September 17, 1952, she added her handprints and footprints to the forecourt of Grauman's Chinese Theater.

(On my daughter Ashley's nineteenth birthday, I took her to see Mom's handprints and autograph in the theater forecourt, located next to Natalie Wood and just below Jack Nicholson and Henry Fonda. I also took Ashley to see Mom and Dad's stars on the Walk of Fame. Dad's star is at

6374 Hollywood Boulevard, and Mom has two stars, one honoring her work in motion pictures at 6607 Hollywood Boulevard and one at 1620 Vine Street, honoring her television work.)

So, yes, the years I was in boarding school were very busy, productive, and artistically important years for Mom. Every morning she left the house at five-thirty for the Warner Brothers Studio, where she was under contract. She was tremendously successful precisely because she was so intensely focused on her career. As a child, however, I didn't know about such things. All I knew was that I missed my mother. I think Maureen knew how miserable I was being away from Mom, and she would visit me and try to comfort me whenever she could.

I admire Mom's accomplishments as an actress. She once asked me what I wanted her to leave me in her will, and I could only think of one thing: the Best Actress Oscar she won in 1948 for *Johnny Belinda*. That golden statuette represents a level of achievement that few people in this world ever reach. She was nominated for best actress in a lead role four times (the other three: *The Yearling*, 1947; *The Blue Veil*, 1952; and *Magnificent Obsession*, 1955). I think that's neat!

Had my mother tried to be a full-time mom while being a full-time actress, she probably would have failed at both careers. Though I can't forget those lonely nights in the Chadwick dormitory, I'll always be grateful that Mom adopted me, made me a part of her family, and taught me some of the most important lessons of my life.

When I was a child, I thought Mom was a failure as a mother. I was angry and hurt because she sent me away to boarding school. But as I look back, I see that she was a great success as a single mother. She not only did the best she could do; she did the best that anyone could have done under the circumstances.

Mom not only sent me to the finest schools, but she also sent me to schools that would supply what she couldn't— discipline and a structured environment. Since I could only visit Dad twice a month, Mom put me in a place where I could be held accountable by a headmaster and the dorm mothers. Though I was miserable and angry then, I praise my mother today for what she did because I can understand it now. Boarding school is where I received the discipline I needed so much.

You'd think, after all the loneliness, misery, and anger I felt because I was sent away to boarding school, that I would never send a child of mine to a place like that! Well, you'd be wrong.

When my son Cameron was little, I got a bunch of brochures from different boarding schools and started reading them. My wife Colleen saw what I was reading and she asked, "What are you doing?"

I said, "I'm looking for a boarding school for Cameron."

She said, "Oh, no, you don't! You're not putting any child of mine in a boarding school!"

I thought, *What is she talking about?* When I was a kid, boarding school was all I knew. Colleen had grown up in a big family in Nebraska, and she knew what family is all about. But I just assumed that when you had kids, you sent them away. I honestly didn't know any better.

Thank God, Colleen stopped me!

## DRIVE-BY PARENTING

If I were a kid today, my parents would probably take me to a doctor and the doctor would say, "Michael has severe separation anxiety. I'm prescribing thirty milligrams of this and a hundred milligrams of that. Give Michael these pills every morning, and he'll be right as rain." As if drugs are the solution to every problem a child has.

What is separation anxiety? It's that perfectly normal sense of panic and dread a child feels when you separate him from his parents, his home, and his sense of security. Children who suffer from severe separation anxiety can experience a whole range of symptoms: headaches, nausea, stomachaches, vomiting, diarrhea, crying jags, bouts of anger, extreme worry, nightmares, and clingyness around parents.

What causes separation anxiety in children? That's easy. Little kids don't like to be placed in the care of strangers. They like being with their mom and dad. That's a normal reaction! What's *not* normal is tossing kids into a strange environment and expecting them to be OK with it.

Yet kids are being placed in the care of strangers at an ever-increasing rate. According to the Bureau of Labor Statistics, only 13 percent of families fit the classic *Father Knows Best* format—dad goes to work while mom stays home and cares for the house and the kids. In 62 percent of two-parent families, mom and dad both work outside the home. In 1980, fewer than half of mothers with children under age six were employed outside the home; by 2000, that proportion had grown to two-thirds.

So who's looking after the baby when mom goes to the office? About half of the child care in our society today is done by parents or family members (mom, dad, grandparents, aunts, and so forth). Of the other half, 26 percent of child care takes place in a home day care, 16 percent in an institutional day care center, and 7 percent is conducted by a hired nanny. According to the Children's Defense Fund, thirteen million kids of preschool age are in some form of day care—and six million of those are infants.

Now let's face it: Day care is rarely a parent's first choice. Frequently, day care is a last resort. For single moms it is frequently the only option available. I don't want to inflict any guilt on a working mom who has been left with the responsibility of providing for both the material and emotional needs of a child.

Life is hard for working moms, and in some cases day care is simply a necessity. There are cases where divorce, death, or persistent poverty make it impossible for mom to be the primary caregiver of her own children. That mother deserves praise for courageously doing what she has to for the sake of her kids. She should not be condemned for putting her kids in day care.

My quarrel is not with single moms who use day care as a

necessary stopgap measure. My quarrel is with those parents who have made "stranger care" of their kids a normal part of their lifestyle. My quarrel is with those moms and dads who are guilty of drive-by parenting—a lifestyle choice of parenting by proxy. Day care is not a valid substitute for genuine hands-on, hugs-and-kisses, mommy-and-daddy parenting.

It used to be that only "underprivileged kids" had to undergo the kind of institutional warehousing that takes place in day care. By "underprivileged kids," I mean children who were orphaned or removed from an unfit home or placed in an institutional home because their parents couldn't afford to keep them. But today we have a whole new class of underprivileged kids. They are deprived of affection and time with their family because mom and dad are too busy with their careers to be full-time parents.

Opponents of day care often raise the fact that day care centers are breeding grounds for infectious diseases of all kinds. Kids go to day care, and they come home sick. To tell you the truth, that's a side issue. Kids always get sick, and they eventually get over it. That is certainly one of the downsides to day care but a very minor downside in my view. There are much bigger issues to consider.

For example, we know that the standard of child care kids receive from strangers in day care is far below what a caring parent can give. It just stands to reason. Day care centers hire low-wage workers and experience a high turnover rate. Day care workers put in long hours, receive no benefits, and are frequently poorly trained and poorly screened.

Kids placed in these facilities see caregivers come and go, and they don't receive any semblance of the kind of nurturing, stability, and security that kids need at that age. There are usually too many children for too few workers. The level of child care in these centers is often inattentive; in some cases it is downright abusive. And how can a parent tell if the quality of care is good or not? The parent is never around to know.

Another much overlooked consideration: Kids need hugs. Because of today's legal and liability environment, because of some highly publicized incidences of molestation, hugs have been legislated out of the equation. Day care workers can no longer give children the kind of affirming, caring, loving touch that all kids need because they are afraid of being accused of molestation.

So kids in day care don't get enough hugs. And when kids don't get hugs, they'll go out and find hugs. And where will they find those hugs? They may find them in the arms of a child molester. That's right—the very laws and regulations designed to protect children from molesters may actually make kids more emotionally needy. And emotionally needy kids are more vulnerable to molesters.

In July 2003, the federal government's National Institute of Child Health and Human Development (NICHD) released the results of its "Study of Early Child Care and Youth Development." The study showed that the more time children spent in nonparental child care from birth to age four and a half, the more assertive, aggressive, and noncompliant (disobedient) behavior they showed (the study appeared in *Child Development,* July-August 2003).

The study identified "aggressive" behavior as including bullying, fighting, and defiance of adults. The harmful effects of nonparental child care were present whether that child care was classified as high quality or poor quality, whether it took place in a private home or a day care center. These findings applied equally to boys and to girls, to kids from poor backgrounds and well-to-do backgrounds.

What's more, kids who spent thirty or more hours a week in nonparental child care were almost twice as likely to exhibit problem behavior as kids with ten or fewer hours in nonparental child care. So we have to ask ourselves, By placing our kids in day care, are we placing them at greater risk for becoming angry, embittered, and hostile?

Parents who place kids in day care so they can work two or more jobs and bring in extra income need to do the math and see if their decision truly pencils out. The fact is, it is expensive for both parents to work outside the home. There is the cost of day care itself. There are restaurant meals, travel expenses, car maintenance and insurance, and other costs. That second job may bump your family into a higher tax bracket. By the time you figure in all the overhead that comes out of that second income, you might discover it's just not worth the price that you and your children are paying.

And the heaviest price of all may be this: Day care may cause your kids to doubt your love for them or to doubt their own worth. I remember how I felt watching the day school kids getting picked up after school by their moms and dads while I had to stay at school for two weeks at a time. I remember thinking, *Those kids get to be with their parents every night. I don't. What's wrong with me? Why don't my parents like me?*

That situation, where some kids seem to get more parental time, attention, and affection than others, really works on a kid. Children notice when other kids get more of something than they get. The way I was thinking in boarding school is the way many kids think in day care. They see other kids getting picked up at three o'clock while they have to wait until five or six. If you think kids don't notice things like that, think again. I guarantee kids are noticing, and they are wondering why other kids get picked up earlier. And they are thinking, *What's wrong with me?*

If we do not absolutely have to put our kids into the care of strangers, then we should avoid doing so. We don't do our kids any favors by placing them in a "kiddie kennel" while we pursue our grown-up plans and goals.

## What kids need

There was a time a few decades ago when child development authorities considered babies to be rather simple and uncomplicated little creatures who really didn't interact all that much with their environment. According to this school of thought, babies didn't perceive much that was going on around them and didn't really have any emotional needs to speak of. Infants were thought of as having a level of aware-ness somewhere between a cabbage and a hamster.

We now know that babies are extremely sensitive and attentive to their environment. They are constantly seeking, sorting, and responding to sensory stimulation. A newborn who is just ten minutes old will prefer a picture of a face over a picture of a blank oval. A newborn will even prefer a pic-ture of a face over a picture that is facelike but with scram-bled features. Ten days after birth, a baby clearly knows and prefers mom's face to the faces of other people. At two weeks the baby also knows and responds positively to dad's face.

A one-week-old baby can recognize his mother by smell alone. Newborns will respond to a poem that their mothers read to them before they were born. Experiments have shown that when a one-month-old child is shown a photograph of mom accompanied by the voice of a woman who is *not* mom, that child will become upset and agitated. From the very beginning of life, there is a lot more going on inside a baby's head than we realize.

While I don't view the issue of day care as a political issue, it does have a political component. Liberals and feminists have, over the years, tended to portray full-time mothers as victims of gender stereotyping, male oppression, and cultur-ally reinforced guilt. Full-time moms have been ridiculed by the left for trying to live according to an unrealistic role model exemplified by 1950s TV moms like Donna Reed and June Cleaver.

Feminist leaders from Hillary Clinton to Patricia Ireland to Eleanor Smeal to Ellen Goodman have pressed the case that, in order for women to enjoy equality, they need to be able to balance the demands of both motherhood and a full-time career, and they expect society to foot the child care bill. *Society*, of course, means you and me, the taxpayers.

The *grande dame* of the feminist movement, Betty Friedan, has even gone so far as to advocate federally mandated, federally sponsored "compulsory preschool" for children starting at two years of age. Friedan even urged President Clinton to establish such a program by executive order in exchange for feminist support for him during the impeachment crisis.[1]

Political forces seek to agendize this issue. For me, however, the child care issue is not political. It's personal. I remember what it felt like to cry myself to sleep in the dorm at Chadwick School. I know from personal experience that children need their moms. Not just want. *Need*.

When you put a child in the care of strangers, issues arise that most grown-ups would never even think about. But I think about them because I remember my own childhood with such clarity. Topping that list of issues is communication.

Your parents are the people you are supposed to share everything with, including the things you would never tell anyone else. But when you have so little time with them, you want it to be a good time, a happy time. You don't want to do or say anything that will rock the boat. You don't want your parents to get mad because of something you've done or because of something somebody else did to you.

So if your time with your parents is limited, what do you do? You keep secrets. You watch what you say. You shut down communication.

I know this is the way it works because that's what I did.

Kids need a lot of time with their parents, especially in those crucial early years. There is a saying—and I can tell you it's absolutely true—that children have a special way of spelling *love*: T-I-M-E. For many years people have been buying into the myth of so-called "quality time." According to this myth, it's not important how much time you spend with your kids; what really matters is that the little bit of time you do spend together is "quality time."

That's like saying that it doesn't matter how much time you spend working out in the gym or jogging on the treadmill, you can stay fit and trim with ten minutes a week of "quality" exercise time. It's like saying that it doesn't matter how much time you spend at the office—your boss will still give you a paycheck if you give him twenty minutes of "quality time" each week. It's like saying that Tiger Woods could have become a great golfer or Joe Montana could have become a great quarterback with just a few minutes a week of "quality time" practice; they didn't really need to put in hundreds and hundreds of hours of practice, perfecting their skills.

See how silly that sounds? Why, then, do we think we can do an adequate job of parenting by giving our kids just a few minutes of "quality time" a week?

Kids need a big, heaping *quantity* of our time every single day. Quantity time *is* quality time. We need to spend time together with our kids, talking to them, reading to them, listening to them, playing with them, praying with them, singing with them, hugging them, tickling them, getting silly with them, watching cartoons with them, getting to know them, and telling them ridiculous stories about the good old days: "When I was your age, I had to walk through ten-foot snowdrifts to get to school, twenty miles there and twenty miles back, and it was uphill both ways!"

Kids need this from us! And you know what? We need this from them! There's nothing that does your heart good like really spending gobs and gobs of time with your kids.

In the fall of 1997, Brenda Barnes, president and CEO of PepsiCo, shocked the world when she submitted her resignation in order to be a full-time mom to her three children, ages seven, eight, and ten. "I'm not leaving because my children need more of me," she said. "I'm leaving because I need more of them." Called "one of the highest-ranking women in corporate America" by *The Wall Street Journal,* she had devoted twenty-two years to reaching the top of her profession; then she tossed it all away for the sake of her family.

She said she made up her mind to leave PepsiCo the day one of her children told her it was OK if she kept working as long as she promised to be home for their birthdays—that innocent plea for just one day a year of "quality time" with mom just broke Brenda Barnes's heart. It made her realize just how much of her children's lives she had already missed and how much more she stood to lose if she didn't make some changes in her life. So she made a change. She gave up her position as head of a $7 billion multinational corporation, and she went home to become mom—just mom.

Kids depend on their parents, and they need a lot of time with the adults who matter most in their lives. When we, as parents, spend significant amounts of time with our kids, we communicate to them in a powerful way, "You matter to me! You're my number one priority! I really love you! You're OK!" Time spent with your kids shouts louder to them than any words you can say, and it builds their confidence, security, and self-esteem in a way that nothing else can.

Jesus told his disciples, "Let the little children come to me, and do not hinder them, for the kingdom of heaven belongs to such as these" (Matt. 19:14). If he made a priority of spending time with little children, so should we. Here are some focused, proactive things you can do to make the most of the quality time and quantity time you spend with your kids:

1. *Try to see the world through the eyes of your child.* Kids don't think and perceive the way adults do. Try getting down at child level and putting yourself in your child's place. Don't assume that your child understands the grown-up things you say or the grown-up things you do. Don't assume that your child feels loved or secure. It takes effort to think like a child, so make the effort.

2. *Practice continual two-way communication with your child.* Talk and listen, and use lots of direct eye contact when you talk and when you listen. When your child tells you something, don't just say, "That's nice, kid, now go somewhere and play." Get down at the child's level, look her in the eye, listen

carefully, nod, repeat back what you've heard, ask questions, and engage that child in a conversation. Show your child that what she says is important to you, and you will communicate to her that *she* is important to you. Don't use TV as a baby-sitter—instead, *you* be the babysitter and take time to talk!

3. *Use touch to communicate caring.* Kids love hugs and kisses. Sometimes as little boys get older, they may resist hugs and kisses, but you can still pat your boy on the back, rub his head, or rub his shoulder. A touch communicates, "I like you, I value you, I want to be close to you." A touch is an affirm-ing act that builds a child's sense of self-worth.

4. *Communicate love, even in the tough times.* A child who feels loved, accepted, and emotionally connected is gen-erally easier to discipline. During tough times with your child, the tendency is to shout, warn, criticize, and punish. If you can say, "I love you, I care about you, that's why I'm disci-plining you," even when there is a lot of friction in the rela-tionship, you can often transform an argument into a productive exchange of feelings—and even an exchange of love. By surrounding tough times with love, you help your child feel connected to you, and a child who feels connected is more motivated to want to please you and obey your rules.

5. *Make time for family meals together.* Mealtimes are important moments when the entire family comes together to talk, to pray before the meal, to reconnect with one another after a busy day, to enjoy good food together, to laugh and relax. Mealtimes together build warm memories.

6. *Do chores and housework together.* Children love working alongside mom and dad. It makes them feel useful and grown-up. It teaches them how to be responsible adults. It gives them a role model to emulate. To this day some of the happiest memories I have stored up in my soul are memories of working alongside Dad at his ranch.

7. *Make a date with your child.* Each parent should set aside regular individual time with each of the children. Go out for a burger and a movie together. Play miniature golf with your little kids or real golf with older kids. Just take a drive and talk. Take time to know each of your children as an individual.

One of the most meaningful traditions in our family is the annual father-son and father-daughter weekends I've had with my kids at Hume Lake Christian Camp in the California Sierras. In 1988, when my son Cameron was ten, he and I attended a father-and-son event called Fisherman's Conference. During the weekend our speaker challenged us to a deeper commitment to Christ; on Saturday night he invited all of us fathers and sons to go forward and sign a pledge to seal our commitment.

I leaned over to my son and said, "Let's go, Cameron." He gave me a horrified look and whispered, "In front of all these guys? You've gotta be nuts, Dad!"

I said, "Come on. It would be great if we could do this together."

After a little more coaxing, he finally groaned, "OK! I'll do it." He got up out of his chair and trudged up the aisle with me. We signed our commitment card and dated it: April 30, 1988. I have that card in my Bible to this day.

Cameron and I went back to our seats. For me it was a great father-son moment. For Cameron—well, I wasn't sure.

That night in our cabin, we shared a big king-size bed. I turned out the lights, and it was quiet and dark. I was drifting off to sleep when I heard Cameron say, "Dad?"

"Yeah?"

"How long has Hume Lake Christian Camp been here?"

"Oh," I said, "twenty, thirty years at least."

"Do you think this place will be here, like, twenty years from now?"

"Probably," I said. "Why do you ask?"

"That was really neat tonight," he said. "Maybe someday I can take my son forward like you took me forward tonight."

I went to sleep with tears in my eyes and a prayer of "Wow! Thank you God!" in my heart. I have kept that moment stored in my memory ever since.

Another heartwarming incident occurred in 1998. Pastor Scott Bauer of the Church on the Way had put together a dinner reception at the Beverly Wilshire Hotel. The reception was to honor the mayor of Nablus, the largest city on the West Bank in Israel. Steve Forbes and a number of other dignitaries would be there. Pastor Scott asked me to come and said it would be a small group of people, about twenty people or so.

Well, I really didn't want to go. The reception was on a Sunday night, and I knew I would just be getting back from a father-daughter retreat with Ashley at Hume Lake

Christian Camp. I would be dog-tired from the trip, and the reception would be about as exciting as watching paint dry. I wanted to say no, but I felt God prodding me to help Scott out because he was a good friend. So I promised Scott I would go.

The weekend came, and Ashley and I had a great time at Hume Lake together. Sunday at noon we packed up the car and raced back to LA. Arriving home, I asked Colleen, "Do we really have to go to that stupid reception?"

"Scott invited us," Colleen said, "and you promised."

So we got to the Beverly Wilshire, and, just as expected, we sat through the most boring dinner of my life. I was overjoyed when it was finally over. Colleen and I walked out to wait for the valet to bring our car around. Then I heard Scott calling my name.

I turned and he approached me. "Mike," he said, "I need to talk to you about my daughter, Lindsey. She and I have been having some trouble lately. I've been so busy in the ministry that every time I make an appointment to do something with her I seem to break it. I've broken so many promises that our relationship just isn't what I'd like it to be. Mike, do you know any place that I could put on the calendar where I could take Lindsey for a father-daughter weekend?"

He had no idea where I had just been! I grinned and said, "Now I know why God put me here tonight because it certainly wasn't for that boring dinner! Yes, Scott, I do know where you and Lindsey can go for a really great father-daughter weekend."

Just then they brought my car, and I reached in and pulled out some Hume Lake brochures and gave them to Scott. I said, "Here's the date for the next father-daughter weekend. Put it on your calendar, and as of tomorrow morning, it's all paid for."

The following year Scott and Lindsey went with Ashley and me to the Hume Lake Father-Daughter Weekend. Scott later told me that it began a new bond of relationship between him and Lindsey. She has grown-up to become a fine Christian young lady, and she's very involved in Christian ministry.

These relationship-building times with your kids are so important. You never know how long you have to build a relationship with your kids. My friend, Pastor Scott Bauer, was suddenly stricken with a brain aneurysm and died on October 24, 2003. I have no doubt that Lindsey's grief is more bearable today because Scott took the time to make a date with his daughter.

And there's another lesson in this story: If we commit ourselves to God and ask him to use us, he will do so even when we don't know it, even when we aren't paying attention. Little did I imagine that God would put all of these different puzzle pieces together—a father-daughter weekend in the mountains and a boring dinner reception at a Beverly Hills hotel—in a way that would produce blessing in the lives of Scott Bauer and his daughter Lindsey. But that is how our awesome God works in our lives!

One final question: When was the last time you made a date with your child?

8. *Enjoy your children!* Make a tradition of a weekly family night, such as a movie night, game night, or music night. You may think teenagers are too cool to enjoy family night, and it's true, they may seem to have a "whatever" attitude toward the rest of the family's activities. But inwardly, they want to stay connected to their parents and their family. Teenagers are going through a lot of changes and stresses, and they need the sense of stability and security that a strong, intact family gives them. Let teenagers have a say in what the family will do on family night, and they will probably enter in and enjoy it.

When I was a boy, I wanted my dad to take me to a football game or a baseball game, but he never did that. When we were together, we always went to the ranch and did what he wanted to do, not what I wanted to do. Don't get me wrong —I loved being at the ranch with my dad. But I also loved football and baseball. Today I understand that he avoided public events, like football and baseball games, to keep from being mobbed by fans. But he didn't explain that to me, so I was always angry and blamed Dad because we never did the things I wanted to do. I didn't feel that he enjoyed spending time with me.

One time when Ron Jr. was in his twenties, Dad came to me for advice. He said, "Michael, I've been having trouble with Ron. He seems to be angry with me, and I don't understand why. You're closer to his age. Maybe you understand what his problem is."

I said, "Dad, take out a piece of paper and draw a line down the middle."

He wondered where I was going with this, but he did it.

I said, "On the left-hand side of the line, write the word *football*. On the right-hand side, write *baseball*." He did. "Now, under *football*, write down the number of times you've taken him to a football game. Under *baseball*, write down the number of times you've taken him to a baseball game."

He didn't. He couldn't. Because he had never done it. He had made the same mistake with Ron that he made with me: he had never explained why he couldn't take his kids to games. Many parents make the mistake of thinking that their kids will understand the reasons by osmosis.

One of the happiest memories I have is of the times Mom took me to the Ice Capades. I absolutely loved it! Mom always got great seats, close to the ice. To this day I love watching ice skating because it brings back that warm feeling of spending time with Mom.

There's a tongue-in-cheek saying: "Choose your parents wisely." You can make your kids feel that they have chosen wisely if you spend time with your kids and if you show them you love them by giving them the precious gift of your time.

## KIDS NEED DADS TOO

In December 2003, eighteen-year-old Lee Boyd Malvo was convicted of murder for the October 2002 killing spree that left ten dead and three wounded in the Washington, D.C. area. In all, Malvo and his forty-two-year-old mentor in crime, John Allen Muhammad, have been linked to twenty shootings (including thirteen deaths) in the District of Columbia,

Virginia, Maryland, Louisiana, Alabama, and Georgia. John Allen Muhammad was convicted and sentenced to death the previous month; Malvo escaped the death penalty.

Malvo's trial revealed that one of the underlying causes of the shooting spree was the youth's fatherless childhood and his sense of being unloved. During the summer of 2002, Malvo wrote a rambling three-page letter to Muhammad's niece, LaToria Williams. That letter, filled with grammatical errors, contained such heartbreaking lines as: "Why I am here, there seems for me no purpose. . . . I'm perceived as a walking time bomb waiting to explode. . . . I've had a hard life believe it or not, no father and a mother who hates [me]. . . . All I ask is to be loved for me."

I don't know about you, but I find those words painful to read. My heart goes out to this fatherless boy who was drowning in loneliness and rage. His pain doesn't excuse mass murder; he deserved to be prosecuted to the full extent of the law. But I can't help grieving over the loss of so many lives, including Malvo's own lost potential, because of a void in his fatherless life. Nature abhors a vacuum; so does human nature. The void in Lee Malvo's life cried out to be filled with a father. Instead, it was filled by a ruthless manipulator named John Allen Muhammad, who became the boy's twisted substitute father.

Every child needs a father. That doesn't mean I'm critical of single mothers; after all, I was raised by a single mother. Single parenting is sometimes the only option a parent has, but no matter how you slice it, a single-parent home is not the best environment for kids. It's true that not every kid can have a dad. But it's also true that every kid *needs* a dad and should, ideally, *have* a dad.

Boys need fathers to teach them what manhood is all about—how to work, build, provide, and protect. A boy learns how a man is supposed to treat a woman by watching how dad relates to mom. A good father affirms and validates a boy as he emerges toward manhood. When fathers are not available to perform these functions in the life of their sons, the results are often disastrous—as in the case of Lee Boyd Malvo. And the young D.C. sniper is not an isolated case.

According to statistics from the US Census Bureau, the Centers for Disease Control, and the Department of Justice, 70 percent of long-term prison inmates—including 72 percent of adolescent murderers and 60 percent of all rapists—grew up in fatherless homes. Fatherless children account for roughly 90 percent of all homeless and runaway children, 85 percent of all youth in prison, 75 percent of adolescent patients in chemical abuse centers, 71 percent of high school dropouts, and 63 percent of youth suicides.

Nearly 24 percent of all American kids—almost seventeen million kids—live in fatherless homes. Alysse Michelle Elhage of the North Carolina Family Policy Council writes, "One of the most dangerous influences for fatherless kids, specifically boys, comes from the threat of gang involvement. In fact, most gang members come from fatherless households."[2]

Kids look to fathers to be their role models and their guides to such issues as morality, character, responsibility, conflict resolution, duty, and honor. If kids don't have fathers to teach them these life lessons, they will find father substitutes. The gangs will become their families, and gang leaders will become their father substitutes. Their only morality will be the morality of the mean streets: kill or be killed. By allowing kids to grow up in fatherless homes, we have abandoned them to the gangs and the streets.

And what about girls? Do they need fathers in their lives? Absolutely! Girls need fathers every bit as much as boys do but for different reasons. Good fathers exemplify a healthy image of manhood to their daughters so that their daughters will make wise choices in a life partner. A father who is affirming and appropriately affectionate with his daughter enables her to feel confident and good about herself.

A teenage girl with high self-esteem is better equipped to say no to peer pressure, drugs, and unmarried sex. Girls with low self-esteem—and particularly girls who were starved for a father's love—are more likely to give in to any boy with a clever line and an active sex drive. When that boy is through using her, she'll be left feeling more hurt, more used, more worthless than ever.

So fathers are indispensable to both sons and daughters. Even when a marriage breaks up, kids need their dads, and dads should always be there for their kids. If you are a divorced dad, if you only get to see your kids every other weekend, you still have something crucial to give them: your affirmation, your values, your example, your guidance and support, your love, and your time.

Sure, pay your child support check on time and without complaints; that, too, is a demonstration that you love your kids. But those kids of yours need more than just a monthly check. They need you. They need their dad.

Fathers are indispensable.

## HOW TO FIND A SUBSTITUTE FATHER

What if your children don't have a father? What if their father deserted the family? Or what if he died? What do you do then? I hope you're sitting down because I'm about to tell you something that's going to shock and panic you.

You need to be both mother and father to your kids. And that's a near-impossible task. Moms are the nurturing ones, and dads are the tough ones—the disciplinarians, the ones who keep the kids in line ("Just wait until your father gets home!"). Guess what, mom, you've got to toughen up and become the disciplinarian.

If you're going to be both mom and dad to your kids, you've got to know something about sports and how to throw a ball and how to tie a necktie. You need to teach your little boy how to use the toilet standing up. You need to teach your little girl what a man's admirable traits are. You, the woman of the house, also need to be the man of the house.

If you don't think you're up to the task, I don't blame you. Nobody is. Nobody could possibly be up to the awesome task of being two parents at once.

So what do you do? Well, you find your kids a substitute father. Understand, I'm not talking about getting yourself a new boyfriend. A boyfriend is interested in you, not the welfare of your kids. Your children need your undivided attention right now. Having a boyfriend will only divide your attention and take away from your kids the very things they need most right now: your time, your focus, your friendship, your thoughtfulness, your attentiveness to their problems and challenges. When your youngest turns eighteen and leaves home, then you can start thinking about your love life again. But right now just think about your kids.

If you are a single mom, you need to find some people who can help you be both mom and dad to your kids. Get your kids involved in youth league sports where they can receive coaching and encouragement from male authority figures. Involve your kids in Boy Scouts, Girl Scouts, Big Brothers and Big Sisters, Junior Achievement, 4-H Clubs, or other programs that provide mentoring and encouragement from male sponsors and volunteers. Involve your kids in your church's youth group. Take time to be involved and get to know the coaches, youth advisors, mentors, and volunteers. Make sure they are people of good character who are only interested in building young lives.

It's tough being both mom and dad to your kids, but you can do it if you have a little help.

## WARM MEMORIES

Even though Mom was an Academy Award-winning film star, she was struggling to pull off the toughest role of her career—the role of a single mom with a full-time career and two kids to raise. It was a flawed performance, but she still carried it off well. Mom is the one who gave me my strength and my ability to persevere. She's the one who taught me never to give up on myself. So much of what I am today, I owe to her.

And then there is Irene Flaugher, my birth mother, who gave me up for adoption; I owe my very existence to her. She, too, loved me and sacrificed incredibly for my sake.

And there is my wife Colleen, who opened my under-standing to the love and grace of God. She took over from Mom the job of making me strong for life's challenges. I'll tell you more about Colleen later in this book.

And then there is my sister Maureen—my friend, my nur-turer, my overseer, and my protector while I was at Chadwick.

I believe that God put these four wonderful women in my life for a reason. God has used them to bless my life in ways that I have only recently begun to appreciate.

Mom really had her work cut out for her. I was not an easy kid to have around the house. I was active, adventuresome, prac-tically fearless. I enjoyed getting into mischief. Though I wasn't a mean or malicious kid, I definitely caused a lot of trouble.

I did things just to get attention—any kind of attention. To me, attention and affection were roughly equivalent. If I couldn't get Mom to put her arms around me and say, "I love you, Michael," I would get her to take a riding crop to the back of my legs. I was pretty good at that.

Do I have any good memories of those days? Absolutely! During some of the weekends that Maureen and I were home from Chadwick, Mom would take us out to my favorite restaurant, the Brown Derby at the corner of Wilshire Boulevard and Rodeo Drive in Beverly Hills. The Brown Derby was owned by Mom's dear friends, Bob and Sally Cobb, the inventors of the Cobb salad. Whenever we visited the Brown Derby, I would order my favorite—an avocado cocktail with Thousand Island dressing.

I also have warm memories of being sick. That's right, sick. When I was physically miserable, Mom was wonderful. I have nothing but fond memories of the time I had the measles. Mom sat on the edge of my bed, massaging my back with calamine lotion until I fell asleep.

And there was that summer vacation we spent in New Jersey with Mom's friends, Sonny and Lea Werblin. Sonny was the owner of Madison Square Garden, the New York Islanders hockey team, and the New York Jets football team. (Sonny signed Joe Namath's paycheck.) That trip to New York was my first ride in an airplane. We stayed in an opulent hotel in Manhattan, and I discovered the joys of room service. I could have a burger and a chocolate shake sent to the room at any time of the day or night. Incredible!

We did all the touristy things on that trip—the Empire State Building, the Staten Island Ferry, the Statue of Liberty. (Maureen and I raced each other up the stairs to the crown.) I also saw my first Broadway musical on that trip—*Top Banana* starring Phil Silvers.

On the flight home Mom had me put my head in her lap, and she covered me with a blanket. I can close my eyes and still feel her stroking my hair with her fingertips as I started to get sleepy. I remember thinking that this had been the best vacation I had ever had and that Mom was the best mother anyone ever had. I didn't want it to end, and I didn't think it ever would. When I was away from Chadwick, I could almost make myself believe I would never have to go back.

But, inevitably, I did.

I was in Chadwick for two years, first and second grade. When I entered the third grade, Mom enrolled me at the Warner Avenue School, a day school in Beverly Hills. No more boarding school! I would finally be living at home with Mom! I even dared to hope that my dreams of a perfect family were finally coming true.

At that same time Mom enrolled me in an after-school day camp program in Rancho Park. I thought that was great. I'd go to school, finish the afternoon at day camp, then come home for dinner with Mom, living my life like a normal kid in a normal family, just like I saw on TV.

I couldn't have been more wrong. The worst thing that could possibly happen to a child was about to happen to me.

# 4

# THE END OF INNOCENCE

The after-school day camp in Rancho Park was run by a man named Don Havlik. Everybody liked Don. He was around thirty years old, was loaded with natural charm, and had great rapport with kids. At the day camp he taught us all how to trampoline, how to throw a football and a baseball, and how to shoot a bow and arrow. In short, he taught all the little boys at that camp the skills they needed to make their fathers proud.

I was exactly the kind of kid Don Havlik wanted in his day camp. People like Don can spot kids like me a mile away. I was a lonely kid whose parents were divorced. I only saw my father a couple times a month, and my mother was busy with her career. He could probably tell at a glance that I was hurting, that I hated myself, that I felt angry and inadequate.

And he knew I was vulnerable.

I wanted my family to love me, but I didn't feel worthy. With my childlike reasoning ability, I figured that maybe I could get my family to like me if I succeeded in athletics. If

I could be the best swimmer, the best football player, the best baseball player, then maybe my family would love me. Being illegitimate and adopted, I didn't feel secure in my home. I was trying to impress my family in the hope that they would keep me and not send me away.

Don Havlik could see this in me. He didn't know the details. He didn't need to. All he needed to know was that here was a kid who was emotionally needy, emotionally empty, and emotionally vulnerable. He could see that I had no self-esteem and that I was desperate to have people like me.

Don seemed to like me, and he soon became my idol and even a father figure to me. I wanted to win his praise and attention, and he knew exactly how starved for attention I was. I set out to prove that I was the best at trampolining, the best at somersaults and backflips, the best at sports like baseball and football. I worked hard to impress him. I believed that if I could impress Don, then maybe I could impress Dad, and I could finally earn my way into the Reagan family.

On one occasion Don Havlik held a yo-yo championship for the kids at the camp. I practiced hard and learned lots of yo-yo tricks—walk the dog, around the world, rock the cradle, over the falls. The day of the championship, a dozen or so kids competed, and Don was the judge. I took second place, but amazingly no one took first place! I wondered how you could have a competition without a first-place winner, but Don explained that to us.

"You kids are all good," he said, "but you still need more practice before one of you is good enough for first place."

Well, that made sense—sort of.

Only after I became an adult and saw what a manipulator Don Havlik was did I figure out what this ruse was all about: Don was setting me up.

After the competition Don took me aside for a talk, just him and me. "Mike," he said, "you're a great kid. I know you really want to make your dad proud."

He had my attention.

"I tell you what," he continued, pointing to the second-place Duncan Yo-Yo Championship patch in my hand. "You give me that second-place patch, and I'll give you the first-place patch. You can show it to your parents, and they'll really be proud of you."

So we did as Don said: we exchanged patches. I took the patch home and showed it to Mom, and I could see in her eyes how proud she was. The following Saturday, I showed it to Dad, and he grinned, clapped me on the back, and congratulated me. It worked just as Don had promised. That patch had made my parents proud.

Mom framed the yo-yo patch and hung it in my room alongside the blue ribbons I had won in swim meets. Years later Dad hung it over my bed at Yearling Row, his ranch in Malibu. I was proud of that patch, and I often showed it off to people, as if to say, "Look at my accomplishments! I'm great!"

Looking back, I see how cleverly Don set me up. He made sure that nobody won first place. That way he could do me the big "favor" of secretly giving me the first-place patch when nobody was looking. If I had won the first-place patch outright, I would have felt I had done it on my own. If some other kid had won it, he couldn't have worked out a trade; the other kid would have cried foul. But Don had it all figured out so that I would feel indebted to him, and he and I would share a secret. He wanted to get me used to the idea of keeping secrets.

Don was lavish with compliments, and I ate them up. He told me how proud he was of me and that I was the best student at the day camp. He always helped me get the attention I craved—even if it took a little cheating.

One time I entered a football throwing competition at the day camp. Each kid was allowed one throw. I got nervous, and the ball slipped out of my hand as I threw it. Don let me have another throw, and I won the prize. It was the yo-yo patch all over again.

Every day when the camp was over, Don would let me sit next to him in the front seat as he drove the other kids home. I was always the last to be dropped off. When he and I were alone in the car, he'd drive slowly, his arm around my shoulder, mussing my hair and telling me what a great kid I was.

One day as he was taking me home, he said, "Mike, you want to do something to make me feel good?"

Well, he had done so much for me, and we were such good friends, what else could I say but, "Sure!" It never occurred to me that Don would do anything bad to children. After all, he was not only an adult; he was my friend and my father figure. I spent more time with Don than with my father.

I didn't know what Don wanted me to do. Even when he started unzipping his pants, I couldn't imagine what was coming next.

## INTO THE TRAP

After that first incident of sexual abuse, Don continued molesting me every time he took me to day camp. Looking back, I realize that it truly doesn't matter if you are molested once or a thousand times; it's the first incident that does the damage. That first sex act solidifies the molester's ownership of you.

Don wanted to touch me, or me to touch him, every time we went someplace, whether it was just the two of us or in a group. For example, he'd take a bunch of kids to the movie theater, and he and I would sit someplace away from the other kids. He'd put his coat over our laps, and it would happen again. I didn't know how to get out of the situation.

I was just in the third grade. I didn't understand that this was a sexual act. I sensed that it was wrong somehow, but I didn't understand why. Don made clear that it was to be our secret. He continued to praise me and compliment me, and that made me feel good about myself. I thought of him as my best friend, and he assured me that what we were doing was something friends do to make each other feel good. But deep inside I was terribly frightened about what we were doing, and I didn't know why.

Molesters know how to affirm a child in those areas where he doesn't feel affirmed by his parents and other people in his life. Molesters make you feel good about yourself for a while, but once the molestation takes place, they own your soul. You don't know how to get away from it. You never think the molester did something wrong. You think *you* did something wrong.

I didn't have any words in my vocabulary to describe what was happening. If I had wanted to tell anyone about it—and I didn't—I wouldn't have known what to call it. I didn't know words like *molestation* or *seduction* or *masturbation*. I didn't understand how Don had carefully maneuvered me into a place where I would feel indebted to him. I didn't understand what a manipulator he was and that he had carefully steered me right where he wanted me.

I had walked right into his trap, and he was about to clamp it shut, and I didn't even have a clue.

One day Don took a group of campers for a weekend hike in the Santa Monica Mountains. He had come up with an unusual form of hide-and-seek. He told the other kids that he and I would be partners and that they should all count to a hundred, then come looking for the two of us. That, of course, is not how hide-and-seek is played—unless the one who makes the rules is a child molester.

So while the other kids counted, Don and I took off by ourselves to a place that Don had scouted in advance— a place, I'm sure, where he had taken other boys. He led me by the hand up the mountainside to an outcropping of rocks— a great hiding place.

"They'll never find us here!" I said as we went behind the rocks.

"Nope," Don said, taking out his camera, "they sure won't. Here, let me take your picture."

So I leaned against a rock and Don took a few pictures. Then he said, "Take your clothes off, and let me take a few more."

I was shocked. Mom and Dad had raised me to be modest. "I can't do that!" I protested. "If the other kids come and see me—"

"But Mike," he said, "you just told me they'll never find us here. Tell you what, while you get undressed, I'll keep an eye out and make sure nobody's coming."

"I can't do it," I said.

At that Don frowned and looked very disappointed. "I thought we were friends, Mike. I thought you trusted me."

Well, I didn't want to disappoint my friend. I didn't want him to think I didn't trust him. So I undressed, and I let Don take the pictures. After a few clicks of the shutter, I thought I heard voices approaching. I threw my clothes back on as fast as I could.

At that point I knew that what Don and I had done was wrong, but I didn't exactly know what we had done or why it was wrong. I didn't understand that Don had manipulated me into that position. I felt guilty, as if I was bad, as if I had done something dirty. I wondered how long that guilt would last.

I had no way of knowing it would haunt me for the rest of my life.

A few days later I once again rode in the front seat while Don dropped off other campers at their homes. Finally, it was just Don and me. As we drove, Don tried to carry on a conversation with me. I didn't feel like talking. I couldn't stop thinking about those pictures Don had taken of me. What if someone else saw those pictures?

We pulled up in front of my mother's house on Beverly Glen. I started to get out of the car, but Don said, "Wait here. I want to talk to your mom."

I froze. Talk to my mom? What about?

Don went up the walk, and Mom met him at the door. I strained to hear what he was saying to her. "Miss Wyman," he said, "if it's all right with you, I'd like to take Michael out tonight for dinner and a movie."

"Oh, Don, that would be great!" Mom said. She waved to me as I sat in the car. "Have a nice time, Michael!" she called.

I just sat there, my brain paralyzed.

Don got back in the car, and we started driving, but we didn't go to a restaurant or a movie theater. We went to Don's apartment. When I walked in, I was immediately struck by an impression that has stayed with me for years: The room was dimly lit by a faint green light. It was as if there was a green tint over everything.

I didn't know what it meant at the time, but now I know that Don had converted his apartment into a darkroom for developing and printing pornographic photographs. Most darkrooms use red safety lights to avoid fogging the film and papers, but some film emulsions are sensitive to red light, so you have to use green.

As I looked around, I saw that everything in the room had a green tinge. The furniture was green. Don's face was green. My own skin was green. I'll never forget the weird feeling I had in that place.

There were what I now know to be negatives hanging from a clothesline. Along one wall were three trays filled with liquid. There was an acid smell. Don led me over to the trays, and he took a piece of white paper with a pair of tongs and placed the paper in the first tray, then moved it to the second tray, then to the third tray. An image magically formed on the paper right before my eyes. It was a photo of the Santa Monica Mountains.

Don smiled at me and said, "Mike, would you like to try it?" I said, "Yeah!"

So Don put the tongs in my hand and put a paper in the tongs. Then he placed his hand over mine and guided it. As he leaned over, the stubble of his beard scratched my cheek. The paper went into the first tray, then the second, then the third. Again an image magically emerged before my eyes.

I stared at the picture. It was me. It was one of the nude pictures Don had taken when we were up in the mountains a few days earlier.

In that moment my life completely changed. I knew there was no recovery for me. That picture—and what Don was about to do to me—would affect all of my relationships for the rest of my life, especially my relationships with my family. From that point until I accepted Christ, he owned my soul.

As I stared at that picture, I literally shook with fear. Don put his hand on my shoulder, and what he said next filled me with panic. He said, "Wouldn't your mom like to have a copy of that picture?"

The trap slammed shut.

I knew my life was over. If God didn't hate me before, he would certainly hate me now. And so would Mom if she ever found out.

Until that moment I had thought that Don was my friend, even like a father to me. I had thought that he cared about me. But when I saw that picture and heard his implied threat of showing it to my mother, I felt violated. I felt raped.

I was shaking violently, and tears were rolling down my face. Don saw how afraid I was. So he did something to calm me down. He said, "Come here."

What he did next would haunt me for the rest of my life.

I can't tell you how I got home that night. I can't even tell you how I got out the front door of his apartment. I don't remember the rest of that year. At that point my memory just stops.

## BLAMING MYSELF

I was interviewed on a daytime talk show one time in the 1990s. After I told my story, a call came in from someone I had known years earlier at the day camp. He told his story on the air. He, too, had been molested by Don Havlik. Instead of keeping the secret, he told his father, and his father called the police. As a result, Don Havlik did jail time, but as soon as he was released, he moved out of state and ran another camp for kids!

As the caller told his story, I thought, *Boy, my life would have been a lot different if I could have communicated with my parents.* The difference between me and the caller was that he came from an intact family. I did not.

After Dan had me develop that picture, I couldn't stand living in my own skin. My self-esteem, which had been low before, hit rock bottom. I kept hearing Don's question in my ear: *Wouldn't your mom like to have a copy of that picture?* What if she ever saw that picture?

I couldn't let that happen. So I made a conscious decision to get away from Mom before she found out about those nude pictures. I loved my mother, and I wanted to protect her. But how? I needed to figure out a way to get Mom to kick me out of the house. I needed to find a way to get her so fed up with me that she would send me away—

But at the same time, I didn't want Mom to hate me. I wanted her to love me, but I didn't believe I was worthy of love. I thought I was bad, and those photos proved just how bad I was. But I didn't want her to know I was bad. I didn't want her to send me away because of those photos.

If all that sounds confusing, it's because it *was* confusing. I was a very confused and conflicted third grader, trying to take control of a situation that was completely beyond my control. I was all alone with this huge burden, and I had no one to talk to.

I blamed God and hated him for the fix I was in. I was sure he had sent Don Havlik into my life to molest me and shame me as a punishment for being born illegitimate. I told God, "I couldn't help the way I was born! Why are you doing this to me? What did I ever do to you?"

I blamed and hated myself for being born a bastard because that meant I was bad, and when you're bad, God lets bad things happen to you. In my mind, I figured that some people were just destined for heaven and others for hell. I just happened to be one of the ones destined for hell, and there wasn't a thing I could do about it.

I was angry with my birth mother for letting me be born illegitimate, for causing me all this pain, and for sending me away. I blamed her for the fact that I wasn't going to heaven.

I also blamed Mom for sending me to that day camp.

When I tell my story, people sometimes ask, "Why didn't you tell somebody? Why didn't you get help?" That's an adult question from an adult perspective, and even many adults who are in similar situations don't get help. After all, why do so many battered wives submit to humiliation and violence and even death before asking for help?

Part of the answer to that question is that I thought it was my fault that this had happened to me. Molesters always set it up so that their victims think that the molestation is their own fault. A common message that molesters tell their victims is, "You enticed me. You seduced me." They lay the blame on the victim, and the victim usually believes it.

If you believe it's your fault, you don't dare tell anyone. You don't dare tell your parents or someone else in authority because you are scared to death that they will condemn you and confirm your greatest fear.

John Geoghan, the notorious Boston priest who molested at least 150 children in half a dozen parishes, was typical of many molesters in that he continually turned the blame for his own crimes back onto the children and their families. "It was not the intention of these innocent youths to arouse me," he once told a psychiatrist. "They were just happy to have a father figure [since] their own father [was] so angry and distant from them."

Do you see how slick (and sick) that rationalization is? Sure, Geoghan calls the children "innocent," but in the very next breath, he says that *they* aroused *him*. He wasn't a predator—oh, no! He was a victim of these "innocent youths" who aroused him.

And who does Geoghan single out for blame? The parents! Geoghan said he was just trying to be a father to these kids whose own fathers were too angry and distant to be involved in the kids' lives! Molesters commonly portray themselves as innocent victims and the victims as the guilty ones, and they frequently get their victims to believe it too!

One thing that's hard for people to understand is that I really didn't know I was a victim. I felt that I was a guilty party to what happened because Don Havlik made sure I felt like a guilty party. I didn't learn until years later, until I was well into adulthood, that everything I had been feeling—my guilt, my self-hate, my anger, my fear—is common to nearly all sexually exploited children. I thought I was the bad person. I didn't understand that I was the wounded one.

## A GAME OF TRUTH-OR-DARE

Kids who have been molested can't even express what happened to them. They don't have the understanding or the vocabulary to put it into words. Big people think little seven-year-olds can just go to an adult and say, "Hi, Mom. Hi, Dad. I was molested." But kids don't know words like *molested* and *sexual abuse* and *child pornography.* They don't know how to explain to their parents that they have been raped.

When I was molested, I knew that what I did was wrong, but I didn't know why it was wrong or even what it was called. But I was scared to death that if anyone ever found out about it, I would be labeled. What would that label be? I didn't know. I had never heard the word *homosexual.* But I knew that the label, whatever it was, would mean I was bad. It would mean that I had been touched by a man. It would mean I'd be hated and condemned for the rest of my life.

As I look back and remember the guilt and fear I went through at that time, I realize that this experience I went through relates to something our society is going through today, more than fifty years later. I'm talking about the controversy over same-sex marriage. As I write these words, it unfortunately looks like our society is on the verge of accepting gay marriage. Let's look, for a moment, at what that means.

If same-sex marriage becomes accepted as having equal validity with traditional heterosexual marriage, what kinds of social pressure will our children and grandchildren have to face? The gay community will tell you that the reason they want to be accepted is that they are born gay. There is no evidence to support that claim, but let's accept it for the sake of discussion.

Now, if homosexual marriage becomes accepted as the moral and legal equivalent of traditional heterosexual marriage, then a time will come in the future when our children and grandchildren will no longer have to be born homosexual to engage in homosexual behavior. Because homosexuality and heterosexuality are equivalent, sexual practice will become a matter of choice not orientation. Guys can marry guys, girls can marry girls, or anyone can marry the opposite sex if they choose—these choices will all be on an equal footing.

There will come a time, not too far down the road—and the beginnings of this trend can already be seen—when the gay community will make young people feel guilty about stepping into marriage with the opposite sex until they have tried it with the same sex once. You've heard of the game of truth-or-dare. It's a popular party game among teenagers. The player must choose a challenge—to tell the truth (usually of a sexual or embarrassing nature) or accept a dare.

If our society goes down the road that I see ahead of us, then a lot of kids will be enticed into having a homosexual experience on a dare. They will be told, "How can you know if you're straight or gay if you never tried gay sex?" And why shouldn't they try gay sex? There is no stigma to it. Gay sex and gay marriage are the exact equivalent of straight sex and straight marriage. There will only be one response that carries a stigma, and that is the response called "homophobia." If kids don't at least try a homosexual experience once, they'll be labeled "homophobic."

What happens to your kids or grandkids after they try a homosexual experience on a dare? They will experience guilt and pain in the aftermath, just as I did. The second they have had a sexual relationship with the same sex, in their own minds and in the view of society, they will be labeled homosexual. They'll never rid themselves of it. They will live with the guilt and the pain that I have lived with all my life.

That's why today I can honestly say on my show, "I admit it; I am homophobic. If I wasn't homophobic before, I am today. I have a great fear of a homosexual community teaching my grandchildren that it's OK to be gay even if you don't think you're born that way."

## THE GREEN FEAR

Soon after the incident in Don's darkroom, I became obsessed with proving to myself that I was heterosexual. I didn't know the words *homosexual* and *heterosexual,* but I knew that it wasn't normal for males to touch other males in a sexual way.

It is common for boys, after they have been molested by a man, to become preoccupied with questions about their sexual orientation. In my case, that meant that I became obsessed with having a girlfriend. I went over to the next street, where Connie Frieberg lived. Her backyard adjoined our backyard. I knew Connie had a crush on me, so I figured she could help me prove to myself and everyone around that I was a healthy eight-year-old who liked girls.

Connie and I would go in her bedroom by ourselves, or we'd go sit in her front yard, with all the neighborhood kids gathered around, and we would kiss. No passionate, slurpy kissing or French kissing—we weren't sophisticated enough for that. We would just sit across from each other and press our mouths together and hold our breaths until one of us would almost pass out. It was more of an endurance test than a kiss, but I liked it, which was reassuring. The neighborhood kids thought they were watching some sort of theatrical performance—and in a way, I suppose it was. I was playing a role, desperately trying to keep anyone from finding out my secret.

The reassurance I got from Connie Frieberg would last an hour or two, and then I would start to remember the horrible things Don and I had done, and the doubts and confusion would creep in again. So the harmful emotional effects of the molestation set in immediately—and many of those effects have stayed with me throughout my life.

One of those effects was my hatred of the color green.

Don Havlik took me into his apartment, and everything in the apartment had a green tint to it. So for years afterward

I equated green with trouble. I'd see green, and I'd think, *Oh, that's bad, that's dangerous.* Green brought back the terror I felt when I first saw that nude photograph of me. Like everything else in the room, it had a green tint to it.

When I was growing up, my parents and sister noticed that I didn't like green, but they didn't know why. I never told them. When I bought tennis shoes, I'd always check the soles. Blue rubber was fine, but I refused to wear tennis shoes with green soles. When I was racing boats in the 1960s, I refused to race a boat with so much as a speck of green paint on it. People thought it was just a superstition. There's an old tradition among race-car drivers that green is a bad-luck color. But for me it was primarily the fact that green meant danger and trouble. If I was racing at a hundred-plus miles an hour, I didn't want that color anywhere near me.

Ever since I purged the secret of the molestation in my first book, *On the Outside Looking In,* green has been my favorite color. I absolutely love green! But to get to that point, I had to get this secret out of my system.

I suffered so much harm from that molestation. The shame, guilt, and fear that were inflicted on me by the molester dominated my emotions, poisoned my relationship with God, and distorted my family relationships for decades. I went through a hell that I wouldn't wish on anyone else, not even an enemy.

The reason I am writing about it today is that I want to keep as many kids as possible from going where I've been. If I can help even a few young people to avoid that trap, then the horrors I went through will have served their purpose.

Let me tell you something that scares me to death: According to the United States Department of Justice, there are *four million child molesters* living in the United States. Studies indicate that roughly 57 percent of child molesters were molested themselves as children. That means that when molesters abuse children, they are producing a whole new generation of child molesters.

Here's how it works: When children are sexually abused at a young age and over a period of time, abuse seems like the norm to them. They don't know that this is not the way to treat children because it's all they've ever known. So they grow up and repeat the cycle, becoming abusers themselves.

It's like when I wanted to send Cameron to boarding school. I had grown up in boarding school, and even though I was miserable there, I simply assumed that kids belong in boarding school because it's virtually all I ever knew.

Somehow, we have to break that cycle. We have to get kids off of that merry-go-round so that victims of sexual abuse do not become perpetrators of sexual abuse. That's why the rest of this chapter is devoted to preventative and healing solutions to the crisis of child sex abuse.

## WHAT YOU CAN DO

Was it Mom's fault that I was abused? Absolutely not.

I first told her about the molestation in 1987, when I was working on my autobiography, *On the Outside Looking In.* That was thirty-five years after the molestation took place. She was terribly hurt when I told her, and she blamed herself.

"Michael," she said, "if only I hadn't sent you to that day camp, this never would have happened."

But how could she have known? Mom thought she had put me in a safe place. She couldn't teach me how to throw a baseball or a football, so she trusted someone who could. Don Havlik seemed like a safe and caring man, the kind of guy you would trust on sight. Almost nothing appeared in the media about child molestation in those days, so people didn't give a lot of thought to such risks. Mom missed the warning signs because she didn't know the warning signs.

A lot of American parents today are in the same place my mother was in the 1950s. I look around at middle-class America, and I see a lot of parallels to Hollywood in the 1950s. What we call "middle class" today is actually an extremely abundant and affluent lifestyle. Like Hollywood in my childhood years, middle-class America is characterized by parents who are too busy, moms in the workplace, divorced families, and kids in day care.

We tend to assume our kids are safe when they are being cared for by "nice" people. But Don Havlik was nice. He was charming and personable and incredibly evil. Molesters look like normal people, nice people. That's how they get their hands on our kids—by winning our trust.

If we put other grown-ups in charge of our kids for long periods of time, we need to be involved; we need to make "surprise inspections." We need to talk to our kids and make sure they know what to do if anyone touches them inappropriately. We *want* our kids to be involved in worthwhile programs like

Boy Scouts, Girl Scouts, YMCA, summer camps, and more. Those are all great programs, but there are risks. As Dad used to say about the Soviet Union, "Trust but verify."

Let's be clear, first of all, what kind of behavior we are talking about when we use terms like *sexual abuse* and *molestation. Child sexual abuse* may be defined as "the sexual exploitation of a child or the exposure of a child to sexual information or stimulation that is inappropriate for that child's age, level of development, or role in the family." Sexual abuse may consist of one act or many. Sexual abuse can take place even if both the offender and the child are fully dressed. Victims may range in age from infants to teenagers.

Examples of abusive acts include intercourse, oral-genital contact, fondling of private places, indecent exposure, sexual propositions or enticements, incest, forcible rape, exposing a child to pornography, taking pictures of the child for child pornography, and child prostitution. By its very nature, sex abuse is a crime that brings embarrassment and shame to victims and their families, and that makes it hard for kids to come forward and report that they were abused.

Sexual abuse is much more rampant in our society than we would like to think. Because crimes of this kind are vastly underreported, there are no reliable statistics. But some authorities have estimated that one-third of all girls and one-fifth of all boys will be sexually molested during their lifetime. There are no cultural, ethnic, or socioeconomic barriers to abuse. If a rich kid from Beverly Hills was vulnerable, then every kid in our society is at risk—including your kids.

What can you do to protect your own children and the children around you from going through what I and so many other kids have suffered? The following are some specific, effective actions you can take.

## STEPS TO PREVENTION

1. *Be aware.* Know where your children are and who they are with at all times. Don't take anything for granted, even if you think you know the person your child is with. Most victims of sex abuse are molested by someone you and your child know and trust. Abusers usually take their time, building trust and learning the child's vulnerabilities, before they initiate sexual contact. The abusive behavior is usually called a "game" by the molester. Sometimes the child is told that it's a form of teaching about the body. In virtually every case, the child is told, "It's our secret. Don't tell anyone."

2. *Be watchful.* Look out for adults or teenagers who pay an unusual amount of attention to your child, spend large amounts of time with your child, or give gifts to your child. Such people are not necessarily molesters, but don't be complacent. Be careful and be on guard at all times.

3. *Check everyone.* Make sure you know all that can be known about anyone who spends time with your children, including babysitters, neighbors, relatives, youth leaders, teachers, and coaches.

4. *Talk to your children.* Make sure your children know how to recognize inappropriate touching if it happens to them, and make sure they know what to do. Discuss these

matters calmly but frankly. Don't beat around the bush. Reinforce and repeat the discussion at least a couple of times a year because kids forget over time. Also, the way you explain it to kids will change as they mature.

5. *Teach your children to be careful on the Internet.* I once invited officers from the sex crimes unit of the LAPD to come on my radio show and talk about the threat from child molesters on the Internet. While one officer was on the air with me, discussing the problem of pedophiles on the Internet, a second officer set up a laptop computer and logged into the Internet. He went into a chat room and posed as a twelve-year-old girl. Do you know how long it took him to make contact with a pedophile? Three minutes! That's right. In just three minutes, the officer had made contact with a guy who was flirting with the "girl" and asking for "her" picture, and trying to set up a place for them to meet. Don't assume for a moment that your kids are safe on the Internet. Make them aware of the dangers.

## WHAT TO TELL YOUR CHILDREN

Here are some messages you should repeat to your kids on a continual basis:

1. *"Respect your own body."* Tell kids that some parts of the body are private, and should not be seen or touched by anyone (except, of course, for medical reasons).

2. *"Respect the bodies of other people."* Tell them it is wrong and harmful to touch other people's private places.

3. *"Don't take your clothes off in front of other people."* Kids should be told it's wrong to take their clothes off for

other people unless the parent is there and it is for reasons of a medical exam (or, with very small children, bathing or changing clothes).

4. *"Never keep secrets from mommy and daddy."* Tell them that if anyone wants them to keep a secret from mommy and daddy, that person may be doing a bad thing. Tell them you need to know right away. Molesters almost always swear the child to secrecy.

5. *"If someone wants you to do something that seems wrong, don't do it."* Tell them to tell you right way. Encourage kids to listen to their feelings. The molester will say it's all right, it's good, but something within the child knows better. Tell your children to listen to that warning voice inside.

6. *"If a stranger asks you for help, get away from that stranger!"* Teach your kids that some adults try to trick children by asking them for help. These adults may smile and seem nice, but *stay away* from them. Teach your kids to stay far out of reach of anyone who asks them for help. Teach them not to approach an adult who pulls up at the curb in a car and calls out to them. If a stranger says, "I lost my puppy" or "I need directions," the child should run away and get help from mom or dad.

7. *"Be careful around strangers but not just strangers."* Eighty percent of molestation victims are abused by someone they know and frequently by the last person you would suspect—a relative, a neighbor, a priest, a day camp counselor, even good old Uncle Charlie. Make sure your children know that people who do bad things often seem like nice people. Tell

them, "Just because someone smiles and gives you a present doesn't mean that person is nice inside. He or she could be acting nice in order to get you to do something you shouldn't do."

8. *"You don't need to be afraid."* Give kids a message of reassurance: Most grown-ups are good people who want to help children and protect them. We only tell kids these things to make sure they'll be safe. It's a lot like a fire drill: you'll probably never need to escape from a fire in real life, but it's good to know how to be safe if it ever happens to you.

9. *"It's OK to say no when adults tell you to do something that is wrong."* We all want our kids to respect adults, but even more we want them to respect themselves and their own bodies. We want them to do what's right—even if it means saying no to an adult (including Uncle Charlie).

10. *Play "What if—?" with your kids.* Help them practice what you have taught them. Ask, "What if a grown-up you know tickled you a lot and you didn't like it. What would you do?" Or, "What if a grown-up offers you money or presents if you'll take your clothes off?" Or, "What if a stranger comes by our front yard and says, 'Will you come with me and help me find my puppy?'" Come up with various scenarios that fit situations your children might actually face. Use your imagination. Let your kids practice giving one simple answer, "I can't talk to strangers," then getting away *fast*.

11. *"Some grown-ups may try to trick you by saying that mommy or daddy got hurt."* People sometimes lie to kids in order to get them to go along with them. Tell your kids not to go anywhere with that person unless he or she knows the

secret code word. Choose a family code word that kids can remember. Make sure they know it's an absolute secret and that if you ever send a grown-up to pick up your kids for any reason, you will give that person the code word. Say, "If the grown-up doesn't know the code word, don't go with that grown-up. Instead, run and find a grown-up you can trust."

12. *"If someone tries to force you to go with them, run, scream, and yell."* The best thing a child can yell in order to attract attention is "Fire!" Kids often yell "help" when they play, and adults ignore playful-sounding screams. But people usually come to investigate when they hear shouts of "Fire!" A child's screams will often be enough to scare off an abductor. Tell children that they should run from people who try to grab them, but they should not hide. Instead of hiding, they should find a place where there are lots of people, and they should ask grown-ups to help them.

13. *If you have teenagers, tell them to be on guard against people who use authority and power to get sex.* This includes clergy, high school teachers and coaches, college professors, and employers.

14. *Warn kids to beware of grown-ups who promise them glamorous jobs, such as acting or modeling.* Some molesters use such promises as a lure to get kids to pose for photographs. The first few photos will be innocent enough. Then comes a casual statement like, "And we'll need a few shots with your clothes off, of course." The seduction is always gradual. Make sure you are always present when your child is with someone who is supposedly helping your child's "career."

## Information your child should know

Your child should know:

1. His or her full name, address, and phone number.

2. The family emergency code word.

3. How to make an emergency call: "Dial 911." (Don't say "nine-eleven." In panic situations kids have sometimes been unable to dial the emergency number because they were looking for a button with the number eleven on it.)

4. How to make a collect call if they are away from home.

5. How to answer the phone properly. (A child should know never to indicate to a caller if he or she is home alone.)

6. The parents' full names and places of employment.

7. Names of relatives and how to contact them.

## Signs that your child may have been abused

Your child may have been abused if one or more of the following signs are present:

1. *Evidence that a child is focused on sex.* For example, the child seems to have sexual knowledge beyond her age and developmental levels; the child exhibits sexualized behavior; the child tells stories of a sexual nature; the child acts out sexual behavior, such as fondling himself or herself.

2. *The child has money or possessions and you don't know where they came from.* Find out where your child got them because they could be gifts from a molester.

3. *The child seems withdrawn, destructive, angry, guilty, ashamed, or fearful.*

4. *Infantile (inappropriately babyish) behavior.*

5. *The child becomes rebellious and attempts to run away from home.*

6. *The child seems obsessed with protecting siblings, especially from one particular individual (who might be the molester).*

7. *The child has a sudden change in eating habits.* Some victims of molestation lose their appetite; others increase their consumption to fill a hole in their souls created by the guilt, shame, fear, or anxiety of the molestation.

8. *The child has physical symptoms that could be associated with a molestation.* These could include: pain, itching, or bleeding in the genital or anal areas; difficulty or discomfort when sitting or walking; torn, stained, or bloody clothing or underclothing; bed-wetting; bruises or bleeding, especially in the genital or anal areas; venereal disease or pregnancy.

9. *The child avoids a certain person or certain people.* The person the child avoids may be the molester. Ask yourself, "Why is my child so nervous around good old Uncle Charlie?"

10. *The school-age child does not want to change and shower in the gym or doesn't want to participate in physical education class.*

11. *The child exhibits sexualized or seductive behavior around peers and adults.*

12. *The child has chronic depression.*

13. *The child experiences excessive bed-wetting.*

14. *The child talks about or attempts suicide.*

## HOW TO RESPOND IF YOU SUSPECT ABUSE

Here's what you should do if you suspect your child has been sexually abused:

1. *Don't panic.* Don't act shocked; don't express anger. Your first response is critical to how the child will heal from the experience. Make sure your child feels believed, supported, loved, and protected.

2. *Reassure your child that he or she did the right thing in telling you.*

3. *Reassure your child that he or she is not bad.* Say, "What this person did to you was bad. This person knew better; you didn't know. We'll make sure that this person can't do that to you again."

4. *Focus on your child's emotional needs, not your own embarrassment.* Once you begin to wonder, *What kind of parent will people think I am?* you are already on the wrong side of the issue. Get back on your child's side and don't worry about what anyone thinks. The only thing that matters is what your child feels and needs right now.

5. *Encourage the child to talk about what happened in his or her own words.* Avoid a lot of questions or pressure. Make sure the child doesn't feel interrogated.

6. *Don't confront, accuse, or threaten the offender in front of the child.* Keep adult issues away from the child. Kids should be made to feel, as much as possible, that everything is

going to turn out OK. They don't need to be made to feel more upset, disturbed, and scared right now.

7. *Be aware that children may not have adequate vocabulary to explain what happened.* Be patient and allow the child to describe the incident in his or her own way.

8. *Believe your child.* Even if your child accuses someone you have always trusted, someone you can't imagine as a molester, tell your child, "I believe you." It takes a lot of courage for a child to speak up because kids are afraid they won't be believed, especially if it's their word against an adult's. Kids need to hear that you are on their side, that you will take their word over that of the molester. It is extremely unlikely that children could imagine sex acts unless they have experienced them. Your child will be more likely to tell you the truth if he or she feels supported by you.

9. *Report the molestation to the authorities.* Call the police. Law enforcement agencies in your area have trained investigators who will talk with you and your child and who know exactly how to handle the situation to protect your child and prevent the molester from hurting other children. Don't call Child Protective Services; investigating crimes is not the function of CPS.

But what if the molester is a member of the family? What if it's good old Uncle Charlie? Call the police! I don't ever want to hear you say, "But we can't have Uncle Charlie arrested! We can't have Uncle Clarlie put in jail!" If you say that to me, I'm going to reach right out of this book, grab you with both hands, and shake you till your teeth rattle! If Uncle

Charlie is molesting your kids, then turn him in and *protect your kids!*

Again and again I have heard horror stories of parents who protected good old Uncle Charlie (or granddad or stepdad or some other predatory, sexually abusing adult) instead of protecting the innocence of their own children! This is an issue where you should have absolute moral clarity: *Molesters belong in jail.* If you don't call the police when you find out that Uncle Charlie is a molester, then you are forcing your children to carry the burden of Uncle Charlie's crimes. If you do that, you are an accomplice and no better than a molester yourself.

After you call the police, you can also call the ChildHelp National Child Abuse Hotline at 1-800-4ACHILD (1-800-422-4453). The ChildHelp counselor will listen to your concerns, answer your questions, and direct you to local support services.

10. *If the suspected molester is a member of the clergy, do not report the abuse to church authorities.* Call the police immediately. Unfortunately, some churches worry more about lawsuits and bad publicity than the emotional and spiritual needs of abused children. Go to the police first so that crucial evidence is preserved and the molester is prevented from hurting other children.

If you or someone close to you has ever been sexually abused by a member of the clergy (whether it took place yesterday or fifty years ago), contact SNAP, the Survivors Network of those Abused by Priests. SNAP was founded in 1989 and has helped thousands of survivors. SNAP is the nation's oldest and largest support organization for men, women, and children who have been abused by religious authority figures, regardless of denomination (priests, ministers, bishops, deacons, nuns, youth workers, and others). For information on how to contact SNAP, see the organization's Web site at http://www.snapnetwork.org/.

Every child is at risk. Don't assume your child knows how to respond when a dangerous situation presents itself. These predators can be amazingly charming and persuasive. Even if your child has been abused, you can limit the damage and begin the healing process—

If you act now.

## WHEN DO YOU GET OVER IT?

People sometimes ask me how long it took for me to get over being molested. My reply: I have never gotten over it. Some effects of the molestation continue to this day. By the grace of God, I have a *great* life today; but that scared, hurt little boy is still there inside me. I can tap into those memories and feelings at any time. The moment I do, I'm seven years old all over again. Let me give you an example:

A few years ago I became acquainted with Deputy District Attorney William Hodgman, head of the Sex Crimes Unit for LA County. I first met Bill Hodgman over lunch at an Italian restaurant in Sherman Oaks. We met to talk about a case that was making headlines in the *Los Angeles Times,* the story of a Jesuit priest in California who had molested numerous children, including members of his own family.

During this period of time, I was talking to Bill Hodgman about the possibility of filing charges against Don Havlik— not so much because I thought he needed to be brought to justice for what he had done to me as a child, not because I wanted him to suffer for what he did in my life. Rather, I wanted to be a lightning rod to other victims who may have been wondering and agonizing over whether they should file charges against their molester. Victims know that if they come out publicly and there is no one there to support them, their life is over.

I wanted victims to know that if Michael Reagan could come forward, they could come forward too. Only one question held me back: *Would this hurt my mother? Mom doesn't need to feel any blame for what happened to me because she was not to blame.* However, I did call the sex crimes unit in the city where he lives, and they told me that he was already on their watch list.

In the course of my conversation with Bill Hodgman, he asked me to come speak to his attorneys at the Sex Crimes Unit about the long-term effects of child molestation. So I went to the LA County Courthouse and went into a mock courtroom, a place used to help prepare children for giving testimony in open court. Bill Hodgman's attorneys were seated in the courtroom, and I stood before them and told them the story of what Don Havlik did to me. Bill wanted the people who prosecuted sex crimes to understand what those crimes were all about, including the lasting scars those crimes leave on a human psyche.

I told my story and I answered questions. Later Bill said that as I was telling my story, I seemed to *become* that little boy again. It was as if I was back in 1953, inside that dimly lit apartment, describing exactly what I was seeing and feeling from moment to moment. When I talked about how the molester made me develop that picture, it was as if it was all happening to me in the present tense.

I said, "Bill, when I start talking about it, I'm there. Remembering it takes me back. I can close my eyes and see that green tint over everything. I can feel the fear and the guilt it put inside me. It's like no time at all has passed."

So when do you get over it? It's been more than half a century since I was molested, and I'm still not completely over it. And that's OK because God is using that experience in my life to help and heal other people.

In November 2003, I got up before my church and told my story. That night, twelve people accepted Christ. Afterward, a man came up to me and said, "God has given me the gift of healing. I saw the hurt inside you as you were talking about being molested, and I want you to know that God can heal you of that hurt. If I pray for you, God will heal you."

I said, "I appreciate that, but I believe God has already healed me. I think God wants other people to see how serious the crime of sexual molestation is. I think God wants people to see that these effects last a lifetime. When I get up in front of audiences and tell my story, and people can see how much the abuse still hurts me after all this time, then they can see how serious an issue this is. I think the pain inside me is God's gift to me so that my pain can help other people."

One night when I was doing my radio show, I talked about the molestation incident. I said, "People sometimes tell me that I shouldn't be affected by it anymore. They say, 'It's been fifty years! Get over it!' But when you keep it a secret, you have no way of dealing with it and no one to talk to about it. You can compartmentalize it, but you can't make it go away. It haunts you. It affects your relationships. It affects the way you treat your parents, your wife, your kids. It affects your ability to trust people. It affects every part of your being.

"For a while, everything will be just fine, but the moment something bad happens, those old feelings will come right back. The molestation will once again become your excuse to fail in life."

Well, right after I said that, I took a call from a man who, from the sound of his voice, was probably in his fifties or sixties. "The same thing that happened to you," he said, "happened to me. I was molested when I was a boy, and I never told anyone. Tonight I'm sitting in this chair, and all I have is my dog." At that point he started to cry.

"I lost my wife," he said, sobbing. "I lost my kids. I lost everyone I ever cared about. You're right, Michael. When you've been molested, it affects your whole life. I never told anyone about it before, and I was never able to let it go. I kept it a secret, and I let it destroy my whole life. But when you told your story tonight, you gave me the courage to pick up the phone and tell you what happened to me. I was never able to tell anyone else, but I knew you would understand."

I do understand. Believe me, I do. And I pray that this man will continue to unlock his secret and find God's healing and peace.

What about your kids? And what about you? What are the secrets that need to be unlocked in your life or in your family so that the healing can begin?

I waited thirty-five years to tell anyone that I had been molested, and it was thirty-five years of living hell. Don't wait for years or decades to begin the healing process. Don't wait another day.

Let the healing begin right now.

# 5

# SLAYERS OF THE SOUL

A bout a year after Don Havlik took those photos, Mom
decided to convert to Roman Catholicism. She was
attracted to the Catholic faith largely because of the influence
of her best friend, actress Loretta Young. Mom hoped that if
she became a serious Catholic, God would bless her marriage
to Fred Karger.

My sister Maureen also wanted to convert, and I decided
to get baptized with Mom and Merm in order to make my
mother happy. I hadn't forgotten what Deuteronomy said.
I hadn't forgotten that, according to my interpretation, an illegitimate child like me could never enter heaven. But I was
playing a role. I felt I could pretend to be a good little Catholic
if it would please Mom.

On December 8, 1954, the day of the Feast of the
Immaculate Conception, Mom, Maureen, and I were all
baptized together. After that, we went to Mass every
Sunday together. I crossed myself and prayed. I studied the

catechism—all of which made Mom very happy. I loved her so much that I wanted her to be happy.

Sometimes the parish priest, in his homily, would mention God's judgment against various sins, including the sin of males having sex with other males, and I would squirm and feel condemned. In my own mind I was already condemned by God. I thought that the priest was telling me I was condemned because I was molested. The church only reinforced my worst fears. I thought, *Oh, thanks a lot, God! That too, huh? Sure, why not? Just pile on the judgment, God! What else are you gonna throw at me?*

Throughout this time the molestation dominated my emotions and distorted my relationship with Mom. I continued to play the blame game. As my rage and bitterness grew, I threw tantrums, yelled, and berated my mother. We would get into horrible shouting matches, and she didn't have a clue what I was angry about!

Mom didn't know that I was trying to break up my relationship with her, that I was trying to get her to send me away so that she would never find out about those pictures. I was determined to get her to send me away for something I could control—angry, obnoxious behavior—not for the pictures or the molestation. It was my disturbed way of taking control of my life.

Thirty-five years later, when my first book, *On the Outside Looking In,* was published, Mom read my book and then she said to me, "Now I know why you were so angry." In all those years she had never understood why I was the way I was.

## IN THE CLUTCHES OF THE SISTERS OF MERCY

When I entered the fourth grade, Mom sent me to Good Shepherd School, a Catholic school in Beverly Hills. Mom hoped that the nuns would straighten me out and deal with my anger and rebelliousness. She wanted me to become a good little Catholic, which I really tried to do. But I also knew that God wasn't going to let me anywhere near his heaven, no matter how good a Catholic I pretended to be.

I loved my mother, and I wanted her to love me; yet at the same time, I also was battling her and trying to get her to send me away. I was angry with myself for the way I treated her, but I couldn't tell her why I was treating her that way. So out of love for her and to make up for my hurtful behavior, I went to church, I knelt at the rail, and I took the wafer.

During my fifth-grade year, while I was at Good Shepherd, Mom debuted in her own dramatic TV series on NBC, *The Jane Wyman Theater*. Suddenly she was working even longer hours than she had worked in theatrical films. She was happy with the series because it was a well-produced, well-written show (the writers included Ray Bradbury and Rod Serling), and it was a big hit with the audiences.

Because Mom was so busy with her TV series, she felt she needed to make yet another change in her children's schooling. She enrolled Maureen at Marymount Girls' School, a Catholic school in West Los Angeles. She placed me in a Catholic boys' school in downtown LA, St. John's Military Academy—or, as I came to call it, St. John's Miniature Alcatraz.

When Mom told me I was switching to St. John's, I naturally assumed it would be a day school like my last school. It never occurred to me that she was sending me to a boarding school.

On the Sunday night after New Year's, Mom took me out to the Brown Derby, where we had a nice dinner. I had my usual avocado cocktail with Thousand Island dressing. Then Mom took me to St. John's Military Academy at Tenth and Washington in LA. Classes started the next morning, and I thought we were going to sign some papers. Well, she signed me in, all right. Then she turned to me and said, "Well, Michael, I'll see you on Saturday." That was the first I knew that I was back in boarding school.

Mom and I had been having a lot of fights at home, and this was how she dealt with it—by leaving me in the clutches of the Sisters of Mercy (who had none!). All of my fighting and arguing with Mom had, of course, been part of my deliberate strategy. I was trying to get sent away so that Mom wouldn't find out about the pictures. But getting sent away to boarding school wasn't part of my plan!

I bawled like a baby as Mom drove away and I was led to my dormitory. I didn't want to be separated from her again. As painful as it was for me then, I know now that I really needed the discipline and structure that St. John's provided. (By the way, my classmates included two of Bob Hope's sons, Tony and Kelly, and the son of singer Billy Daniels, famed for singing "That Old Black Magic.")

The thing I hated most about St. John's was that it was an all-boys school. I was already in a state of confusion about my sexuality. It wasn't that I felt attracted to guys. No, what scared me was the question, "Is there something about me that attracts guys to me?" I wondered if there was something about me that marked me, that would make me a target for more guys like Don Havlik.

So, with those kinds of thoughts already going through my mind, living in an all-boys school turned my state of confusion into a state of full-blown panic. Living in Dormitory C with a lot of other boys made me obsessively modest. I avoided taking showers with the other boys. I learned to take a complete shower in sixty seconds or less because I didn't want any of the other boys to come in and see me with my clothes off.

Because St. John's was academically more advanced than my previous school, Good Shepherd, I had to repeat the fifth grade. One of my teachers was Sister Mary Cyprian, who was like a Marine drill sergeant in a nun's habit. She had injured her arm before the start of the school year, so on her forearm she wore a hard leather cast, reinforced with a metal bar.

The classrooms had no air-conditioning, so on hot, muggy, slumber-inducing days, I sometimes found myself jolted awake by a whack between the shoulder blades by Sister Mary Cyprian's steel-and-leather cast. We also wore neckties as part of our school uniform, and the nuns would yank on those neckties whenever they needed to get our undivided attention. As I look back, I'm grateful to this day for those hard-nosed Sisters of Mercy and the order and discipline they imposed on my unruly personality. Thank you, Sister Mary Cyprian.

I can tell you this right now: I will never be elected president. Why? Because if I were, the first thing I would do is sign an executive order requiring a nun in every classroom of every school in America. I would order that each nun carry a paddle in one hand to administer corporal punishment. And I would order that each nun carry a blackboard eraser in the other hand—because there isn't a nun in the country who couldn't hit a kid with an eraser at forty paces. I speak from personal experience.

Sister Mary Cyprian had between thirty and forty boys in that class. We all knew who was in charge in that classroom, and it wasn't us. Even though I acted up and was the class clown, I paid the price every time. Within that class were some ten to fifteen boys, me included, who had what would today be classified as attention deficit disorder, but it only took Sister Mary Cyprian about three weeks to knock it out of us. And she did it without Ritalin.

So if I were president, I would begin by putting discipline back into the schools. I am convinced that the number one education problem in America today is not a lack of money but a lack of discipline. I don't expect to be inaugurated any time soon.

## THE ALTAR BOY

The emotional residue of the molestation and the stress of living in an all-boys school kept me in a state of continual anxiety. I had horrible dreams at night, and I became a chronic bed-wetter. I awoke almost every morning in a wet bed. The other kids teased me cruelly for it, but I soon found a solution: I became an altar boy.

As an altar boy, I had to serve Mass at six in the morning. That meant I had to rise at five, before any of the other boys were awake. Every morning, I got up, stripped the wet sheets off my bed, and put clean sheets on my bed. Then I headed for the showers. At that time of the morning, I had the showers all to myself—another advantage of rising early. Then I took off to serve Mass.

Mom came to see me serve my first Mass, and I have never seen her more proud than she was that day. The boy who was supposed to serve that morning was sick, so I got to serve High Mass my very first time. Talk about nervous! Wow! I was so happy Mom was there, and it gave me a warm feeling to see the joy and motherly pride shining in her eyes. I knew I had made the right decision in becoming an altar boy. As I saw it, being an altar boy was one more way of covering up how bad I was inside.

One of the worst things about St. John's was that it severely limited the time I could spend with Dad. Boarders like myself weren't allowed off campus until 4:30 Saturday afternoon and had to be back by 7:00 o'clock on Sunday night. Dad and Nancy had given me my own horse to ride at the ranch (I named him Rebel). The restricted weekend hours meant I could only visit Dad (and ride my horse) during holidays, long weekends, and before or after my eight-to-ten-week stretch at summer camp. At a time when I really needed my Dad, I felt almost completely deprived of him. And I blamed my mom.

I was so miserable at St. John's that, one Sunday afternoon, I hid from my Mom so that she couldn't take me
back to school. She was all ready to drive me back, but she
couldn't find me. She searched and called all over the house,
all over the yard, but I wouldn't answer.

You know where I was? On the roof. I was sitting on top
of the house, listening to my mother call my name. Even
though Mom and I battled continually when I was home,
I preferred living in a conflict-ridden home with Mom to living in a boys-only concentration camp guarded by nuns.

When Mom finally figured out where I was, she called to
me and pleaded with me to come down. No way—I wasn't
going back to that school. Finally, Carrie our cook—truly the
only person I trusted at that time—talked me into coming
down. I grimly climbed down from the roof and trudged to
the car, and Mom whisked me back to St. John's Miniature
Alcatraz.

## DASHED HOPES

You never outgrow the effects of sexual molestation. Time
doesn't heal all wounds; in fact, the wound of molestation
tends to fester and grow worse with time, not better. Left
untreated, the wounds of sexual molestation can destroy a
human life.

Bill Hodgman told me about a case he encountered in his
duties as head of the Sex Crimes Unit for the LA County DA's
office. "There was one incident," he said, "that really demonstrates the lifelong trauma that child sexual assault victims

suffer. This took place early in the investigation of the Archdiocese of Los Angeles—an investigation that at one point involved allegations against more than a hundred suspects, mostly priests.

"One of the woman detectives assigned to the Catholic clergy sex abuse cases was interviewing a victim who had come forward with allegations against a certain priest—call him Father X. The detective asked this victim if he knew of anyone else who had been molested by this priest.

"The victim said, 'There was this one guy. I don't know if he was molested, but he sure spent a lot of time with Father X.' And the victim gave the detective a name.

"The detective was very diligent in tracking the individual down. It wasn't easy, and she was surprised when she finally located this man. He was an inmate at Chino State Prison, east of LA. She went out to the prison and made arrangements to interview the inmate. She was ushered into the prison visiting room and sat down on the visitors' side of the glass barrier.

"After a few minutes, the inmate came in and sat down on the other side of the barrier. He had long hair, a bushy mustache, bulging muscles from lifting weights, and plenty of tattoos. He looked like a Hell's Angel—as tough a customer as this detective had ever met.

"The inmate looked at the detective with suspicion. He had no idea why she wanted to talk to him, and he clearly did not like detectives. He said, 'Why the @#$% should I talk to you?'

"'I'm here to talk to you about Father X,' she said.

"Instantly, the inmate fell on the floor, as if he had been felled by an arrow. He just sobbed like a baby. Here's this tough Hell's Angels type guy, and all it takes to mentally put him right back in the clutches of his molester is hearing the name of Father X.

"The interview resumed after the guy composed himself. He told the detective a story about the downward spiral of his life after being molested by this priest. As a boy, this guy had been a good student, a bright kid with a future; but after the molestation, he slipped into delinquency, petty crime, and finally serious crime. This priest took his whole future away from him. I think it's fair to say that this priest condemned a once-promising child to prison.

"With clergy sex abuse, we see this phenomenon over and over again. Many victims of abuse grow up to have problems with alcoholism, drug abuse, failed relationships, and self-destructive behavior. Some commit crimes. Some commit suicide. Many have sought therapy. A lot that haven't sought therapy really need it. These people grow up with an inability to trust anyone or anything. They lose faith in people, institutions, government, the police, and particularly God and the church."

Let me interject here that one of the reasons molestation victims tend to have problems with alcohol, drugs, and other self-destructive behavior is that we (the victims) would rather have you (our family and society) think of us as drunks and addicts than as molestation victims. To us, being a drunk or an addict is nowhere near as awful as the thing we are living with inside. So we hide behind a bottle of gin or a line of coke or a syringe of heroin to keep you from finding out what we went through, so that you won't discover our *real* secret and uncover our shame.

Bill Hodgman continues: "In clergy sex abuse cases—in any molestation case, in fact—when the child sex abuse victim grows to become an adult, he or she still bears the scars of what happened in childhood. Some victims are more successful than others in processing and releasing the hurt of the molestation.

"But as a general observation based on my own experience as a prosecutor, victims of sexual molestation are wounded in one way or another forever. The memories may be repressed, jammed into a little box, and tucked into the recesses of the mind, but those memories never go away. The victim may be more or less successful in achieving a happy life, but the memory is always there."

I asked Bill Hodgman, "Isn't it hard dealing with molestation cases every day, week after week, year after year?"

"Yes," he said, "living with it is hard. You have to deal with heartbreaking stories all the time. But there's a lot of satisfaction in helping to get justice for these victims."

But along with the satisfaction, there are frustrations. One of the toughest frustrations Bill has had to deal with was a U.S. Supreme Court decision in the case of *Stogner v. California*—a narrow five–four decision that caused convictions to be overturned or charges to be dropped involving more than eight hundred molesters throughout California. (The four dissenters to the decision were Justices Anthony Kennedy, Antonin Scalia, Clarence Thomas, and Chief Justice William H. Rehnquist.)

For many years California had a three-year statute of limitations in molestation cases. That means that if a five-year-old child was molested but didn't report that molestation by the time she was eight, her molester couldn't be prosecuted. A 1994 law closed that loophole by removing the statute of limitations for sex crimes. Then came *Stogner v. California.*

Marion Stogner, a man in his seventies, was accused of molesting his two daughters when they were children. The two daughters told police about the assaults during a 1998 investigation of alleged child sexual abuse by Stogner's two sons. The daughters said that Stogner began molesting them when they were younger than five years old, and the abuse continued for years.

Stogner's attorney argued that he could not be prosecuted because the 1994 law amounted to a violation of the *ex post facto* provision of the US Constitution. Stogner claimed the elimination of the statute of limitations for his alleged crimes allowed him to be prosecuted retroactively, in violation of the Constitution. A California appeals court ruled against Stogner and upheld the 1994 law, but when Stogner appealed to the Supreme Court, he prevailed.

One of Stogner's daughters said that the Supreme Court ruling made her "feel like I've been molested all over again. I was four years old, and I was supposed to know the law on this?" The American Psychological Association agreed, observing that child molesters are rarely exposed until the statute of limitations has expired because kids either don't know they are victims of a crime or they are afraid to report it.

The Supreme Court ruling not only wiped out the case against Stogner, but it also dismantled scores of prosecutions that were being pursued against molesters in the Catholic priesthood. At the time of the ruling, more than three hundred priests had either resigned or retired after being accused of molestation or sexual impropriety.

(The case also has implications for the war on terror. The Bush administration argued before the high court that a decision against California would threaten the Patriot Act, which retroactively eliminated statutes of limitations in cases involving terrorist hijackings, kidnappings, bombings, and biological weapons.)

"We had eleven cases against molesting priests at the time," Bill Hodgman recalls. "We were developing many more and would have filed—cases in which victims had been abused by priests many years earlier. When the Supreme Court ruled, those victims felt as if they were being abused all over again. The system had denied them justice.

"I attended one gathering of fifty or more victims in Long Beach just days after the Stogner decision was handed down. The mood in that room was one of grief and shock, much like the mood you would find in a roomful of people who had all lost loved ones in a plane crash. Tears, anger—all the stages of grief were evident in that room. The victims were absolutely devastated.

"They had just started to hope that their molesters would finally be held accountable, and then their hopes were dashed by the Supreme Court. It was just heartbreaking. I still get a physical reaction to this day. I was sick about the result, but I had no choice. I had to dismiss the cases and let those guys go, even though I had no doubt of their guilt."

## "I'LL NEVER BE COMPLETELY HEALED"

One family whose hopes for justice were dashed by the Stogner decision was the family of Larry Lindner, a longtime police officer with the Los Angeles Police Department, now retired. "I arrested a number of child molesters when I was a policeman," Larry told me. "I once investigated a burglary at a school teacher's house. I looked around and saw Polaroid photos all over the floor—pictures of nude children. I thought, *This sucker's a pedophile!* Suddenly, I wasn't investigating a burglary, but a child molester. I got a search warrant and we found that this guy had been molesting kids in a ten-block radius of his house.

"It turned out that the house had been burglarized by a boy who had been victimized by this teacher. The boy and his younger brother had both been molested, and the guy was using photos of the younger brother to get the boys to do what he wanted: 'Do what I say, or your parents will see these pictures.' So the boy had broken in to get the pictures back.

"The molester was convicted and put away. One day, during roll call, my commander said, 'After roll call, there's someone who wants to see you.' So I went out and there were about fifty kids and their parents. They had a cake for me, and they thanked me for saving their kids from that monster. The kids were getting therapy and they were doing well. I still get choked up thinking about it, but all I did was my job."

One of the tragic ironies of Larry Lindner's life was that, after he had put a number of child molesters behind bars, he was horrified to learn that his own brother, a Jesuit priest and a teacher at Loyola High School in LA, had molested his children, his sister, and his nieces and nephews. Larry's brother, Father Jerold Lindner (or "Father Jerry," as he was called) was lauded for being unusually devoted to his students. He was also a frequent guest in Larry's home.

One day in 1984, Larry walked into a room and found Father Jerry molesting his eight-year-old daughter, Tiffany. Larry told his daughter to leave the room, then he ordered his brother out of the house. Later, when Larry's kids wanted to know where Uncle Jerry went, Larry said, "I told him to leave. He won't be coming back." At that point, the kids told him that Uncle Jerry had molested each of them.

Heartsick, Larry asked, "Why didn't you tell me when it happened?"

"He's your brother," his children told him, "Uncle Jerry said we'd get in trouble if we told anyone." Larry learned that Father Jerry had been molesting his youngest, Tiffany, since she was four. On one occasion, he had grabbed her hair and yelled, "You're a dirty girl! You made me do these things! If you tell anyone, they'll take you away and you'll never see your Mommy and Daddy again!"

Larry went to Loyola and confronted his brother with the children's accusations. "Were my kids lying about you— or telling the truth?" he asked.

"They're not lying," Father Jerry admitted.

"You're really sick," Larry said, barely keeping his anger controlled. "You either seek help now, or I'll find it for you."

"All right," Father Jerry said, "I'll get help."

That was the last conversation Larry ever had with his brother. Larry believed his brother was in therapy, as he had promised, but Father Jerry didn't keep his promise.

In 1992, Larry Lindner contacted the rector at Loyola High School to find out how Father Jerry's therapy was progressing. "Therapy?" the rector asked. "Therapy for what?"

"For being a child molester," Larry said.

"Whoa!" the rector responded, shocked. "I never heard anything about this!" So Larry told him what Father Jerry had done. Shocked and dismayed, the rector replied that a lot of things suddenly added up. Jerry led a number of clubs on campus, such as the archery club and chess club; he was also a Boy Scout leader. The obvious question: Was he molesting the kids in those clubs as well?

The Jesuits placed Father Jerry on leave and sent him to St. Luke Institute, a Catholic psychiatric treatment center in Maryland. Before leaving for Maryland, Father Jerry had his mother and two sisters write letters to his Jesuit superiors. Those letters accused Father Jerry's brother Larry of lying about Father Jerry. "I have been informed that one of the lies being made against my brother," wrote one sister, "is that he also molested me. . . . I can assure you that in no way is this true." That sister, however, had actually been Jerry's first victim. She wrote the letter at her mother's insistence.

The therapists at St. Luke accepted Father Jerry's denials, which were supported by the deceptive letters from Jerry's mother and sisters. In the fall of 1992, Father Jerry's superiors sent him back to Loyola High School to resume his duties. Five years passed while Father Jerry continued to work with young students at Loyola High. He even took student groups on summer tours to Europe.

Then, in 1997, two brothers filed a civil suit against Father Lindner, accusing him of molesting them some twenty-five years earlier during a camping trip. The brothers had suffered from nightmares, depression, and alcohol abuse; one of them had twice attempted suicide. In 1998, the Jesuits quietly settled for $625,000—with no apology or admission of wrongdoing.

"After this, my younger sister called me up," Larry told me, "and she said, 'I can't keep lying to make Mom happy. I'm sorry I lied to protect Jerry, and I love you very much.'" By this time, Larry's sister had learned that Father Jerry had molested her own son.

Eventually other people, both male and female, came forward and accused Father Jerry of sex abuse. To date, Father Jerry has never been charged with a crime.

In December 2002, the *Los Angeles Times* published an extensive report on Father Jerry and his trail of victims. The day the story appeared in the *Times*, I opened my radio show

with a monologue about the Lindner case and other molestation cases. I related it to my own experience of having been
molested at an early age.

When I went to the phones, my first caller was a woman
who said, "I've been listening to you talk about Father Jerry
Lindner. I'm Cathie Lindner, and Father Jerry is my brother-
in-law. He molested our kids."

We talked on the air about the case and about the pain
that Larry and Cathie Lindner and their kids had suffered.
Cathie was especially concerned about her daughter Tiffany,
who was in her twenties. Tiffany was having a difficult time
with relationships because of memories of the molestation.

At the end of the call, I told Cathie to stay on the line,
and I had my staff give her my private number. Later she
called me on my private line and I talked to both her and her
daughter. Tiffany and I had an instant rapport, because we
were both survivors, and we understood each other's pain.
She told me she was in therapy, and I said, "I bet you don't
get anything accomplished when you sit down with your
therapist."

"Yeah," she said. "They think they know how you feel,
but they've never been through it. I can talk for hours to my
therapist, but she doesn't get it. I talk to you for two minutes,
and I *know* you get it."

Cathie and Tiffany thought it would be good for me to talk
to Larry Lindner, so I called him and introduced myself. I told
him about my own experience of being molested, and he
seemed to appreciate talking with someone who had been down

that road. I asked him if he would like to see Father Jerry prosecuted for molesting his children.

"I would love to bring charges against my brother," Larry said. "But the statute of limitations has expired."

"Well," I said, "why don't you call Bill Hodgman of the Sex Crimes Unit in LA. Maybe something can still be done." I gave him Bill's number, and he followed up right away.

Soon afterwards, a detective from the LA County Sherriff's Office flew to Oregon, where the Lindner family was living at that time. The detective met with Larry, Cathie, and Tiffany, and took down a crime report with dates, times, and details. The Sheriff's office investigated, but by this time the Stogner decision was being appealed to the Supreme Court, so the authorities held off filing a criminal complaint against Father Jerry pending the decision. Once the Stogner decision was announced, Tiffany's case was declared dead-on-arrival. Father Jerry got off scott-free.

Today, Father Jerry Linder lives in the Sacred Heart Jesuit Center, a scenic retreat near Los Gatos, California. Though barred from contact with children, serving Mass, or hearing confession, he is getting on with his life. He sometimes teaches seminarians and has spent a number of months on a sabbatical in France.

Tiffany recently told me, "Father Jerry is sitting up there, living like a king, with all of his meals made for him, with no responsibilities and no punishment for what he's done. Meanwhile, his victims are dealing with nightmares and depression, while having trouble holding down jobs and maintaining relationships.

"I'm only twenty-eight, yet I'm already on my fourth marriage. I have six children by three different fathers. It's only recently that I realized the rut I'm in when it comes to relationships. I was molested by Father Jerry for four years, and that's exactly how long each of my relationships tend to last—four years, then it's over.

"I believe in God, but I don't go to church. And when I see a man in a priest's collar, I feel sick inside. It brings it all back. Father Jerry can just get on with his life, but it's never over for me or his other victims. I'm slowly getting better, but I'll never be completely healed. This will be with me for the rest of my life."

She's right. The pain of being molested doesn't go away after ten years, or twenty—or, as in my case, fifty years. Larry, Cathie, and Tiffany Lindner told me that they wanted their story in this book because they want you, the reader, to know what kind of damage a child molester leaves in his wake. Larry said, "If sharing our story can stop one pedophile or save one child from going through what our kids have gone through, it'll be worth it."

## THE RESPONSIBILITY OF THE CHURCH

"During the priest abuse scandal in LA," Bill Hodgman told me, "an investigator told me about an abuse victim he interviewed. Years before, when the victim was an altar boy, he was molested by the priest in the rectory, the place where the priest lived. The boy had to lie facedown on the bed while the priest sodomized him. While the boy was lying there, suffering this abuse, he looked at the crucifix on the wall, and he prayed, over and over, *Please, God, make it stop!*"

How can any man do that to a child? Worse still, how can a priest do such a thing? After all, what is a priest, according to Catholic doctrine? He represents Jesus Christ to the people. In a worship service he stands at the altar and offers the sacrifice of the body and blood of Christ as the atonement for sin. He administers the sacraments *in persona Christi,* which means that he stands in personal, sacramental identification with Jesus himself. What kind of ungodly monster could sacrifice the body and blood of Christ in the sanctuary, then sexually abuse an altar boy in the rectory, under the very eyes of Christ upon the crucifix?

This man is supposed to represent Jesus Christ to this boy. And what did Jesus tell us about those who would harm children? "And whoever welcomes a little child like this in my name welcomes me. But if anyone causes one of these little ones who believe in me to sin, it would be better for him to have a large millstone hung around his neck and to be drowned in the depths of the sea" (Matt. 18:5–6).

Jesus warned that a special fate awaits those who would mistreat and molest a child. I can't help believing that the penalty is a hundred times worse for those who hurt children while pretending to serve Christ and his church. I'm not only talking about Roman Catholic priests because the problem of ministers who prey on kids goes far beyond Catholicism. It includes Orthodox priests, Protestant pastors and youth workers, Mormon teachers, Jewish rabbis, and on and on.

Just as monstrous as a clergyman who abuses children is a church official who protects abusers, hides the secrets, and allows the body count of victims to rise, year after year. We who call ourselves Christians and who represent Jesus Christ to the world will have to account for the children God has entrusted to our care. When God demands that we give that account, will he say we were his faithful servants, or will he hang a millstone around our necks?

In February 2004, the US Conference of Bishops released a report on its own internal investigation of sexual abuse of minors by Catholic priests from 1950 to 2002. The study showed that, over that fifty-two year period, some 4,450 priests were accused of sexual abuse by more than 11,000 victims. Because sexual abuse of minors is a grossly under-reported crime, these numbers are likely to be the tip of the iceberg.

On July 23, 2003, Massachusetts Attorney General Thomas F. Reilly issued a seventy-six-page report on the findings of a sixteen-month criminal investigation into the priest abuse scandal in the Boston Archdiocese. The report determined that more than a thousand minors were abused by priests over more than fifty years, and the church hierarchy was well aware of it and engaged in a deliberate cover-up. The purpose of the investigation was to determine whether high-ranking church officials (including former Boston Cardinal Bernard Law) should be charged with crimes. Unfortunately, the report concluded, Massachusetts laws were too weak to allow criminal charges to be filed against church leaders.

"The magnitude of the archdiocese's history of clergy sexual abuse of children is staggering," said Reilly in his report. "The mistreatment of children was so massive and so prolonged that it borders on the unbelievable. . . . The choice was very clear, between protecting children and protecting the church. They made the wrong choice."

Reilly added that for more than fifty years "there has been an institutional acceptance within the archdiocese of clergy sexual abuse of children. For decades, cardinals, bishops, and others in positions of authority within the archdiocese chose to protect the image and reputation of their institution rather than the safety and well-being of children."[1]

Among the Boston cases was that of John Geoghan, who preyed on young boys over a period of three decades. Church leaders knew of his crimes against children, looked the other way, and moved him to a half-dozen parishes. Each time he was moved, he was unleashed on a new group of unsuspecting victims. In the end, more than 150 people came forward, claiming to have been molested by him.

In February 2002, Geoghan was convicted of a single count involving a ten-year-old boy in Waltham, Massachusetts. The Boston Archdiocese later paid a $10 million settlement to eighty-six other victims. Geoghan was sentenced to prison and was serving time at the Souza-Baranowski Correctional Center in Lancaster when another prisoner strangled and jumped on him, killing him.

The accused killer, Joseph L. Druce, wrote a letter to the *Catholic Free Press* of Worcester in which he said that he himself had been molested as a child. In the letter (which I'm quoting with the original spelling errors), Druce wrote: "I'm the alledged murdered of Defrocked priest John J. Geoghan, and a victim of Sexual Abuse as a Child. This was'nt a crime to committe a crime, but to let the world no that all child predators must be dealt with with a more stryngent hand, and to stop focusing on Catholoism as the mainstream. Let's look at the crime and not the Church. Joseph Druce says 'Leave the children alone.'"![2]

Richard Sipe, a former priest and author of *Sex, Priests, and Power* and *Celibacy in Crisis,* has made a thorough study of clergy abuse in the Catholic priesthood. Based on his research, he estimates that about 6 percent of all Catholic priests engage in sexual molestation of minors. He says that about 2 percent of priests are pedophiles (involved with pre-pubescent children) and 4 percent are ephebophiles (involved with adolescent children).

Sipe also reported, "The hierarchy of the Catholic Church in the United States, as exemplified by the bishops, archbishops, cardinals and other members of the Bishops Conference of the United States, has known of this problem for some time. . . . Well established studies show that the average pedophile has 250 or more victims over his lifetime."[3]

In an online chat on *USA Today's* "Talk Today" Web site, Sipe was asked if it was true that the Catholic Church had paid out over a billion dollars since 1980 to settle claims of clergy abuse. Sipe replied:

The Church has done everything it could to stem the financial costs of sexual abuse cases, but the money has to be paid out in compensation in accord with jury judgments. The money that is paid silently to keep quiet abuse cases, added to the money insurance companies have had to pay, and the cost of money for the treatment of victims (which is minimal compared to the money spent on priests' rehabilitation—that usually involves 7–11 months of inpatient treatment at $350 a day), plus legal fees, will bring you to a figure close to or exceeding one billion dollars.[4]

As a result of these multimillion–dollar settlements, many people look at the molestation scandal in the Catholic Church as a money issue. I assure you, it's not. The abuse victims don't really want the money. They want the burden of the molestation taken from their shoulders. The problem is that children have been forced to accept the burden of molestation because the church won't accept responsibility. Children have been saddled with the horror, guilt, and shame of these abusive acts because the church refused to hold the perpetrators accountable for their crimes.

A cash settlement is just a token compensation for the wound suffered. It's roughly on a level of getting several million dollars for losing both legs or both eyes. Sure, it's nice to have money, but you'd gladly pay that much and more to get your limbs or your sight back. There is no doubt in my mind that every one of the victims who has received a cash settlement from the church would gladly forego every penny if only they could have the memory of the molestation erased.

And, of course, there is an invisible price tag to sex abuse of children that we haven't even considered yet. Richard Sipe talked about it in an article on his Web site at RichardSipe.com. He wrote, "Men who abuse minors are called 'Slayers of the Soul.' . . . One of the common consequences of abuse by a Catholic priest is the complete loss of the comfort, support, spiritual sustenance, and meaning in life the victim previously experienced. Those who do not understand the nature and depth of this deprivation think that the victim can merely 'forget about it,' 'move on,' or 'find another religion.' Some victims cannot. A part of them is dead—their faith."[5]

The day camp counselor who molested me was not a representative of any church, yet that molestation drove a wedge between God and me that went all the way to the bottom of my soul. I can't imagine how anyone could be molested by a priest, or a pastor or a youth worker, and not have his or her faith irreparably damaged. Just think of the many children who have been raised with a beautiful, trusting, childlike faith—only to have it ripped out of their souls by some monster in a clergyman's robes.

People who molest children truly are slayers of the soul. They kill something inside their victims that can never be made alive again—short of a miracle from God. Abusive clergy not only put their own necks into the millstone of God's wrath, but they also grab children off the path to eternal life and toss them into spiritual darkness—just to satisfy their own lusts. And the problem extends far beyond the Catholic church.

## MAKING CHURCHES SAFE

What happens to kids who are molested, particularly those who are molested by leaders in the Christian church? A lot of them end up in the homosexual community. And I can tell you exactly why that happens. After being molested by a man, a boy questions his own sexuality. He is truly confused about his sexual orientation. That's what I went through after I was molested, and I was not only confused but scared to death that I might be a homosexual.

At the same time, the church and society tell these victims that any male who is touched by another male has sinned. So that young victim not only feels confused but scared and condemned as well! He doesn't feel safe in the heterosexual community, and he particularly doesn't feel safe in the church. He believes that if anyone finds out his secret, he will be condemned and ostracized.

So what does he do? He looks for a safe haven. And what is the safe haven he finds? The homosexual community. He may not truly be a homosexual, he may not have homosexual tendencies, but he has been molested, he has been touched by another male. So he joins the gay community where he knows he will be accepted, not condemned.

For the molestation victim, the gay community seems like a safe haven. Yes, it's the wrong haven, but it feels safe. From the time he's molested, the victim never feels safe or accepted. The church tells him he's a sinner, he's going to hell. The gay community says, "We'll accept you. You're OK. You're safe here." If you give a human being the choice between acceptance and condemnation, between safety and fear, what is he going to choose?

Without compromising the truth of the gospel, without compromising the Scriptures, we need to make our churches a more welcoming, accepting, and safe place for wounded souls. There is an old saying that "the church is the only army that shoots its own wounded." That saying is all too often proven true in the lives of wounded victims of child sex abuse.

Christians should be the most accepting people on earth. After all, we have been accepted by a gracious and loving God, even though we don't deserve his love and could never earn it. He has made us a part of his family. The sacrifice that made our acceptance possible cost us nothing and cost Jesus everything. The grace and love we receive from God is the grace we must now give to people who are wounded and hurting. We need to make the church a safe haven for victims of abuse.

In the church we often talk about the love of God and the grace of God, but do we exemplify his love and grace in the way we live? We love to quote the words of Jesus from the cross, "Father, forgive them, for they know not what they do." Why, then, are we not willing to follow in his footsteps and get up on that cross for our own kids and for other people who have sinned? When sinners and victims come to church to find love, acceptance, and forgiveness, why do we give them judgment and criticism instead? Why can't we pray for sinners the same way Jesus prayed: "Father, forgive them, for they know not what they do"?

Victims of molestation carry the burden of a horrible secret. In almost every case, they are thinking, *I did something wrong. I need this burden lifted from me.* But the fact is that they didn't know what they were doing. The molester knew; they didn't. So we, as Christians, need to become the personification of Christ to these victims. We need to get up on that cross for them and pray, "Father, forgive them, and take away their burden, for they know not what they do!"

The burden of molestation is too heavy for the human soul to bear. It would have been such a healing experience if, at any point in the last fifty years, Don Havlik had come to me and said, "I'm so sorry for what I did to you, Michael. Let me take that burden off your shoulders. What I did to you wasn't your fault. I take full responsibility for it—for the sex acts, the pictures, the secret-keeping, the lies, all of it." I have never experienced that, and I don't expect I ever will. So, despite the progress I've made and the healing I've experienced, I still carry some of that burden.

As the apostle Paul wrote, "We who are strong ought to bear with the failings of the weak and not to please ourselves. Each of us should please his neighbor for his good, to build him up. . . . Accept one another, then, just as Christ accepted you, in order to bring praise to God" (Rom. 15:1–2, 7). So we must make our churches safe for victims by helping to lift their burdens, and by showing them that they are loved, accepted, and forgiven.

Another way we must make our churches safe is by safeguarding our children so that they can't be preyed upon by the soul-slayers around us. This means we must adopt policies and practices in our churches that will make it hard for child molesters to have access to our kids. Sexual predators will swarm to any place they can gain easy access to kids. Since the public schools, the Boy Scouts, and other child-centered organizations have put child safety programs into place, pedophiles have started moving into the churches in search of "fresh meat."

What makes Protestant churches so vulnerable is that much of the child-centered ministry is performed by volunteers rather than clergy or paid staff. In fact, the *Church Law and Tax Report* has found that 50 percent of all sex abuse offenses in churches are committed by volunteer workers; 30 percent are committed by ordained clergy and other paid staff; and 20 percent are committed by other children in the church.

*Christianity Today* cited a case that shows how easily child molesters can slip into a church and wreak destruction. In 1997, youth minister Bryan Buckley was convicted of nine counts of sexual misconduct involving a long-term sexual relationship he had with a girl in his youth group at Christ Community Church, Saint Charles, Illinois. She was fourteen when the relationship began. Buckley was not charged for offenses involving a second girl in the church. The church ended up paying for counseling for the two girls who reported Buckley; the church also pays for Buckley's therapy while he is in prison.

Was the church negligent in hiring Buckley? No. The church had carefully checked his background and even did a criminal record check. He not only appeared clean but also had excellent references. Buckley was even named Youth Minister of the Year at Liberty University.[6]

It's impossible to eliminate completely all risk of child sex abuse in the church. But there is much that we can do to put guardrails in place to discourage molesters from preying on our kids. Mark Hughes, who operates an employee screening company, HR First Contact, also helps screen staffers and volunteers at his own church, Park Cities Baptist Church of Dallas.

"Churches are the paths of least resistance for pedophiles," Hughes told *The Baptist Standard*. "If a church doesn't have a screening program, a pedophile could be working with children in a couple of weeks. Many churches have been successfully sued due to negligent entrustment of employees, clergy or volunteers. The greatest sin is the sin of doing nothing."[7]

Every church should have a child safety program and a screening program in place for all staff and volunteers who would have access to children. Churches should thoroughly educate and train all staff members and children's ministry and youth workers in the prevention of abuse. The most important reason for having child protection policies and programs in place is to protect kids from soul-slaying predators. These policies and programs also protect adults from false accusations, reduce the liability of churches, and help parents to have greater confidence in the church program.

Unfortunately, this also means that every person in the church is treated, to some extent, as if he or she is suspect. It means that, even in the church, children can't get the hugs they need because everyone is afraid of being accused of molestation. But that's the world we live in today.

A church child safety program should include these features:

• All staff and volunteers must be subject to reference checks, including criminal background checks. Background checks should include residency and employment for the past ten years. (Release of information forms are available from the Department of Social Services / Child Protection Services agency in almost every state or Canadian province.)

• All youth and children's ministry volunteers must be members of the church for at least six months.

• All youth and children's ministry staff and volunteers should be interviewed and asked about their history and attitudes toward discipline in the home and should be asked about any incidences of abuse or molestation in their own childhood.

• No staff or volunteers are ever permitted to be alone and unobserved with a minor. Contact with minors can only occur in places where the adult and the child can be observed by two other adults who are not related to each other.

Foolproof? Certainly not—and we should never become complacent just because our church has a policy in place. But if we put barriers in the way, making it hard for child molesters to get access to our kids, molesters will move on in search of easier targets. Also, the mere fact that a church has a child

safety program in place tells the congregation and the surrounding community that this is a church that values and protects children, just as Jesus did.

"Parents have to be vigilant," Bill Hodgman told me. "It's
a sad commentary, but in our society you have to arm yourself with knowledge. You can't turn a blind eye to what can
happen—not where the safety of children is concerned. It's a
shame, but even in the context of one's own church, where
you want to be able to trust those who minister, you must be
very watchful.

"Once a child's trust has been betrayed, it is very hard for
that child ever to give that trust again, even as an adult. After
all, if your own priest or minister or youth worker abuses you,
whom can you trust?

"I've seen instances where parents allowed their kids to go
on camping trips and overnight stays with a clergyman. The
clergyman said, 'Your child is special to me. I've taken an
interest in him.' He gains the trust of the parents, he gains the
trust of the child, and then the seduction process begins. So
parents must be vigilant.

"Church boards, elders, and pastors must be vigilant as
well. They need to screen all applicants with care, and take letters of recommendation with a grain of salt. In the scandal at
the Los Angeles Archdiocese, molesting priests were moved
around from parish to parish and always had glowing letters
of recommendation that didn't mean a thing. Churches have
to do their own background checks, and they need to be very
thorough."

## VICTIMS AND SURVIVORS

People who are casualties of molestation are often told not to think of themselves as victims. "Remember," the saying goes, "you are no longer a victim but a survivor." I know that's true. But there are, unfortunately, many survivors who don't survive.

One of them was James Thomas Kelly of Morristown, New Jersey. Kelly was a member of SNAP, the Survivors Network of those Abused by Priests. He helped found the New Jersey chapter of SNAP, and he often spoke to groups about his experiences. Jim Kelly was well-liked, known as a positive, caring, and upbeat guy who was always willing to help someone in need. He was thirty-seven years old, yet the memory of the childhood molestation continued to haunt him.

Kelly was one of more than a dozen men who claimed to have been abused as children by Rev. James T. Hanley, a priest at St. Joseph's Catholic Church in Mendham, New Jersey. Though Hanley was never charged with any crimes, the diocese removed him from the priesthood, and he has never publicly answered the accusations.

Jim Kelly had worked as a salesman in the telecommunications industry for ten years and also served in the Army Reserves. In July 2002, he was the keynote speaker at the first meeting of Voice of the Faithful, a group seeking to eliminate sex abuse in the church. He also spoke to law enforcement groups, civic groups, SNAP chapter meetings, and anywhere else he could get his message out.

Everybody thought that Jim Kelly was doing fine, even after all he had been through. Well, some days he was doing fine. Other days, he didn't cope with the memories and emotions too well. On one of those bad days, Jim Kelly decided he couldn't cope any more.

Early on Sunday morning, October 12, 2003, Jim walked along the tracks just west of the Morristown train station. At 5:17 a.m., he stepped out in front of the New Jersey Transit train that was speeding eastbound along the tracks. He lived as a survivor, but tragically he died a victim. And I can identify with Jim Kelly because I, too, considered suicide many times.

The slayers of children's souls are all around us. You and I are the only ones standing between those predatory monsters and the souls of our children. Jesus said, "Let the little children come to me, and do not hinder them, for the kingdom of God belongs to such as these." That is his command to us, his servants. Let's be faithful to his command and to the children he has entrusted to our care.

# 6

# THE AGE OF RAGE

*I* earned good grades my first two years at St. John's Military Academy. Being an altar boy, I was quickly rewarded with promotions in my military rank. I was made a corporal my first year and sergeant my second.

Sometime during my second year at St. John's, my sixth grade year, Mom and Fred decided to call it quits. After spending two failed marriages in the house on Beverly Glen, I guess Mom didn't want to live with the memories there anymore. So we moved. Then, less than a year later, we moved again. Fact is, between the end of my sixth grade year and the beginning of the eighth grade, we moved three times. But even though we kept changing houses, one thing remained the same: I was still going to boarding school.

By the seventh grade I had become the class clown. Making the other kids laugh got me a lot of attention, made me feel more important, and alleviated the pain of my bruised self-esteem. It also helped me to mask the constant shame and despair I felt as a result of the molestation.

On one occasion I made a joke in class that everyone in the room thought was funny except the teacher. She proceeded to give me the kind of tongue-lashing that only a nun can give. She called my behavior "the work of Satan" and told me that I needed to dispel Satan from my life. She sent me to the front of the room where there was a bowl of holy water by the door. She told me to dip my fingers into the holy water and cross myself, then she turned and started writing on the blackboard.

I walked to the front of the room with my fingers beside my head like the horns of a devil. Reaching the bowl of holy water, I dipped my "devil horns" in the bowl, then crossed myself. The other kids howled. At the sound of their laughter, the teacher turned and caught my devil impression. Well, that was the last straw!

She reached me in three quick strides, snatched me by the ear, and hauled me straight to the principal's office. The blasphemy was one thing, but the bigger issue was that she had disciplined me for disrupting the class, and I had made a mockery of her discipline by disrupting the class again! When she explained what I had done to our principal, Major Scanlon, he took away my sergeant's stripes. There was even talk of expelling me from St. John's.

Mom donated a set of the *Encyclopedia Britannica* to the seventh-grade class—a very expensive atonement for my stunt. Thanks to her generosity, the school gave me another chance—much to my dismay. I would have been happy with expulsion and a switch to a new school—especially if it was a day school.

Catholic teaching made me miserable because it constantly reminded me of my sins and my downfall—the molestation. The church's teaching about hell filled me with terror. I also learned (or, at least, I interpreted) that illegitimate kids were doomed to a fate called limbo—a place that was neither heaven nor hell. As I understood the nuns' teaching, the Virgin Mary would sometimes travel to limbo, gather up a few lucky little souls, hide them in her robes, and steal them away to heaven—a tiny ray of hope in an otherwise bleak outlook for illegitimate kids like me.

I hated my life so much that I seriously weighed the pros and cons of suicide. On the minus side the church taught that if you commit suicide, like Judas Iscariot, you go straight to hell. On the plus side, if I went to hell for committing suicide, wouldn't that be better for me and my family? To my immature way of thinking, going to hell for killing myself was a lot better than going to hell for being illegitimate or for a homosexual act or for those pictures. In the end I decided I was in no hurry to go to hell. I figured I'd go on living and put hell off for as long as possible.

My attitude and behavior, both at home and at school, continued to deteriorate. I wanted to get kicked out of St. John's because I hated it. I wanted to get kicked out of Mom's house paradoxically because I loved her. I was actually trying to spare Mom the pain of finding out about all the horrible things I had done—especially those pictures. I battled her and fought her in the hope that she would give up on me and send me away for good.

The only relief I had from all my inner turmoil was the times I spent with Dad at the Malibu ranch. I enjoyed helping him with the chores, like painting fences and splitting firewood. There was nothing better than working alongside Dad, or hunting ground squirrels with him, or riding horses with him.

Unfortunately, those golden moments were all too rare.

## WHEN GOD WAS A BICYCLE

When I was thirteen years old, all my friends had ten-speed bikes. If you didn't have one, you weren't cool. Well, I wanted to be cool.

From my friends I had learned the number one rule of being a rich kid: Use guilt to get money from mom and dad. Most Beverly Hills parents were loaded with both cash and guilt, so they handed out guilt money hand over fist. They used money as a substitute for love and time with their kids.

I tried to play that game with Mom. I asked her to buy me a shiny blue Schwinn ten-speed, and I added, "If you buy it for me, I'll love you forever!"

She gave me one of those stern Jane Wyman looks—the same look she gave Hayley Mills in *Pollyanna*. Then she said, "Michael, I can afford to buy anything you want."

Hey, so far, so good! But her next sentence dashed my hopes.

"However," she said, "even though I can afford it, I think it's important that you learn the value of a dollar. And the only way you'll learn that is by earning the money to buy the bike yourself."

"But—" I began.

"If you earn it yourself, you'll appreciate it more, and people will respect you for being a hard worker."

"But—"

"This is an important lesson for you, Michael. If you learn it now, then when you grow up, you'll be a forty-year-old *man*—not a forty-year-old *boy*. I build men. I don't build little boys."

"But," I said, "by the time I save up enough money, I'll *be* a forty-year-old man!"

We negotiated, and she agreed to buy the bike if I promised to earn the money to pay her back in installments. Good deal!

So I got a job selling the Sunday newspaper in front of Good Shepherd Catholic Church in Beverly Hills, where I had been baptized in 1954. When I left the house early each Sunday morning, I told Mom I was going to church—and I was. Sometimes I even went into the Sanctuary and sat through Mass, but usually I only went as far as the vestibule to look at the Daily Missal. I could scan the page, check out the gospel reading, and even find out what color the priest's vestments were that day. When I got home, Mom would quiz me about the Mass, and I had all the right answers.

I was very good at deception. I was good at making Mom think I was going to church, but the reality was that I was convinced that the church couldn't do anything for me, couldn't save my soul, so why should I go? Mom was impressed with my apparent church attendance, and we seemed to get along better for a while—but it didn't last long. Increasingly, every conversation became an argument. I created friction with Mom by complaining that we moved too often and that I didn't get to see Dad enough. It was clear that Mom didn't like Nancy, and I felt she was putting up road-blocks to keep me from spending time at Dad and Nancy's house. Boy, I was sure a pill!

I felt that I didn't truly belong anywhere. I wasn't happy at home. Maureen was attending school in New York state, so it was just me and Mom. I hardly ever got to spend time at Dad's house. I bitterly resented the time I spent at boarding school. There was no nice, safe place in my life that I could call home.

My rage and frustration grew to a point where I had one argument with Mom that really got out of control. It was prompted by her announcement that we were moving once again. I was frustrated with moving, with losing friends as soon as I made them, with my own self-loathing, with the secrets that I kept.

So I lashed out at her and shouted at her and told her I didn't want to move anywhere with her. I wanted to go live with my dad.

Mom picked up the riding crop that she kept handy as a disciplinary tool, and she whacked me on the back of my legs. Then she added a swat in the middle of my back. It was probably aimed at my posterior, but she missed her target. The swat really stung, and it shocked me. She had never hurt me like that before, so I decided to hurt her like I had never hurt her before.

I turned on her and snarled, "I've had it with you, *Miss Wyman!*" Then I slapped her across the cheek. Ever since then I have wished I could undo that slap. I can still see the wounded look in her eyes and the red impression my hand left on her face.

With that the argument was over. But not the hurt.

She knew what I meant by calling her "Miss Wyman." She knew I was telling her that she wasn't my real mother. How mean was that! For a long time I had been stretching the slender and strained cord of love that bonded us together. In one uncontrolled moment, I broke that cord.

We have since rebonded, and we love each other very much as mother and son, but for a long time after that slap and those hurtful words, things were not the same between us.

Soon after that incident, we moved to Lido Isle, a bayside resort in Newport Beach patterned after the Lido section of Venice, Italy. I got my wish in one respect: Mom took me out of St. John's Military Academy and enrolled me in a day school, the Horace Ensign School in Newport, where I finished the eighth grade. So I came home every day after school during the week.

I didn't see much of Mom, however. She was still busy with her television show, and she stayed in an apartment in Hollywood during the week. But there was an occasion that brought me closer to her again.

I was trying out for the track team, and I tried the high jump. I went straight up, then straight down, and I missed the sawdust. I'm probably the only person in history ever to miss the sawdust while doing the high jump. I put my right hand down to brace myself, and I broke my wrist.

The school called Mom, and she rushed over from the studio in her little blue Thunderbird. She picked me up at school and took me to the hospital. That was one of the great days of my young life because that showed she cared for me. It really meant a lot. The problem was that those memories weren't strong enough at the time to overshadow all the bad memories I had of my life.

When Mom was home on the weekends, we had an unspoken truce between us. That truce ended the day she announced her decision to send me to Loyola High School in Los Angeles. She told me it was one of the best Catholic schools in the area, but I didn't care how great a school it was academically. I didn't want to go.

I found the idea of Loyola High School completely intolerable on three counts: (1) it was a boarding school, (2) it was an all-boys school, and (3) it was a Catholic school. Loyola High symbolized everything that was wrong with my life: the agony of again separating from my family, the fear that I might be homosexual, and my continual awareness that I couldn't live up to what Catholicism was. Yet I kept being put in those places.

Catholic teaching left me riddled with guilt. I already knew I was a sinner, I was going to hell, and yet Mom was spending all of this money on Catholic schools in an attempt to straighten out my life. I knew my life was going nowhere, I hated school, I hated everything, including the church.

I told Mom I refused to go to Loyola. She replied that I was going to Loyola, and that was final. What's more, she was going to hire a tutor for me during the summer so I would be ready for school in the fall. I knew that this contest of wills would end as they all ended: I would do what Mom said, and I would resent it.

When I went to bed that night, I was full of rage—rage at my mother, rage at God, rage at my life, which was completely out of my control. Every important decision in my life was made for me by my mother, and I had no say in the matter. I pounded my pillow, trying to pour all my rage into some inanimate object. The harder I pounded, the angrier I got. When I woke up the next morning, I was even angrier than before.

Mom had already left for the studio when I came out of my bedroom. That was a good thing because I was furious with her and ready to pick a fight. The only other person in the house was our Russian cook. I decided to get on my bike and go for a ride. Maybe that would calm me down.

I went to the garage, grabbed my ten-speed bike by the handlebars, kicked the kickstand, and walked the bike a few feet toward the driveway—and then I heard a *clunkety-clunkety* sound. I looked down and saw that the chain was off the sprocket.

Even my bike hated me!

The rage inside me finally boiled over. I stamped into the house, flung open a drawer, and took out a heavy ball-peen hammer. Then I went back to the garage and hammered on that bike with every ounce of fury in my body.

That bike was the man who molested me. And it was Mom. It was Dad and Nancy. It was myself. It was everyone I loved and everyone I hated. It was everyone who had ever hurt me. Most of all, that bike was God.

I took that hammer, and I beat God with it. I smashed God with it, and I hurt God with it, over and over and over again. The whole time I hammered that bike, I cursed God. I was trying to kill all the things that ever hurt me. Today, when kids fly into a rage, they kill people. I killed things. I used things to take the place of people. I killed and killed and killed that bike, my most prized possession.

At one point the cook came out to see what all the noise was. I turned and glared at her with that hammer raised in my hands. Her eyes got big, and she went back in the house like a shot.

I went back to work and hammered that bike beyond recognition. Then I put the ruined bicycle over my shoulders and carried it across the street, walked all the way to the end of the Newport Beach pier, and I heaved my bike, my mother, my father, myself, my molester, and my God into the bay. Then I went back home, flopped onto my bed, and cried uncontrollably.

Hours later Mom arrived home. She noticed that my bike wasn't in the garage, and she came to my room and said, "Where is your bike, Michael?"

I said, "Someone stole it."

"Did you see who stole it?"

"Nope," I said, shrugging.

She didn't ask me any more questions. A few days later Mom replaced the bike. I didn't care. The bike didn't matter anymore. Nothing mattered anymore. I had given up on life, on school, on myself, on Mom, on everything.

## "I CAN'T DO ANYTHING MORE FOR YOUR SON."

I finished the school year at Horace Ensign School, collecting a report card full of well-earned Ds. I figured I had pretty well foreclosed any chance that Loyola would take me. I knew that Loyola had high academic standards, and a straight-D report card didn't come close.

When summer vacation arrived, so did my tutor. He worked with me every day, and I fought him relentlessly. When the summer was almost over, I learned that Loyola High School had accepted me as a student. I couldn't believe it! There was no way on earth that Loyola would take a student with grades like mine.

But I had underestimated Mom. She wanted me to attend Loyola, so she persuaded the school to let me in. I couldn't even control my scholastic destiny by failing on purpose. But maybe if I could move in with Dad, that would all change.

Well, fine. I would take up a seat at Loyola High School, but nobody could make me learn if I didn't want to. That was the one thing in my life I had some measure of control over.

Throughout the school years, Mom coaxed and pleaded with me to give my schoolwork a try, but I remained sullen and unresponsive. Finally Mom sent me to our parish priest for counseling.

I sat in the office of the priest, and he and I endured some long, uncomfortable silences. I didn't tell him a thing. Why? Because I was sure that if I told the priest, he would tell my mother everything, and she would know that I was condemned to hell.

If Mom was going to throw me out, I wanted it to be on my terms, because of my rotten behavior, and for no other reason.

Mom kept taking me to the priest every week, even though we weren't accomplishing anything. She kept hoping for some kind of breakthrough, but no breakthrough came. During one session I asked the priest, "Why do I have to go through you to talk to God? Why can't I go straight to God and talk to him myself?"

He was silent for a long time. Then he said, "But you can. You can talk to God whenever you want." And that ended our session.

I wasn't sure what the priest meant. If I could talk directly to God, then why confess my sins to the priest? The way I saw it, I couldn't talk to God about Don Havlik and those pictures because I had to go through the priest, through the confessional, and I didn't dare do that because I was too ashamed and I didn't want him to tell my mother. Now the priest was telling me I could talk directly to God. But how? The only time I had ever talked directly to God was when I cursed him. I didn't know how to pray to him.

After the session the priest went to Mom and said, "I can't do anything more for your son."

At that point Mom was getting desperate. She decided to take me to a Beverly Hills child psychiatrist. That was scary. Remember, this was a good ten years before it became fashionable for everybody to be in analysis. In those days, if you went to a shrink, people thought you were crazy. Mom took me to the psychiatrist's office four or five times. He gave me inkblot tests and asked me a lot of questions, and I gave him my carefully guarded answers.

I had the impression that the psychiatrist was a friend of Mom's. Even though he promised that anything I said to him was confidential, I didn't trust him. I figured that anything I told him would get right back to her, so I made only one honest, revealing statement to him. I said, "You want to know why I don't get along with Mom? It's simple. She won't let me spend time with my dad. I want to visit my dad more often, and I want to live in his house."

It was sheer manipulation on my part—and it worked. I got the therapist on my side, and I got him to tell Mom exactly what I wanted him to say. He recommended that Mom and I take a break from each other and that I go to live with Dad and Nancy.

I was thrilled. Finally, I was winning. At long last things were working out the way I wanted them to. I was going to move out of Mom's house, and I would save her the trauma of discovering the truth about the molestation and those pictures. I thought, *I can finally put Don Havlik behind me!*

Mom must have called Dad and asked him to make it sound like it was his idea because the next time I saw Dad, he said, "Michael, how would you like to come live with me and Nancy?"

"That would be great, Dad," I said.

On the day I moved out, Mom's only comment to me was, "Good luck—and remember, it was your choice to move." I didn't realize it then, but that comment was a sign of just how hurt she was that I had chosen Dad and Nancy's home over hers.

A recent anecdote shows just how hurtful that episode was for her. In 2002, I was having lunch with Mom at her home in Palm Desert. Our mother-son relationship has grown tremendously in recent years, and we have been able to talk about things we never talked about before. So as we were having lunch, she looked at me and said, "Now, Michael, tell me again—Why did you leave my house when you were fourteen? Why did you move in with your dad?"

Understand, I had moved out in 1959; this was 2002. Forty-three years had passed, and she still didn't understand why I had moved out, and she was finally asking the question. That's how much it affected her. That's how much I had hurt her. Mom, I'm so sorry.

So I said, "I know this sounds crazy, Mom, but I was trying to protect you from the secret I was carrying. I know now that it hurt you when I moved out, but in my mixed-up way of thinking, I moved out because I loved you. I didn't want you to find out about my secret and be hurt by it."

So I moved in with Dad and Nancy.

They lived on San Onofre Drive in Pacific Palisades. Their house was set on a high bluff with a spectacular view of the Pacific Ocean. Dad was in the middle of an eight-year run as host of *General Electric Theater*, which aired Sunday nights on CBS. Because of his position as spokesman for GE, the company had built him a special house called The House of the Future. It was filled with GE gadgets and futuristic prototypes.

In 1959, when I moved into the Reagan household, Patti was about seven and Ron Jr. was a newborn. I was fourteen— the big brother, a role I relished. It meant I was finally accepted and even respected. That was very important to a hurting kid whose sense of self-worth was hanging by a thread. I assumed that since I was now in a two-parent family, I no longer had to go to boarding school. I couldn't have been more wrong.

I soon found out that Mom had made a deal with Dad, and the deal was that I still had to attend Loyola High. She wanted me to receive a Catholic education, and though Dad was Protestant, he agreed to that stipulation. Dad believed that the stability of a two-parent home would be good for me—even if I could only be with the family on weekends.

To me it was like a prison sentence. From the time I started school at age five until I graduated at age nineteen, I spent my entire schooling in boarding school, except my third grade year at the Warner Avenue School and my fourth grade and half of the fifth grade at Good Shepherd.

The house in Pacific Palisades was large, but every bedroom was taken. Because there was no bedroom for me, I slept on a couch in the living room and used the guest bathroom. At the time I thought it was a terrible arrangement. Why couldn't I have a bedroom of my own? I took it as an insult, as a sign that I was a second-class member of the family.

I saw everything in my life in negative terms. I saw nothing in a positive way.

For some reason it didn't occur to me until years later that the couch I slept on should have been a sign of how much Dad and Nancy cared for me. They were willing to put up with a lot of inconvenience in order to make room for me when they really didn't have room for another person in their home.

I thought I had left my problems and my rage behind when I left my mother's house. I hadn't. They were still with me. I still carried the burden of my illegitimacy and the molestation. I was full of adolescent rage, and my anger would continue to tie my family relationships in knots for years to come.

I was a teenage time bomb, waiting to go off.

## A DANGEROUS EMOTIONAL PLACE

December 1, 1997, West Paducah, Kentucky: A group of Christian kids held hands and prayed in the hallway at Heath High School. A fourteen-year-old student opened fire on them, killing three students, wounding five, and leaving one girl paralyzed for life.

March 24, 1998, Jonesboro, Arkansas: Four girls and a teacher were killed and ten others wounded by two boys with guns, ages eleven and thirteen. May 21, 1998, Springfield, Oregon: A fifteen-year-old student, who was expelled the day before, killed both of his parents, then went to school and killed two students at random in the school cafeteria.

April 20, 1999, Littleton, Colorado: Two teens in black trench coats opened fire on fellow students at Columbine High School, killing thirteen innocent students, plus themselves. March 5, 2001, Santee, California: A fifteen-year-old boy walked onto the campus of Santana High School and opened fire, killing two classmates and wounding thirteen.

These are stories of mass murders committed by children, most of them thirteen to sixteen years old, one killer as young as eleven. Where does all of this teenage rage come from? We all know that the teen years are the age of rage, a time when hormones, emotions, frustrations, adolescent crushes, and conflicts with parents combine to produce feelings of alienation, rebellion, and anger. But only in recent years have we seen these emotions become fuel for random mass murder.

I vividly remember the anger I felt in my own teen years. There were times I was so full of rage I could barely control myself, and I had no idea what I might do if I ever gave in to it. If the idea of a school shooting had been planted in my head at just the right time, who knows?

In March 1998, fifteen-year-old Kip Kinkel was sitting in a classroom at Thurston High School in Springfield, Oregon, watching live news coverage of a deadly school shooting that was unfolding in Jonesboro, Arkansas. Kinkel leaned over to a classmate and said, "Hey, that's pretty cool!"

Two months later Kip was expelled when he was found to have a .32 caliber semiautomatic pistol in his locker. The gun was loaded with a nine-round clip. He was taken to the police station, fingerprinted, photographed, and charged, then released to his father's custody.

That afternoon, while Kip's father was sitting at a table, sipping coffee, Kip crept up from behind and shot him in the back of the head with a .22 rifle. Three hours later, when his mother arrived home, Kip met her in the garage, told her he loved her, then shot her multiple times.

The next morning Kip drove his mother's Ford Explorer to school. Dressed in a trench coat, he carried three guns and plenty of extra ammo. He had a hunting knife taped to his leg. He shot two students in the hallway, then he went to the crowded cafeteria and fired fifty rounds. Two students were killed and twenty-five were injured—and more would have been shot if five courageous students hadn't wrestled Kip Kinkel to the ground. When the police arrived, they found the students holding Kip down on the ground as he repeatedly said, "I just want to die! I just want to die!"

Kids have seen the news reports. They know that, with a trench coat on their backs and a gun in each hand, they can shake our society to its core. Kids have always felt alienated and rejected, misunderstood by parents and teachers, angry over boyfriend-girlfriend breakups, criticized and condemned, isolated and powerless. What is new is that they now resort to lethal ways to express their rage.

Psychologists tell us that preadolescent children have a lot of rage, just as adolescents do, but they suppress it because they fear abandonment. But once a child reaches adolescence, that pent-up rage emerges in the form of teenage rebellion. Not only does a teenager no longer fear separation from his parents, but he actively *seeks* separation. Instead of trying to win his parents' approval, he wants to express his anger in ways that will shock and dismay his parents.

So teenage kids rebel. They do all the things their parents tell them not to do. They dress weird, put rings through their flesh, use vulgar language, and listen to rebellious music. They smoke tobacco and marijuana. They drink and do drugs. They have sex. Sometimes, when adolescent rage reaches an unbearable level, the youth will act out his anger through violence, sometimes against others, sometimes even against himself: "I'll show them! I know how to hurt them! I'll kill myself!"

When an adolescent becomes angry, that anger often becomes an obsession. Rage fills the mind, squeezing out every other emotion, every other thought. The young person is unable to focus on other people's good qualities, or on happy memories, or on the possibility that things might get better tomorrow. The rage-filled youth thinks in terms that are all-encompassing and extreme: "Everything that happens to me is bad. Everybody hates me. Everybody's against me. Life is totally unfair. I've always been completely miserable. I'll never be happy. Nothing good ever happens to me."

I remember those feelings. That's a dangerous emotional place for a young person to be. Once a kid starts down that road, the stage is set for tragedy. A young person who is full of rage and who sees the world in such negative terms is like a gun with a hair trigger. Put the slightest pressure on that trigger, and it is liable to go off.

## THE CAUSES OF TEENAGE RAGE

What does a kid who's full of dangerous rage look like? Most of them look a lot like Mitchell Johnson. He's one of the two boys who shot fifteen students and teachers (killing five) at Westside Middle School in Jonesboro, Arkansas. At the time of the shootings, Mitchell Johnson was thirteen years old and living with his divorced mother, a devout Christian woman who attended the Revival Tabernacle in town. He regularly attended church services and youth group. He loved music and basketball. He liked school. He was well-mannered, clean-cut, and well-behaved in school—never a disciplinary problem. Around girls he was a gentleman and even pulled out chairs for his female classmates.

He and the eleven-year-old boy also did things that the grown-ups didn't know about, such as torturing and killing animals—evidence of a suppressed inner rage. According to the police, Mitchell Johnson said that the reason he shot all of those people was that he was angry because his girlfriend had broken up with him.

Bottom line, you can't tell what's going on inside an adolescent's head and heart. You can never be sure whether the next human time bomb to go off is the goth kid with all the rings in his face and the Marilyn Manson CD playing on his headset or the polite, clean-cut kid in your church youth group.

What causes the rage in an adolescent to reach critical mass and explode? Nobody knows, but I'd like to suggest some possibilities.

1. *We are medicating young people instead of listening to them and helping them face life.* I'm worried about the current emphasis on drugging kids in school and in the home. I worry that the drugs we are pumping into these kids to control their moods and their behavior are only masking the *real* problems at the root of their adolescent rage.

Family therapist Michael Gurian, author of *The Good Son: The Moral Development of Our Boys & Young Men* (J. P. Tarcher, 2000), put it this way: "We need to distinguish between that small group of people who are sick and need medication and the vast majority of our boys, who are normal. Our therapeutic profession and our culture right now do not know how to figure it out. Some sixty to seventy percent of our males on Ritalin don't need Ritalin; they need a change in their family system and school system."[1]

When we drug a child, we send that child a message: "You are sick, defective, and flawed." But it may be that what is truly defective is not the child but the child's parents, or the child's school, or the molester who abused the child, or even the society in which the child lives. Many of the teenage school shooters have been on psychiatric medication at the time of their violent episodes.

Kip Kinkel was on Ritalin as a child and on Prozac (the most widely prescribed antidepressant) as an adolescent. Eric Harris, one of the Columbine High School killers, was on the antidepressant Luvox. Fourteen-year-old Elizabeth Bush was on Prozac when she fired at a number of students, wounding one, at Bishop Neumann High School in Williamsport, Pennsylvania, in March 2000. Eighteen-year-old Jason Hoffman was taking Celexa and Effexor at the time he wounded one teacher and three students during a shooting rampage at Granite Hills High School in El Cajon, California.

I'm not saying that these drugs *caused* these young people to become enraged and start shooting people. Millions of people take these drugs and do not go on killing sprees. What I am saying is that these young people had problems that needed to be addressed. They needed to have people listen to them, understand them, and help them understand themselves. It may well be that, instead of taking the time to deal with the sources of their rage, the grown-ups in their lives just medicated their symptoms.

2. *Our corrupt media culture is saturating the minds of our kids with toxic, angry, violent input.* Young people today are exposed to all kinds of rage-inducing influences that you and I never knew when we were growing up. The Internet has spawned thousands and thousands of hate-filled, blood-drenched Web sites aimed at young minds and, in many cases, created by young minds. (Do you know what your kids are seeing on the Internet?) Kids go into Internet chat rooms and verbally assault, abuse, and threaten one another in the most

vile terms imaginable. (Do you know what your kids are saying to other kids on the Internet?)

If you are the parent of an adolescent today, you probably have no conception of the mind-destroying, soul-rotting ideas and images your child has already been exposed to on the Internet—everything from movies of people being gruesomely killed to instructions on how to build a bomb. "Now you have Web sites glorifying [the Columbine killers] and kids chatting with each other about doing another Columbine," said Cornell University researcher James Garbarino. "On the Web, adolescent rage takes on a cultural life of its own."[2]

Violent computer games can also have a toxic influence on our kids. The Columbine High School killers had actually created a scenario for the shoot-and-splatter game Doom that was modeled on the floor plan of their high school. Months before they stalked the halls of their school, shooting at everyone in sight, they were practicing the Columbine massacre on their computer screens.

The music kids listen to today—from rap to alternative to punk to heavy metal—preaches a relentless message of despair, nihilism, meaninglessness, loneliness, alienation, rage, and suicide. If you are not listening to the lyrics of the music on your kids' CDs, you should. Listen to Korn or System of a Down or Metallica. If you can't understand the words, go to the Google page on your computer and type in the name of the band in quotes, the name of the song in quotes, and the word *lyrics*. When you read the words to the songs that are drenching your kids' brains, I guarantee you will be horrified.

3. *We have encouraged teenagers to be preoccupied with themselves instead of involved in helping others.* The teenage years are typically a time when people differentiate themselves from their parents and try to discover who they truly are. As a result, adolescents tend to be self-absorbed and preoccupied with their own feelings, needs, and problems. They focus on issues in their relationships and on their continual power struggles with their parents. That's normal.

But when kids are self-absorbed, they tend to magnify their problems and think their lives are harder than they really are. That's not their fault. It's our fault as parents and teachers. We have become so concerned about their fragile self-esteem and their tender little egos that we have made them hypersensitive to every perceived unfairness. Instead of disciplining kids when they do wrong or correcting them when they make a mistake, we coddle them and worry about bruising their little feelings.

Many kids are never taught to face challenges and problems, to figure them out and conquer them, and to persevere through obstacles and opposition. Instead, we have taught them to dwell on how bad they feel. We have taught them to be offended when things don't go their way. Instead of shielding them from life, we should be telling our kids, "Everybody goes through trials and hurts, but we all get over it. You will too."

Unfortunately, today's self-absorbed kids think that their pain is the worst pain anyone has ever suffered. The result is that even something as temporary as the end of a teenage romance feels like the end of the world. When a teen sees life in such extreme terms, it seems perfectly reasonable that he should get his revenge by picking up a gun and ending everybody else's world.

Our message to kids must be, "Life is good, but life can be hard at times. When you face hurts, problems, and challenges, don't give up on yourself or on life. You will get through it, and life will get better once again."

And there is one more message we should send to young people: "If you want to have a happy life, become a servant to others. Don't just focus on your own feelings, needs, and emotions. Don't just focus on having fun or on material possessions. The truly happy people in life are those who look outside themselves and focus on meeting the needs of others." Self-absorbed people are always miserable, but those who are absorbed in service to others are the happiest people on earth.

4. *We have failed to teach young people the truth about the love of God.* If you are taught to believe things about God that are not true, then you will base your whole life on a lie. It is easy to become bitter, rebellious, and full of rage if you believe that God is always on your back. But it is impossible to be angry if you know that God is on your side.

We need to teach our kids the biblical truth that God is love. He is not arbitrary or cruel but loving and kind. He does not punish us for things that are not our fault, but he gives us grace beyond anything we deserve. If we teach kids the truth about God and his love from their earliest years, we will save them a lot of rage in their teenage years.

5. *We have failed to teach young people that it is OK to be angry with God.* Does that statement shock you? It shouldn't. It's based on the truth of the Bible.

Notice I didn't say it's *right* to be angry with God, but it's OK. It's normal, it happens, and God accepts us where we are and doesn't punish us for questioning him and having feelings of anger toward him. God always knows what he's doing, and his judgments are always right, but they don't always seem right to us, and that's why we become angry with God. He knows that, and he understands and accepts our honest anger.

In the Old Testament a righteous man named Job went through a time of incredible loss and suffering, including the destruction of his possessions, the death of his children, and the loss of his health. How did Job respond? He got angry! He screamed that God was treating him unfairly!

> Even today my complaint is bitter;
> his [God's] hand is heavy in spite of my groaning.
> If only I knew where to find him;
> if only I could go to his dwelling!
> I would state my case before him
> and fill my mouth with arguments. . . .
> He carries out his decree against me,
> and many such plans he still has in store.
> That is why I am terrified before him;
> when I think of all this, I fear him.
> God has made my heart faint;
> the Almighty has terrified me. (Job 23:2–4, 14–16)

In his pain Job was complaining and wishing he could argue his case before God. He thought God was unfair! He thought God was against him! Have you ever felt that way? I have—many times. That's often how people feel when they have been kicked around by life. It's hard to see that "God is love" when you've suffered pain, losses, and unfairness in life.

If you read through the book of Job, you will not find any passage in which God condemns Job for his anger. God corrects Job's false impression, but he never condemns Job. Being angry with God is normal, and God is not threatened or offended by our anger.

But God also knows that it's not healthy for us to stay angry, and he wants us to move beyond our anger to a place of trust. And the way we move beyond our anger with God is by honestly talking to him about it.

When we are mad at God, he doesn't want us to repress our anger. He wants us to express it directly to him in prayer. He wants us to pray through our rage. God would much rather hear an angry, accusing, screaming prayer than silence.

One of the reasons I suffered so much throughout my childhood and adolescence was that I hid from God. I didn't pray to God, I didn't communicate with God, but I would curse God for something I thought he did to me that day. I even tried to trick God. I thought that because the priests talked to God, if I didn't tell the priests, then God wouldn't know! I thought I could keep God from finding out that I was illegitimate and that I had been touched by a man by simply not telling the priests. I was afraid to talk to him, so I stayed as far away from God as I could.

I know now that if I had screamed my questions and my pain at God, even from the depths of my rage, he would have accepted it. And we need to tell our kids that they have that kind of access to God. They need to know they have a place to take their adolescent rage. They can take it to God. He will listen to them and accept them, and he will help them move beyond their rage to a place of trust and healing.

There are many places in the Bible where we see righteous, godly people expressing anger with God. For example, in Psalm 44, the psalmist accuses God of being unfair to the people of Israel. He writes:

> You have made us a reproach to our neighbors,
> the scorn and derision of those around us.
> You have made us a byword among the nations;
> the peoples shake their heads at us.
> My disgrace is before me all day long,
> and my face is covered with shame
> at the taunts of those who reproach and revile me,
> because of the enemy, who is bent on revenge.
> All this happened to us,
> though we had not forgotten you
> or been false to your covenant.
> Our hearts had not turned back;
> our feet had not strayed from your path.
> But you crushed us and made us a haunt for jackals
> and covered us over with deep darkness. . . .
> Yet for your sake we face death all day long;

we are considered as sheep to be slaughtered.
Awake, O Lord! Why do you sleep?
Rouse yourself! Do not reject us forever. . . .
Rise up and help us;
redeem us because of your unfailing love.

> (Ps. 44:13–19, 22–23, 26)

Clearly this is a psalm of anger toward God. It speaks of how the Old Testament people of Israel felt victimized not only by their enemies but by God himself. This psalm also can be personalized as a heartfelt prayer of anger by any person who has ever felt exploited, abused, mistreated, and humiliated. It expresses the rage of all victims, both toward their abusers and toward God.

Let's face it: One of the hardest things to understand about God is the way he allows injustice in the world. It is hard to understand why he allowed sin and death to enter the world. It is hard to understand why he allowed six million Jews to be exterminated in the Holocaust. It is hard to understand why he allowed three thousand people to die in the terrorist attacks on September 11, 2001.

It is hard to understand why he allows people to starve to death or be slaughtered in racial or religious wars all around the world. We can't understand why God allows children to die of horrible diseases like leukemia or why God allows children to be molested. All we know is that God's ways are not our ways, and sometimes his ways make us angry.

Pain, loss, frustration, and rage are normal parts of life and especially of adolescent life. We should encourage young people to make their honest feelings, including their rage, a normal part of their prayer life. When young people realize that God feels along with them, hurts along with them, and even rages along with them at sin and injustice, they will be able to move beyond their rage to a place of faith, hope, and trust in God.

I wish somebody had told me that when I was a child and a teenager. I wish I had known that God loved me and that I could pray out my rage to him instead of cursing him.

I don't want to see other kids go through years and years of rage as I did. I don't want to see other kids destroy their possessions, or destroy human lives, because they are blind with rage and despair. I don't want to see other kids feel hated by God and devalued by the world they live in.

God is love. He understands our pain. He accepts our prayers, even our prayers of rage. Most important of all, God, too, gets angry at injustice. As the psalmist assures us, God *will* rise up and help us. He *will* redeem us because of his unfailing love.

# 7

# SEX EDUCATION

*T*he first time I ever saw pornography was at Dad's Malibu ranch.

I had just turned fifteen and could legally drive a motor scooter, so I asked Dad to buy me one. I had found a used blue Lambretta scooter in beautiful condition for seven hundred dollars. I wanted it so I could ride out to the ranch on Friday nights after school. So Dad bought it for me, and I painted it red.

At the same time he bought me the scooter, Dad also made a deal with me: he'd get me a new car as a graduation present—and that was all the incentive I needed to graduate. He also promised me five hundred dollars cash on my twenty-first birthday if I didn't drink or smoke until I was twenty-one. I graduated and got the car, but Dad kept the five hundred bucks.

On Friday afternoons I couldn't wait to get home from Loyola High so I could ride my scooter out to the Malibu ranch. There was a modest-sized ranch house for our family and a small house for the ranch foreman. I enjoyed Friday nights at the ranch because it was quiet and peaceful, and I had my own room to stay in. There were pictures of race-horses on the walls of my room, as well as the framed ribbons from my swimming competitions and that yo-yo patch.

During my weekends at the ranch, I would often spend time in the cabin, talking with Dad's foreman, Ray Jackin, and Ray's son, Dick, who was about my age. Ray was a stocky man with a pronounced beer belly (which he seemed proud of, because he never wore a shirt). He had a real knack for making chili.

One time Ray took out a stack of magazines he kept under his bed, and he showed them to Dick and me. They were "girlie magazines," pretty tame stuff by today's porn standards, with topless shots of smiling models out in the woods. As I flipped through the magazines, Ray told me something that surprised me: The photo layouts I was looking at were shot right there on Dad's ranch. Looking closer, I saw it was true. I recognized some of the locations.

It turned out that Ray had some photographer friends who did photo shoots for these magazines. Unbeknown to Dad, Ray would let his friends come onto the property and use the scenic spots on the ranch as backdrops for their photo shoots. Ray's only stipulation was that the photographers let him watch while they shoot.

That night, and in weekends to come, Ray would regale Dick and me with stories about those photo shoots. I hadn't gotten much sex education from Mom or Dad or the nuns and priests at school, so Ray's tales of the photo sessions served to fill many of the gaps in my knowledge.

I thought it was funny that there were naked girls on Dad's ranch on a regular basis—if Dad only knew! To me Dick's dad was a really neat guy for showing us those pictures and telling us those stories.

A lot of things have changed since those days. Ray Jackin died a few years ago. Today Ray's son, Dick, has multiple sclerosis. In recent years Dick and I have renewed our friendship from years ago.

These days I have a whole different perspective on pornography than I did when I was fifteen years old. I now realized that I was used and exploited for child pornography.

## A RETAIL TRANSACTION

Like any boy in his mid-teens, I thought about girls during most of my waking hours. For some reason, the fact that all my thoughts were about girls didn't do anything to allay my fears that I might be thought of as a homosexual. Not only was I *not* attracted to boys, but I daydreamed about girls all the time, and I was still excessively modest in the boys' dorm. Yet, despite all the evidence of my heterosexual orientation, the guilty residue of the molestation was so much a part of me that I still felt insecure about my sexuality.

Loyola High was an all-boys school run by Jesuit priests. How about that! From the Sisters of Mercy to the Jesuits! I looked forward to Fridays at the ranch because just down the road, at Malibu Lake, were some girls I had met. My contact with the world outside of school was so limited that they were literally the only girls I knew. After weeks of nothing but guys to talk to, it was a real treat just to be around girls and have conversations with the opposite sex.

Like teenage boys at every high school, the guys at Loyola would sit around in their spare time and lie to one another about their sexual experiences with girls. We all lied. I lied too. Guys would say, "What about you, Reagan? Ever been laid?"

"Sure," I said. If pressed for details, however, I would have to keep my stories a bit vague since I had no experience. If the other guys knew I was bluffing, they never called me on it. Perhaps a few of them had been bluffing too. In fact, maybe all of them were.

When I was around sixteen or seventeen, I began visiting seedy shops on Hollywood Boulevard where I could rent a camera and take nude photos of female models, like the girls I had seen in Ray Jackin's magazines at the ranch. I also visited stripper bars and X-rated theaters in the area.

I was gaining information of a sexual nature, but I still had no experience with sex. And I still had nagging insecurities from the molestation. So I decided to do something about it. I borrowed Dad's station wagon and drove out to Western Avenue and cruised the red-light district. I'd stop at the curb and roll down the window, and girls would come up, lean on the door, and we'd talk. After a few minutes of this, the girls could see I had a serious case of cold feet, and they lost interest and moved on. After all, they had to make a living.

For several months I cruised Western Avenue, talked to

some prostitutes, then went home. Finally, while I was talking to one girl, I worked up the nerve, negotiated a price, and we went to bed. I only did it to prove that I could, to prove to myself that I was heterosexual. I had to.

I found it embarrassing and shameful that I'd had sex with a prostitute. I was afraid of getting caught because if I got caught, there would be questions like, "Why did you do it?" I was afraid that if I had to answer that question, everything would come out, including the molestation and the pictures Don had taken of me.

To this day one of the great regrets of my life is that I lost my virginity to a prostitute, to a girl whose name I never even knew. That first sexual experience with a girl temporarily reassured me that I was not a homosexual, but the reassurance didn't last long. My fears and sexual insecurities continued to haunt me as an aftereffect of the sexual molestation.

I continued to worry about those pictures Don Havlik took. I was scared to death that they would somehow surface and destroy my life. If they did, they would prove that my life was a lie. And it was.

The worry over those pictures drove me back to Western Avenue again and again. When I was with prostitutes, I didn't think about the pictures. But after I had been with a prostitute, I had additional fears to deal with: What if I got caught paying for sex? And then there was the price tag. Going back to the red-light district again and again quickly became more expensive than my teenage allowance would cover. So, when I ran out of money, I stole it from Dad.

At some point it hit me that this urge to get sex from prostitutes was a kind of sickness. If I didn't stop, sooner or later I was bound to get caught, and I didn't want to have to explain why I was so obsessed with proving my manhood with prostitutes. So one day I just quit, and I never went back to Western Avenue again.

## SELLING A DEBASED VIEW OF SEX

I look around, and I see our entire society doing what I did as a teenager. We are drowning in lust and sexual sin. You can't turn on the TV in the evening without seeing immoral behavior played out on almost every channel. Our movies, TV shows, music, books, magazines, and the Internet are barraging us with sexual images and messages. In LA, where I live, you can't drive down Sepulveda Boulevard or any main street without seeing billboards for "gentlemen's clubs." I'm sure it's no different in your town.

You rarely see anything in the media about married sex, sex as God intended it and created it. Most of the media messages about sex have to do with unmarried sex, adulterous sex, group sex, gay and lesbian sex, sadomasochistic sex, and even sex with animals.

And these messages are not just smuggled into the entertainment portions of the programming anymore. The moral polluters in our society have become so arrogant that they are now using smut-laden commercials to sell us products. Ad agencies and corporate heads have concluded that we Americans no longer care about morality and protecting children. And they have decided that there are no longer any boundaries or limits. Almost anything goes.

You turn on your TV and there's Hugh Hefner, age seventy-seven, sitting in his silk pajamas, saying, "People always ask me, 'Hey, Hef, do you have favorites?' I tell them no. It's not about that. I love them all. It just depends what I'm in the mood for." Cut to a buxom young woman in a T-shirt who says, "I feel for Hef. It's so hard to choose." Cut to another young woman who says, "He can have anything he wants. I don't know how he makes the choice." Then back to Hef, who has one of Carl's Jr. Six Dollar Burgers in his hands. The commercial concludes with the announcer telling us, "Because some guys don't like the same thing night after night."

Now even elementary schoolkids who see that commercial know that Carl's Jr. isn't just talking about hamburgers. There's nothing subtle about it; this commercial celebrates promiscuity in no uncertain terms. A company that used to be family friendly now jabs a thumb in the eye of everyone who lives in a faithful, monogamous marriage relationship— a relationship that the announcer derides as "the same thing night after night."

The commercial's not offensive merely because it features the founder of *Playboy,* though that is offensive enough. The *Playboy* philosophy has done enormous harm to our society. It's not just that the commercial blatantly compares women to hamburger—though that's offensive too. It's not just that the commercial suggests that promiscuity equals freedom of choice while monogamy equals monotony.

The commercial is truly offensive on all of these levels at once, and the result is a piece of propaganda that is about a whole lot more than selling hamburgers. It's selling a debased view of sex—and it is a none-too-subtle attack on people who believe in the sanctity of marriage.

Perhaps the most tragic part of this sorry episode is that Carl's Jr. was founded on Christian principles by Carl Karcher, a devout Catholic. My friend Joe Farah of WorldNet Daily.com called Karcher "a good American—a Christian, a family man. But long ago, his family business went public and the ad agencies took over the marketing. Now the company uses Hugh Hefner to promote the *Playboy* philosophy in its commercials. It's not about selling hamburgers anymore. It's about selling irresponsible, care-free sex."[1]

And Rev. Robert H. Schuller, on his weekly *Hour of Power* television broadcast, said that he had spoken with Karcher and that the man was "just heartbroken that a company he founded on Christian principles has taken such an amoral act that can be so dangerous on the impressions left with the children who watch."[2]

The ad sparked a firestorm of controversy and complaints when it began airing in November 2003, yet the company remained unrepentant. Company spokeswoman Caroline Leakan issued this statement: "We're sorry people took offense, but we're standing by our advertising. There's nothing sexual about them." Incredible! "Nothing sexual"! According to Ms. Leakan, we didn't see what we saw, we didn't hear what we heard. It was all in our minds.

Fortunately, some people and institutions are still willing to take a stand against corporate immorality, irresponsibility, and greed. One such institution is Thomas Aquinas College, a Catholic liberal arts institution in Ventura County, California. Carl's Jr. founder Carl Karcher had given generously to the college and served on its board for many years. After Karcher retired as CEO of Carl's Jr. in 1998, he was succeeded by Andrew Puzder, both as CEO of Carl's Jr. and as a member of the Thomas Aquinas College board of governors.

After the Hugh Hefner commercial aired, college president Thomas Dillon contacted Puzder and asked for his resignation from the board. He got it. "Thomas Aquinas College stands for principles that are in direct conflict with those of Hefner and *Playboy*," Dillon said.

The Hefner commercial was one of the first commercials to air during Super Bowl XXXVIII on Sunday, February 1, 2004. That was the infamous Janet Jackson Super Bowl, featuring a halftime show in which entertainer Justin Timberlake danced and sang with Janet Jackson, ending with Justin ripping the bodice of Janet Jackson's costume and exposing her right breast for approximately 2.5 seconds. The whole world went into apoplexy over Janet Jackson's indecent exposure— and rightly so. The Super Bowl is a family sports event, watched by millions of kids, and Ms. Jackson's deliberate attempt to offend and shock the nation to promote her soon-to-be-released CD was without excuse.

But those 2.5 seconds of bare breast weren't the only tasteless, offensive, and antifamily moments in the Super Bowl telecast. To begin with, consider the commercials. For example, there was an ad for Bud Lite in which a talking chimp brazenly invites his human owner, a young woman he calls Babe, to go upstairs and have sex with him. Well, sure! Why not? If a seventy-seven-year-old porn peddler can sell hamburgers, then bestiality can sell beer!

And then there was the commercial for Levitra, a drug that works like a turbo-charged Viagra. Here's a line from the commercial, as seen by millions of kids on Super Bowl Sunday: "Erections lasting longer than four hours, though rare, require immediate medical help." How would you like to have to explain *that* tagline to your kids?

I could cite other commercials, but you get the drift.

At halftime viewers were treated to an MTV-produced show that was (or should have been) an embarrassment to everyone involved. It featured Kid Rock wearing the American flag as a poncho while performing a foul-mouthed rap about forcing a girl to have sex. He was followed by P. Diddy, who also rapped about rape as the dancers in the background simulated assorted sex acts, both straight and lesbian. And then there was rap star Nelly, who accompanied his nasty rhymes with almost continuous crotch-fondling.

And all of this was mere foreplay to Mr. Timberlake's groping and disrobing of Ms. Jackson to the tune of "Rock Your Body." One line from the song should have been the tip-off to the NFL and the CBS television network that something bad was going to happen—the line where Timberlake sings, "Gonna have you naked by the end of this song."

When I saw that halftime show, I was struck by how all of those songs and images blended seamlessly together to present one long, blaring, pornographic message. And don't forget that the whole thing kicked off with Kid Rock jumping and gyrating while wrapped in the American flag. That show was beamed around the world by satellite, sending a message to the entire world: "This is what America is all about—the American flag and filthy lyrics, nonstop sex and on-stage masturbation, men demeaning women and immorality run amok." Any wonder why it's so tough being a parent these days?

You know something else? That was one heck of a great Super Bowl game, one of the best ever played. It was decided by a forty-one-yard field goal in the last four seconds of the game. Yet within hours the game itself was all but forgotten. The following day, and for weeks to come, all anybody talked about was Janet Jackson's right breast.

If there was anything good to come out of that Super Bowl halftime show, it was this: Parents who had never seen MTV before got a glimpse of the crotch-grabbing, sex-drenched "entertainment" their kids have been watching for years. It was quite a wake-up call.

Unfortunately, there was also a lot of hypocrisy in the wake of that Super Bowl show. Janet Jackson's breast flashed by so quickly that a lot of people missed it. No problem—by Monday morning, Matt Drudge had photos (including close-ups) of the breast in question on his Web site. I wonder, how many so-called "conservatives" now have that image on their computers as a screen-saver.

## LURING YOUR KIDS TO XXX.COM

It happened literally millions of times: Schoolkids wanted to write a letter to the president or write a term paper about the government, so they went to the computer and typed *whitehouse.com* into the URL window of their Web browser. Moments later, up popped a pornographic Web site. Why? Because the Web address of the White House in Washington, D.C., is not *whitehouse.com* but *whitehouse.gov.*

Since 1997, the whitehouse.com Web site has been a porn site. It was founded by a man named Daniel Parisi. Clearly he intended to confuse Web surfers and lure unsuspecting people into his world of smut. Just as clearly, Parisi had to know that a substantial number of those who would be snagged by his porn site are children.

In February 2004, after seven years in business, purportedly making a million dollars a year from his whitehouse.com site, Daniel Parisi decided to get out of the smut business. Why? He says it's because he's worried about the impact his porn site might have on his preschool-age son.

Parisi appeared on Neal Cavuto's show on the Fox News Channel on February 11. Cavuto asked him why he had decided to quit the porn business. "Is it because your kid is going to school now," Cavuto said, "and you're embarrassed?"

"Well, yes," Parisi replied. "Obviously, I think next year he's coming to the understanding age. Before, he was a young child, and children that young don't know what is going on. But now he starts going to school. He's going to look around and ask, 'What does Daddy do?'"

"Yes," Cavuto said, "but there's a bad news flash here: There are other kids who went to your site thinking they were getting the official White House site, and instead they got a porn site. So you don't feel bad for those kids, but you feel bad for your own kid?"

"Well," Parisi replied, clearly uncomfortable, "it's not really him going to the Web site. We're doing adult content, you know, not—"

"Yes," Cavuto pressed, "but it doesn't bother you that *other* kids did go to your porn site?"

At this point it was obvious that Parisi wanted to be anywhere but in front of the Fox News cameras. "Well," he said, "I've always thought that has been exaggerated."

So I guess it's OK if mere thousands or hundreds of thousands of kids clicked into his porn site by mistake, as long as it's not millions. The real crime here is not peddling smut to minors but exaggerating the problem.

And what about Parisi's claim that he finally wants out of the porn biz because he's concerned about his son? Well, maybe so. But it's abundantly clear that, for seven years of pimping porn on the Internet, Daniel Parisi never cared one bit about your kids or mine.

The timing of his decision is interesting. Nine months before Parisi decided to get out of the porn business, President George W. Bush signed a law making it illegal to use a misleading Web address to lure children into sites with harmful material such as pornography. For nine months Parisi continued to operate a site that clearly should have been targeted by that law. I don't know why the Bush Justice Department didn't swoop down and close Mr. Parisi's porn site forthwith.

But it is interesting that Parisi's decision came just a week or so after the Federal Communications Commission announced that it was going to investigate the outrageous halftime show at Super Bowl XXXVIII. Suddenly it appeared that the Bush administration might be getting serious about protecting kids from pornographic images, and within days Mr. Parisi decided to bail out of the porn business.

Connection? You be the judge. Maybe Mr. Parisi's real concern was not so much that his son might ask, "What does Daddy do?" but "What is Daddy doing in prison?"

Daniel Parisi says he plans to go into the Internet real estate sales business. I sincerely hope his son never has to encounter what so many thousands of innocent children encountered when they clicked on whitehouse.com. But Parisi is only one ex-pornographer. There are still plenty of other people out there seeking to lure our kids into XXX Web sites. According to a 2002 report by the NOP Research Group, nine out of ten kids ages eight to sixteen have viewed online pornography, and most of them stumbled into it by accident while doing homework.[3]

What can we do to protect our families from these predators? Here are some practical suggestions:

1. *Be aware of what your kids are doing online.* Check the "History" folder on the computer to see which Web sites have been visited on that computer. You also should be aware that

checking the "History" folder is not foolproof; a computer-savvy kid knows that the "History" folder can be altered.

2. *Use Internet filtering and monitoring software.* Programs like Spector, eBlaster, Child Safe, I Am Big Brother, Guardian Monitor, Cyber Sentinel, and ContentBarrier for Mac can give you the ability to block bad sites, track what sites your kids visit, check their e-mail and chat activity, and more. Investigate the features of these programs before you buy. Some monitor but do not filter or vice versa. You may need to purchase and install more than one program to obtain all the features you need to protect your kids.

3. *Keep the family computer in a public area of the house where it can always be observed.* Kids should not have an Internet-connected computer in their rooms where they can use it privately and unobserved.

4. *Limit the time your kids spend on the computer.* Some programs, such as Enuff, give you a parentally controlled timer that limits the amount of time kids can spend on computer games or on the Internet. Once the time limit is reached, Enuff shuts the program down.

5. *Do not give your kids access to the computer when they are home by themselves.* Kids who are home alone after school, latch key kids, are especially vulnerable to Internet porn and online sexual predators. Make sure your computer cannot be started without your password—or, if you must, lock the computer in a closet when you're not home.

6. *Teach your kids about God's gift of sex.* Make sure they understand the difference between true sexual intimacy within

the protective enclosure of a committed marriage versus the commercial exploitation of sex that takes place in pornography. Teach your kids that, though pornography glamorizes casual and perverted sex, it destroys a porn viewer's ability to have healthy attitudes toward sex. It can even damage one's ability to have healthy sexual relationships in marriage. Pornography treats human beings like objects rather than valued and unique human beings made in the image of God.

7. *Teach your kids that pornography exploits and abuses women and children.* The people who are depicted in pornography often participate because they are forced to. (Child slavery is a major factor in child porn.) Many are drug addicts, and the porn makers supply them with money or drugs to feed their self-destructive habits. Organized crime is a huge factor in the porn business. Kids need to know that when they view porn, they are viewing the destruction of human lives. I know about that destruction firsthand.

8. *Help your kids build strong biblically based convictions about pornography.* It's one thing to build external barriers around your kids, such as Internet filtering software. But it is even more important to strengthen their inner convictions against pornography. Young people need to know that pornography is both sinful and destructive to the viewer. It has the power to take over a person's life, just like a drug addiction. Pornography can even destroy one's marriage, one's family, and one's entire future.

Teach your kids what Jesus said: "The eye is the lamp of the body. If your eyes are good, your whole body will be full of light. But if your eyes are bad, your whole body will be full of darkness. If then the light within you is darkness, how great is that darkness!" (Matt. 6:22–23).

And the psalmist David wrote, "I will be careful to lead a blameless life—when will you come to me? . . . I will set before my eyes no vile thing. The deeds of faithless men I hate; they will not cling to me. Men of perverse heart shall be far from me; I will have nothing to do with evil" (Ps. 101:2–4).

9. *Talk to your kids and hold them accountable.* Never assume that your child would never get involved with Internet porn. Even kids who are "good kids" in every other way can fall prey to lust and pornography. Ask your kids, "When you use your computer, do you ever surf the Internet in places you shouldn't? Are you honoring God through the way you use your computer?" Don't be timid about talking candidly with your kids about these issues.

10. *If you find your child has gotten into pornography, take it seriously, but don't panic.* Many parents take a lackadaisical "kids will be kids" attitude toward pornography. Others get hysterical. As Christian parents we need to find the firm yet loving balance in dealing with this issue.

When you discover your children are viewing pornography, you must talk to them about it. You can expect them to react with shame, defensiveness, and even lies. You should respond by firmly stating that you know what they've been doing, so denials won't work. Then state that you love your kids and you want only the best for them. This is going to be hard to talk about, but you and your kids *must* talk about it.

If you discover porn on the computer when the child is not present, talk to your spouse and decide together how to approach the subject. Should one of you talk to the child or both? If just one of you, which one? Make sure you have a well-thought-out plan before you talk to your child. Also, pray together for guidance and the ability to communicate God's grace and forgiveness to your child.

Set appropriate consequences and hold your kids accountable. Children need to know there is a price to pay for misusing the privilege of a computer and for disobeying God's law about sexual purity.

Set boundaries for the future. Decide what kind of guardrails you need to put in place to prevent porn from coming into your house again. Then stick to that decision. Those guardrails should include regularly talking to your child and holding him or her accountable to you for using the computer in a proper and godly way.

Don't be afraid to "invade" your kids' privacy in order to protect them from pornography. Parents have a duty to know what their children are doing, especially if they are doing something harmful to themselves. Go in their rooms and look around when they're at school. Check in their dresser drawers and under their beds. Listen to their phone conversations. You are the parent, and you have a duty to know what your kids are doing. So act like a parent, not a best friend.

One more thing we should all do: Write to the president, your senator, your congressman, and tell them you want all sites that feature pornographic content to be required to register with a special domain extension, such as dot-xxx, dot-sex, or dot-adult. Urge our nation's leaders to address this problem and to call upon the entire world to follow suit.

Pornographers oppose the idea of a special "dot-xxx" domain. They resist being segregated into a "red-light district" on the Internet. They propose, instead, putting all kid-friendly sites into a safe "green zone" with a "dot-kids" extension. But what about sites that should be safe for both adults and kids, such as government sites, research sites, magazine/newspaper sites, online encyclopedias, e-texts of classic books, and so forth? Why should we put kids in a ghetto? It makes much more sense to make the entire Internet into a nice neighborhood, while putting the red-light district safely to one side, available to those who want it but safely out of the reach of kids.

As we confront the pornographers who are trying to increase the hit count on their Web sites by luring our kids into their lairs, we need to realize that porn merchants are under the same judgment as child molesters. As Jesus warned, "But if anyone causes one of these little ones who believe in me to sin, it would be better for him to have a large millstone hung around his neck and to be drowned in the depths of the sea" (Matt. 18:6 NIV).

## THE XXX FACTS

Charles R. Swindoll is senior pastor of Stonebriar Community Church, chancellor of Dallas Theological Seminary, and the author of more than thirty best-selling books. He has written an open letter to churches in which he calls "pornography, especially Internet pornography" the "number one secret problem" in our churches.

"Without your knowing, it could be eating your church alive," he wrote. "The most recent studies available suggest that one out of every two people—that's fifty percent of the people sitting in our pews—are looking at and/or could be addicted to Internet pornography. The struggle is going on among those who volunteer in your church and mine. Chances are good that some of our full-time staff members, even some who faithfully serve on our boards, may be losing this secret battle. And while I'm listing these possibilities, let's not overlook our young adults—married and single—who provide instruction among our junior and senior high youth. Truth be told, that statistic could be even higher."[4]

Here are some of the X-rated facts:

N2H2, a software publisher specializing in Internet filtering products, says that, as of September 2003, there were 260 million pornographic Web pages in the company's filtering database. That is an 1,800-percent increase over the 14 million pages N2H2 had in its 1998 database. The company reported that more than 28 million new porn Web pages appeared on the Internet in the month of July 2003 alone. N2H2 also reported that a Google search of the word *porn* yielded more than 80 million pages, and a search of the term XXX returned more than 76 million pages.

An MSNBC Survey conducted in 2000 found that 25 million Americans spend from one to ten hours a week visiting porn Web sites. According to the *Wall Street Journal*

(26 November 2001), online pornography now generates an estimated ten to twenty billion dollars of revenue per year.[5] A 2003 ABC News report put that figure into perspective. If even the low end of that estimate is correct, ten billion dollars, then that is more revenue than is generated by the NFL, the NBA, and Major League Baseball combined. "And," the ABC report adds, "some of the nation's best-known corporations are quietly sharing the profits. . . . Companies like General Motors, AOL Time Warner, and Marriott earn revenue by piping adult movies into Americans' homes and hotel rooms, but you won't see anything about it in their company reports."[6]

Pornography victimizes every life it touches. Children are victimized by porn when they stumble into a hard-core Web site and see images that they are not emotionally and developmentally ready to see. Often, the victims become predators themselves. I recently heard of one boy who discovered his parents' cache of hard-core videos while he was home alone. He watched them and learned sexual techniques from them, and then he molested his little sister and several of her neighborhood friends.

Women are victimized by pornography in a variety of ways. Wives lose the genuine affection of their husbands who have become addicted to pornography and masturbation. Women are often sexually harassed and even assaulted by men who form their impressions about women from the dehumanizing, depersonalizing porn they view on a regular basis. Hard-core porn often presents women as tied up, physically abused, and raped—and it depicts women as enjoying these degrading, painful experiences. There should be no doubt in anyone's mind that hard-core depictions of rape inevitably stimulate some men to act out what they see.

Young women, as young as eighteen, sometimes become trapped in a sex industry that exploits them and often leaves them filled with shame and infected by AIDS or other venereal diseases. An ABC News *Primetime* segment profiled a porn actress named Belladonna, who was raised in a Mormon home in Utah and got her start in porn films at eighteen. According to the *Primetime* report, she was required to perform anal sex without condoms, a very risky behavior. In one film she had on-screen sex with twelve male partners and later contracted chlamydia, a serious sexually transmitted disease. Though she is paid a lot of money to have sex for the camera, she is still a victim.

At one point in the program, interviewer Diane Sawyer asked Belladonna why she always smiled. At that point the porn star's smile trembled, and tears welled up in her eyes. "Because I like to hide," she said. "I hide everything, you know?" She broke down and cried, then added, "I'm not happy. I don't like myself at all." Describing what she felt like while having on-camera sex, she said, "My whole entire body feels it when I'm doing it, and I feel so—so gross." Though she pretends to enjoy the sex while the camera is rolling, she told Sawyer that she usually imagines herself being outside her body, as if the debasing sex acts are happening to someone else. That's what pornography is like for the women who are exploited by it.[7]

Men, too, are victimized by pornography. Sure, they're willing victims, but they're still victims. Pornography plants a totally false image of what their own sexuality is about, what women really want out of sex, and what God intended true sexual pleasure to be. Pornography robs men of the joy of true sexual union with a loving partner. It cheats men and reduces their sex life to a joyless, lonely experience of self-gratification in front of a computer screen or a magazine.

Our culture is spinning down a sewer drain of depravity, and individual lives—and entire families—are being destroyed in the process. Both adults and young people are allowing themselves to be drawn into a spiraling cycle of addiction to pornography. Gene Edward Veith, cultural editor for *World Magazine,* observed in the March 10, 2001 issue:

> The reason that the jettisoning of sexual morality leads to such a slippery slope has to do with the nature of sinful pleasure. The Bible describes the process of the "hardening" of people's hearts, which is both the psychopathology of sin and God's judgment against it. Those who persevere in a particular sin after awhile no longer feel guilty about doing it. Whereupon they take up another vice, and the process continues, as they grow worse and worse and more and more depraved. . . . When the heart becomes hardened, the thrill is gone, and like a drug addict having to shoot up higher and higher doses to get the original high, sinners have to go to ever greater extremes in order to get the old forbidden pleasure.[8]

The cycle of addiction begins when people discover pornography, sometimes by accident on the Internet and sometimes out of curiosity. They experiment with it and are soon hooked. The need for increasingly extreme sexual fantasies grows until just seeing nudity and sex is not enough. The addict craves more and ends up getting hooked on bondage, sexual torture, rape, bestiality, or sex with minors. In the process he soon becomes desensitized. Sex acts that were once shocking and repulsive are now acceptable and arousing. Pornography and normal married sex are no longer enough to satisfy. The addict must act out his fantasies through promiscuous behavior, soliciting prostitutes, voyeurism, and more.

In the end pornography owns the porn addict's soul. Many people—people you would never suspect, even people in your church—end up losing their reputations and their self-respect. Some lose their families.

## DEALING WITH TEMPTATION

No one is immune from temptation. I'm not. I'm sure you're not, either. In our media-saturated society, the problem of temptation becomes far more difficult than ever before because hard-core porn is now available with the click of a mouse or the TV remote control.

"Part of the problem is that the search for adult entertainment is so easy," writes Henry J. Rogers in *The Silent War: Ministering to Those Trapped in Deception of Pornography.*

Go to a convenience store to buy a gallon of milk and you have to deal with the temptation of a magazine rack. Go to a video store to rent a family movie and you have to deal with the temptation of a back room filled with adult videos. Drive down the road past billboards for strip clubs and you have to deal with the temptation of a reclining, scantily-clad woman on the billboard. Walk into a motel room while you are away from your family and you have to deal with the temptation of turning on an adult movie. It seems to have no end.[9]

We can't remove ourselves from society, and even if we could, the temptation would still be with us. Ultimately, the problem is not outside. It's in our own hearts. Christ said, "For out of the heart come evil thoughts, murder, adultery, sexual immorality, theft, false testimony, slander. These are what make a man 'unclean'" (Matt. 15:19–20).

Throughout the Bible we see the terrible sorrow and disgrace suffered by people who give in to sexual temptation. Some of the greatest heroes of the faith suffered shame and incredible loss when they allowed sexual temptation into their lives.

There was King David, whose sin started with voyeurism, simply watching from his rooftop as a woman took a bath in her backyard—essentially no different from viewing pornography today. But what began as voyeurism ended in adultery and murder. There was Judah, the son of Jacob, who had sex with a veiled woman, thinking she was a prostitute. Then he was disgraced to learn that she was his own daughter-in-law, Tamar. There was Samson, who thought he could outwit temptation in the form of a woman named Delilah, and he lost his strength, his eyes, and ultimately his life.

If some of the great heroes of the Bible gave in to temptation, then what hope do the rest of us have? Actually, we have all the power we need to overcome the temptation of pornography, lust, and sexual sin. Now we just need a strategy for relying on God's strength at all times, and especially in times of sexual temptation and moral weakness. Here's a biblical strategy for defending yourself against temptation:

1. *Make a firm commitment.* Promise yourself, your spouse, and God that you will not view pornography or commit any sexual sin. Author and radio host Dr. James Dobson *(Focus on the Family)* says that his marriage is based on an absolute commitment to his wife. "Honestly," he once wrote, "I have never even considered cheating on Shirley. The very thought of hurting her and inviting God's judgment is more than enough to keep me on the straight and narrow. Furthermore, I would never destroy the specialness we shared for all these years."

A commitment doesn't make you immune from temptation, but it does strengthen you against the attack of it. Dr. Dobson described how his commitment to his wife and his integrity protected him at a vulnerable time in his life:

> Shirley and I had been married just a few years when we had a minor fuss. It was no big deal, but we both were pretty agitated at the time. I got in the car and drove around for about an hour to cool off. Then when I was on the way home, a very attractive girl

drove up beside me in her car and smiled. She was obviously flirting with me. Then she slowed down, looked back, and turned onto a side street. I knew she was inviting me to follow her.

I didn't take the bait. I just went home and made up with Shirley. But I thought later about how vicious Satan had been to take advantage of the momentary conflict between us. . . . That is typical of his strategy. He'll lay a trap for you, too, and it'll probably come at a time of vulnerability.[10]

2. *In times of emotional stress, rely on the Holy Spirit.* In his book *Experiencing Spiritual Breakthroughs*, Dr. Bruce Wilkinson, author of *The Prayer of Jabez* and founder of Walk Thru the Bible Ministries, notes that temptation is often greatest in times of emotional stress. So he offers a simple prayer that he calls the "Three-Minute Temptation Buster"— a prayer addressed to the Holy Spirit, whom the Bible calls "The Comforter." Dr. Wilkinson's prayer is simple: "Dear Holy Spirit, You've been sent to me to be my personal Comforter. I am in desperate need of comfort. I don't want to sin. Please comfort me. In Jesus' name, Amen."[11]

Now that seems too simple, doesn't it? Yet Dr. Wilkinson says that the first time he used that prayer to ward off temptation, he took off his watch to see what would happen. "Slowly," he writes, "I became aware of something—I was comforted. My soul felt soothed and no longer in pain. When I turned back toward that temptation, I discovered it had miraculously slithered into the darkness, far away from my senses. I was free."

Wilkinson adds that, over the years, he has often prayed that prayer and checked his watch to see how long it would take for the Holy Spirit to respond. Every time, without exception, the Comforter removed his stress and his temptation in three minutes or less.

3. *Be accountable to someone.* Find a group in your church who will meet on a weekly basis to pray together, study the Bible together, and hold one another accountable in an atmosphere of trust and confidentiality. Tell the others in the group that you have a struggle with temptation. You don't have to be specific or detailed, but be honest. Tell the others in the group that you want them to ask you every week how you are doing and to call you during the week or even every day, if necessary. Knowing that you have to answer to someone for the way you live your life can be a powerful reinforcement against temptation.

4. *Regularly remind yourself of the terrible cost of giving in to temptation.* When we sin, we grieve Christ and dishonor his name. In Romans 14:12, Paul says, "So then, each of us will give an account of himself to God." When we look the Lord in the eye someday and give an accounting for ourselves, what will we say?

Sexual sin, including viewing pornography, harms not only our relationship with God but our most important human relationships as well. It can cost you the trust and love of your wife, the respect of your children, your reputation and credibility as a Christian, and your own self-respect. The risk and the cost are too great.

5. *If you find you can't resist temptation, then remove it from your life.* Get rid of cable TV and cut off the Internet, if you have to. These things are conveniences, not necessities. If you can't handle having these connections in your home, then cut them off and spend more time reading good books (including the Bible) and building relationships with your family and friends.

6. *Avoid temptation when you travel.* When you book a hotel room, ask if the hotel offers in-room pornography because you won't stay there if they do. In-room porn is a $500 million-a-year sideline for the hotel industry, but some hotel chains have made a courageous decision to get out of the smut business.

In 1999, the Omni hotel chain stopped offering in-room porn, citing a commitment to family values. That decision costs the company an estimated one million dollars a year, but the Omni chain also has received more than fifty thousand messages of support, including a note from a traveling businessman who said, "Thank you for taking away the temptation."[12]

7. *Use Scripture to cleanse your mind on a daily basis.* Focus on passages of the Bible that will strengthen you against temptation. Some good examples:

"I made a covenant with my eyes not to look lustfully at a girl" (Job 31:1).

"You have heard that it was said, 'Do not commit adultery.' But I tell you that anyone who looks at a woman lustfully has already committed adultery with her in his heart. If your right eye causes you to sin, gouge it out and throw it away. It is better for you to lose one part of your body than for your whole body to be thrown into hell" (Matt. 5:27–29).

"Therefore do not let sin reign in your mortal body so that you obey its evil desires. Do not offer the parts of your body to sin, as instruments of wickedness, but rather offer your-selves to God, as those who have been brought from death to life; and offer the parts of your body to him as instruments of righteousness. For sin shall not be your master, because you are not under law, but under grace" (Rom. 6:12–14).

"Finally, brothers, whatever is true, whatever is noble, whatever is right, whatever is pure, whatever is lovely, what-ever is admirable—if anything is excellent or praiseworthy—think about such things" (Phil. 4:8).

"Marriage should be honored by all, and the marriage bed kept pure, for God will judge the adulterer and all the sexually immoral" (Heb. 13:4).

Pornography and sexual sin isolate us and ruin our rela-tionships, including our relationship with God. We can't live in a state of integrity and inner peace as long as we are slaves to shame and sexual addictions. The great irony of God's gift of sex is this: In its rightful place, sex brings children into the world and creates families; wrongfully used, sex hurts children and destroys families.

How will you use God's gift of sex?

# 8

# RACING TO NOWHERE

*I*n 1961, I was a sixteen-year-old high school student at Loyola, living with Dad and Nancy in Pacific Palisades. I had a lot of turmoil going on inside. Here I was, the son of Ronald Reagan, adopted into a family that everyone idolized, yet I felt I didn't belong because I was the black sheep of the family. I felt like an absolute failure to the Reagan name, and I didn't deserve to be called Michael Reagan, but I didn't know anything else to call myself.

To give you a perspective on just who my parents were, let me put it this way: When they were married in 1940, Ronald Reagan and Jane Wyman were the Ben and J-Lo of their day. That's a lot of fame to live up to, and I didn't think I was much of a credit to those illustrious Hollywood names.

I had succeeded in getting out of Mom's house, only to discover that I was just as uncomfortable and unhappy in Dad's house. So now I began trying to work my way out of Dad's house.

The strategy I used was this: I would pick a fight with Nancy, and I would badger her and tell her I wanted out of the Reagan family. "Just tell me what name I should use," I told her, "and I'll go be somebody else. I won't be a Reagan anymore."

Do you see what I was doing? The molestation had made me hate myself, yet at the same time I loved my parents, and I didn't want to hurt them. So, in order to protect my parents from the secret inside me, I did everything I could to get them to dislike me and send me away. If I could get them to send me away, then I could spare them the pain of finding out what a bad person I was because of the molestation and those pictures.

In effect, I was doing the same thing to Dad and Nancy that I had already done to Mom, only I used a different strategy for getting them to dislike me. With Mom, the strategy I used was bad behavior, anger, picking fights, yelling, and arguing. With Dad and Nancy, the strategy I used was badgering Nancy for the answer to the question, "Who am I?"

Do you see how distorted my thinking had become because of what Don Havlik did to me? Out of my love for Mom and Dad, I was deliberately doing everything in my power to make them miserable!

And there was another reason I kept pushing Nancy to get that information: I really wanted to know who I was and where I came from. I wanted to find my birth mother and ask her, "Why? Why did you give me up? Was there something wrong with me?"

I wanted to tell my birth mother, "You don't give up on children! You raise them!" I wanted to tell her how much pain

I had gone through because she had given me up. I kept thinking that if my birth mother hadn't given me up, none of these bad things would have happened to me—the molestation, the pictures, the boarding schools, and on and on. At that time in my life, I was screaming inside, "Tell me why! I need to know why you gave me up!"

So I kept badgering Nancy and demanding that she find the information about my birth name. At first she refused, but finally I pushed her to the point where she decided to take me up on it.

At the time, Dad and Mom used the same business manager, David Martin. So Nancy prevailed upon him to get my birth information out of Mom's files.

One weekend I came home from school, and Nancy was waiting for me with a piece of paper. "I have the information you wanted," she said. "If you want to change your name and move out, that's up to you. Here's the information. You can do what you want with it."

We sat down in the living room, and I felt like all my internal organs had jumped into my throat. All these years I had thought I wanted to know who I was and where I came from. But now that the moment had finally arrived, I wasn't so sure.

"The name you were given at birth," Nancy said, "was John L. Flaugher. It's spelled F-L-A-U-G-H-E-R. You were born at Queen of Angels Hospital in Los Angeles. Your father was a corporal in the army."

I had to know the answer to the question that had haunted me for almost ten years. "Were my parents married?" I asked.

"No," Nancy said.

With that one word she confirmed my worst fears. I got up and walked out of the room. All I could think was, *I'm a bastard and I'm going to hell.*

## FOUR HUNDRED MILES FROM HOME

A few days later I visited Mom. She and Maureen were at Fred Karger's apartment, and I joined them there. In casual conversation I happened to throw out the name *John Flaugher* to see if it would get a reaction.

I expected at least a look of shock from my mother, but she didn't say anything, didn't even look up. If Mom recognized the name, she gave no indication. But I noticed that Maureen was staring at me wide-eyed.

Later Maureen took me aside and said, "Where did you hear that name?"

I said, "That's the name I was given at birth."

"I know it is," Maureen said. "Mom told me a long time ago. But where did you hear it? How did you find out?"

"Nancy told me."

Maureen gasped. "Nancy! How did *she* find out? Those records are supposed to be sealed!"

I shrugged, and I began to cover my tracks. "I don't know how Nancy found out," I said. "She just found out."

I didn't tell Maureen that I had pestered and badgered Nancy for the information. Instead I tried to make Nancy look bad. I told Maureen that Nancy was trying to throw me out of the house, and I suggested that Nancy had obtained my birth information in order to get me to leave home and go searching for my birth mother.

(I told that cover story so many times that it was even turned into a scene in the TV smear-movie about my family, *The Reagans*. During the controversy about that movie, I appeared on *Hannity and Colmes* on the Fox News Channel, and Alan Colmes asked me about that particular scene, saying that the movie portrayed Nancy as scheming to move me out of the house. I had to set Alan straight. In real life I was the one scheming and manipulating to get Dad and Nancy to throw me out!)

After hearing my story, Maureen said, "Listen, Michael, don't you ever bring up that name again! And not another word about this to Mom because it would kill her!"

My relationship with Nancy continued to deteriorate. We spoke to each other only when necessary, and sometimes the tension was so thick you could cut it with a chainsaw.

My grades were in free fall. One Sunday night as Dad drove me back to Loyola High, he said, "You know, Michael, every time a report card comes out, it's like D-day."

"Yeah, I know," I said. I had been trying for months to get sent away from Dad and Nancy's home, and I finally saw an opportunity to make it happen. Choosing my words carefully, I said, "If you really want to do something for me, send me to a coeducational school. In fact, if you'll send me out of state to a coed high school next year, I promise I'll pull my grades up."

"OK, Michael," Dad said. "It's a deal."

Nancy's mother and father lived in Phoenix. Her father, retired neurosurgeon Loyal Davis, talked to some people at Judson School, a prestigious boarding school in Scottsdale, Arizona, and he got me in. I dropped out of Loyola and went to Judson, where I had to repeat my junior year (academically, I had wasted my junior year at Loyola anyway). I didn't mind being a junior again; at least there were girls on the campus.

One thing I noticed right away was that the Judson student body had a distinct mind-set. It was an exclusive school for rich kids, and the students on that campus all hated their parents, felt their parents hated them—and, like me, most of them hated themselves. It was a campus full of kids who were not wanted, who were sent away by their parents.

And the greatest irony of it all was this: *I had won!* I had accomplished exactly what I set out to do. I had gotten away from Dad and Nancy's house and had made it all the way to Arizona. Yet, soon after I arrived at Judson, I fell right into the Judson mind-set: I started blaming my parents for sending me away!

The school was run by Henry and Barbara Wick, and they became substitute parents to all the kids at Judson. They were some of the nicest people I ever met, and they were mentors to me.

I enjoyed myself at Judson. I organized poker parties to supplement the meager allowance I got from Dad. There were plenty of rich kids at Judson with money to burn and not much poker sense. I was more than happy to separate them from their allowances. I always won enough money every week to afford dinner and a movie with my girlfriend of the moment.

Dad and Nancy came by train every Easter to visit the Davises in Phoenix, and they came to the school to see me perform in my first school play. I was nervous with two professional film actors in the audience, and I felt like I was pretty terrible in the role of a prosecuting attorney. Maybe it's because my whole life was an act. After the show Dad generously praised my performance.

I went out for sports and lettered in football, basketball, and baseball. My grades shot up, and I became an honor student. As an honor student, I was entitled to live in a cottage with three roommates instead of living in a dorm, and that meant no more gym-style showers. I was still dealing with those old insecurities.

Dad couldn't believe the change in my grades. He asked me what I wanted for Christmas. I said I wanted a gun to hunt with during the season—either a shotgun or a deer rifle. When I came home for Christmas, I found he had gotten me *both* guns. The rifle was a .243, and the shotgun was an absolute work of art—a beautifully engraved double-barrel Winchester with a gold trigger.

I used the rifle to hunt boar, and I shot the biggest wild pig taken in the state of Arizona that year. Dad had it mounted for me. Ugly as that pig was, I thought it was a beautiful trophy. I hung it on the wall in place of the yo-yo patch. At last, I no longer had to see that reminder of the molestation.

## SABOTAGING MYSELF

Every summer between my eighth and eighteenth birthdays, I spent eight to ten weeks at summer camp, usually at Mountain Meadow Ranch near Susanville in northern California. I had my horse Rebel with me, and I did a lot of horseback riding and hiking there. The camp directors were Jack and Jacquie Ellena (their son, Jack Jr., runs the camp today with his wife Jodie). I stayed at the ranch not only as a camper but also volunteered on the work crew.

Jack Ellena was one of the great steadying influences in my life. He had played for the Los Angeles Rams in the 1950s, so he was a man's man, the kind of guy I truly respected. He and Jacquie took me to church, taught me good values, and disciplined me when I needed it, which was often. They reinforced a lot of the lessons Mom and Dad tried to teach me about faith, values, and working hard to get ahead in life. I didn't appreciate what a good friend and role model Jack was when I was a teenager, but more than thirty years later, I dedicated my book *Making Waves* to several of my mentors, including Jack.

Jack and Jacquie were two people I really loved. I had been going to their camp since I was small, and they had been mentoring me forever. They were absolutely wonderful people, yet I ended up doing the same thing to them that I had done to Mom and Dad: I tried to make them dislike me so they would send me away. It was as if I couldn't let anything good happen to me for too long. In the end I figured out a way to get *them* to kick me out. If nothing else, I was consistent! Here's what I did:

Near the end of my last summer at Mountain Meadow Ranch, the summer before my senior year at Judson, I provoked an argument with Jack. Once I got the argument going, I took a swing at him. Jack countered with a jab that knocked me on the ground. That ended the argument, and it also ended my stay at Mountain Meadow Ranch. Jack put me on a plane and sent me home.

Are we beginning to see a pattern here? I got Mom to send me away, I got Dad and Nancy to send me away, and now I got my dearest friends—Jack and Jacquie Ellena—to send me away too. Once again, I had won! But what had I won?

And that wasn't the only way I had sabotaged myself at that camp. When I was a camper at Mountain Meadow Ranch, I wanted to earn a camper's belt and buckle. You had to do ten activities to earn it. One of those activities was shooting. Understand, I was trained to shoot by my dad. Rifle marksmanship was one of my best skills.

While I was at camp, I did nine of the ten things I had to do in order to earn that belt and buckle. What do you think is the one thing I *didn't* do? You guessed it. I didn't go to the range and shoot! I failed to do the one thing I did best!

It was as if I failed on purpose in order to prove to myself and everyone else that I really was a bad person. It was typical of so many things I did in life. Again and again I would fail to finish a task; I would fail to follow through on a commitment. In the process I missed so many opportunities and good things in life because I continually sabotaged myself.

Recently I was talking to Jack on the phone. (His wife, Jacquie, passed away in January 2002.) I told him, "I would give up a year's salary for a chance to earn that camper's belt."

And Jack said, "If you want to come back to camp, shoot at the range, and finish qualifying for it, I'll get you that belt and buckle."

And you know what? I'm going to take Jack up on it.

## "YOU NEED TO BE OUT ON YOUR OWN"

The last few weeks of my summer vacation, I painted fences at Dad's Malibu ranch. Then I returned to Judson a couple of weeks before the start of my senior year so I could get ready for the football season. That year, I took our football team to a state championship—Judson's first and last championship—and I was named Football Player of the Year.

In the spring Nancy's mother, De De Davis, came to one of my baseball games. It was really neat. De De had been a Broadway actress before World War I, and she was a wonderful, enthusiastic lady. She sat in the stands, whooping and cheering for me. Her support inspired me to hit a home run. I really clobbered that ball! It was the first (and last) home run of my high school baseball career. Also that year I pitched a no-hitter in my last high school baseball game.

After my successes in both football and baseball, I thought, *Boy, will my family be impressed!* And they were. Dad congratulated me, and Mom said she was proud of me. Yet I still felt empty inside. Even with all the positive things that were happening in my life—my good grades, my success in sports, and a successful dating life—I still felt that my life was pointless and unsatisfying.

I was living a lie, and I was the only one who knew it. People would tell me they were impressed with my accomplishments, but I wasn't impressed with myself. I still hated myself. I still carried the burden of a molestation I had suffered over a decade before. I was angry inside, and I carried that anger with me wherever I went.

I started thinking about college while I was at Judson. Dad suggested his alma mater, Eureka College in Illinois, where he had graduated in 1932. He told me he could talk to some people in the administration and get me in. Eureka is a liberal arts college affiliated with the Disciples of Christ denomination. I didn't want to tell Dad, but I would have rather crawled on broken glass than attend a Christian college. I was enjoying life in Arizona, so I applied to Arizona State and was accepted.

In May 1964, I graduated from Judson School as a member of the National Honor Society. Just as Mom and Dad had promised, they bought me a car—a brand new Ford Galaxy 500, black with red vinyl interior.

After spending the summer working at Yellowstone National Park, I started at Arizona State University. I started out with the same good academic intentions that got me on the honor roll at Judson, but soon I was at it again: I sabotaged my own success.

Near the end of my first semester at ASU, Nancy sent me money to pay my way home for Christmas. I took that money and spent it at The Library. No, not the ASU Library. There was a bar a few blocks from campus *called* The Library, but the only books in that library were painted on the walls. Whenever Mom or Dad would call and ask, "Where's Michael?" my roommates would answer, "He's at The Library." That answer, though deceptive, was technically accurate.

So I spent the money from Nancy on good times at The Library. When the money ran out, I called Nancy and said, "I need more money so I can come home."

"I already sent you the money for your trip home," she said. "Where is that money?"

"I had expenses," I said.

"Well," she said, "if you spent it, then I guess you're not coming home."

So I ended up going with Mom to Lake Tahoe for Christmas. After Christmas break, I returned to ASU, but I never went to another class. That was my twisted way of punishing Dad and Nancy for not sending me the money. When Dad and Nancy found out about my academic meltdown, they pulled me out of college.

Having sabotaged my scholastic future, I had to come home to California. At that point Mom called Dad and said, "Mike's coming back to LA and he's going to want to live with one of us. We both have to be strong and say no. We can't coddle him. He needs to get a job and take responsibility for his own life." Mom was determined to make a man out of me if it killed me!

Dad agreed that the situation called for tough love. So Mom and Dad hung tough and refused to take me in. Robert Frost once wrote, "Home is the place where, when you have to go there, they have to take you in." According to that definition, I didn't have a home!

Meanwhile I got in my car and headed for California. Since I couldn't go to Dad and Nancy's house or to Mom's house, I went to see Maureen. She was married at that time to Marine Captain David Sills. I went to their house, and they sat me down for a talk. It was one of those "Mike, you need to get your act together" talks that I had heard so many times in my life. I got the impression that Maureen had been talking to Mom, Dad, and Nancy.

Then Maureen told me something that really floored me. She said that Nancy had asked David to call the marines and tell them I was available to be drafted into the corps. David had to explain to Nancy that the marine corps didn't take draftees. But that didn't stop Nancy. She called every branch of the service until she finally found one that was interested, and I soon received an induction notice.

I couldn't believe it! Nancy was trying to get me drafted!

The last thing I wanted was to end up in a military barracks, surrounded by nothing but men. It was like St. John's Military Academy and Loyola High all over again—only this time with a real shooting war to boot! It was 1965, and the Vietnam War was heating up.

I called Mom and told her what Nancy had done, and Mom went nuts! "I can't believe she did that!" Mom said.

"I can't believe it either," I said, "but she did."

I reported to the induction center, took my physical, and was classified 1Y (unfit for service) due to medical problems—a duodenal ulcer and a pilonidal cyst (and if you want to know what *that* is, you can look it up yourself).

## "TELL US, MIKE—DO YOUR PARENTS LOVE YOU?"

I ended up rooming with some friends in LA whom I'd known for years in summer camp. I enrolled in morning classes at a junior college. (I figured that would make a good impression on Mom, Dad, and Nancy.) And Maureen introduced me to a friend of hers whose father owned Asbury Trucking in Vernon, just north of Watts. The owner gave me a job loading oil-well freight from five in the evening until one-thirty a.m.

I toiled away at that loading dock as Dad revved up his campaign for governor of California. I was all in favor of Dad's becoming governor—not because I cared about politics but because I imagined how great life could be for the son of a governor! There was only one thing that worried me, and it worried me a lot.

Those pictures.

I didn't know where Don Havlik was or what he had done with those pictures. Sometimes I would lie awake imagining what would happen if those pictures ever surfaced. I was sure they would shame me for life and ruin Dad's chances of getting elected.

So I was afraid to have any visibility in the campaign, afraid even to show my face. At first Dad or people from his campaign would ask me to make an appearance, give a speech, or be interviewed. I always found an excuse not to do it. After a while they quit asking me.

The night my dad won the election, I went and saw my dad, and I thought it was going to be so neat. I thought his election as governor was going to change my life. I took Dad aside and told him that I was looking forward to a job in his administration—you know, something cushy, a desk to prop my feet up on, a secretary at my beck and call, and a big fat paycheck from the State of California.

Well, Dad wasted no time in popping that bubble. "Michael," he said, "you might as well know right now that I don't believe in nepotism. You'd better keep that job on the trucking dock."

So I went back to the trucking dock. The guys I worked with couldn't figure out why the son of the governor of California and an Academy Award-winning actress was doing manual labor for $2.85 an hour. One time they came to me and said, "Tell us, Mike, do your parents love you?" They thought they were being real funny. They didn't know how many times I had asked that question myself.

The guys had their joke, and they went back to work. But in my own mind, I tried to tell myself: *Yes, my parents love me. Sure, they must love me. The only reason they refuse to help me is because they want me to make something of my life.*

As time passed and my life didn't get better, I began to wonder if those guys on the dock were right.

## CURSING GOD

One night I left the loading dock long after midnight, feeling beat down into my socks. By this time I had traded in my Ford Galaxy for a Volkswagen Beetle. I was driving that VW down the Golden State Freeway in LA when I fell asleep at the wheel. The car veered off the road, took out one hundred fifty feet of chain-link fence, and slammed to a halt against an upright fence rod.

At that point, believe me, I was awake.

I looked around and saw that the windshield had popped out. My glasses had flown off, and I had a big gash in my head that was leaking lots of blood. I got out of the car and looked at the mess. The front left wheel had been welded to the fence rod by the impact.

I checked myself over. My clothes were getting soaked with blood from the gash in my head, but otherwise I seemed to be all right.

The police arrived, and they had an ambulance take me to the hospital. While I was lying down in the emergency room, waiting to be seen by a doctor, someone gave me some papers to fill out. The doctor wouldn't examine me until I filled out the forms. I looked at the forms, and there were numerous questions about my family history.

Being adopted, of course, I didn't have a family history. I didn't know the answers to any of those questions. Yet it said right on the form: "Fill In All Blanks."

I was furious. How was an adoptee supposed to fill in all the blanks? I had been trying to fill in all the blanks of my life for some twenty years without success.

I walked out of the hospital without being treated.

I needed transportation to get to my job, but my VW was totaled. Mom told me she didn't want me driving such a small car anymore, so she bought me a new Oldsmobile Cutlass Supreme. I was proud of that car, and I couldn't wait to show it off at work.

Not long afterward, I drove the Olds to Dad's Malibu ranch and stayed overnight by myself. The next morning I went out and got into the car to start it up. I turned the key, but it wouldn't start. The battery was dead. It was like that ten-speed bicycle all over again!

I pounded on the steering wheel and cursed that car. Then I got out of the car and slammed the doors as hard as I could, then kicked the doors until they came off the hinges. I pounded the hood with my fists. I kicked the hub-caps off.

The whole time I was pounding on that car, I was cursing it up one side and down the other. The next thing I knew, I was cursing God! Then I cursed Mary! Then I cursed Jesus! Then I cursed the whole Trinity!

It was my twisted, pathetic way of taking control of my eternal destiny. I couldn't help it that God was going to send me to hell, but at least I could control the reasons he was sending me to hell. I wasn't going to let God condemn me for being illegitimate or for being molested. I was going to curse God so bad that he would have to send me to hell for cursing him! That way no one would ever find out, even in eternity, all the horrible things that were going on inside Mike Reagan.

I was so furious with God that I went into the barn, and I got a sledge hammer. I took that hammer, and I absolutely destroyed that car. I burst all the windows and smashed all the lights. My beloved Oldsmobile Cutlass Supreme had become my most bitter enemy—God himself—and in my mind I was taking God apart, piece by piece, bumper by fender.

Finally, when my rage was spent, I sat down on the steps of the foreman's house, my body wringing with sweat, and I just cried and cried until there were no tears left in my body. Then I went into the house and called Dad. I told him that some thieves had come on the ranch and wrecked my car.

In the end the insurance company replaced the car and paid the price for my years of anger.

## WIN OR DIE

Around this time I became hooked on boat racing. When I was out on a speedboat, life was good. For me the sensation of speeding across the water was not only exhilarating; it was truly relaxing.

As the boat-racing son of famous parents, I received a lot of media attention, which stroked my wounded ego. Boat racing also enabled me to leave my $2.85 an hour job and travel around the country, living the life everyone expected me to live—the life of a playboy. Whenever I wasn't racing, I was playing tennis or picking up girls. I spent money faster than it came in and steadily racked up a mountain of debt.

Because of who my parents were, people were eager to extend credit to me. They thought that giving me credit was a safe bet because my parents would always bail me out. Well, they thought wrong!

I started racing boats with inboard engines, and I competed around the country alongside some famous names, including astronaut Gordon Cooper, oil-well firefighter Red Adair, and oil magnate John Meekham, owner of the New Orleans Saints. Though I never won any inboard races, I always finished near the front.

Even though I was new at boat racing compared to most of the competition, I quickly became one of the better drivers. I was a tough competitor for the simple reason that I never worried about getting killed. I already saw myself as having no future, and I figured that if I won, I would finally prove myself to my family. And if I got killed, it would be just as good as winning because I'd die a hero.

My boat racing worried and upset both Mom and Dad. I had a long conversation with Dad and he told me he was concerned about my safety out on the water. "Racing at those speeds," he said, "you're bound to get hurt sooner or later." I could see by the look on his face that his concern for me was genuine. Because of all the times I had doubted his concern for me, I was touched by that.

But his concern didn't keep me from racing. I didn't just want Dad to be concerned about me. I wanted him to be *impressed* with me. In fact, I wanted the whole world to be impressed with me. And in my mind there were only two ways to accomplish that: win a big race or die trying. I believed that if I could win a big race, then the world would love me, and that love would be so strong that it would overcome all the shame and self-hate inside me.

In 1967, at the urging of chain-saw magnate Robert McCullough, I entered a two-day race at Lake Havasu, Arizona. It would be my first outboard race, and I would go up against some of the greatest names in racing, including Craig Breedlove, Caesar Scotti, and Renato Molinari. No one expected me to do well in my first outboard race. The promoters wanted me there simply because my name was Reagan and I was the governor's kid.

The next day, Saturday, I joined my partners, Bill Cooper and boat builder Rudy Ramos, on the waters of Lake Havasu. We put in eight grueling hours on the two and a half mile course. Our first day of the two-day race silenced all the snickers. Our boat was tied for first place. The only problem was that the boat was falling apart and we had another full day of racing ahead of me.

Ours was the only boat still in contention with Mercury motors, so the Mercury team—who had ignored me before the race—swarmed around me and offered to help me stay in the race. They worked all night on our motors while our support team made repairs on the fiberglass deck and hull.

The next day, with me driving the final two-hour leg, we won the Outboard World Championship of 1967.

I had never known such a thrill before. I was on top of the world! I went to bed that night feeling like a winner.

The next morning I woke up and picked up the sports pages. The story on the race was headlined "Ronald Reagan's Son Wins Race." My first name wasn't even mentioned. All that effort, everything I was trying to attain, was all for naught.

Later that year, I was named Inboard Rookie of the Year. I got media attention and popular acclaim. As usual, it was nice for a while, but the warm feelings didn't last.

## "THERE'S NO FUTURE IN IT"

"You're bound to get hurt sooner or later," Dad had told me. And he was right.

In 1969, I entered the two-hundred-fifty-mile Speed Classic Circuit at Offut's Bayou near Galveston, Texas. I was in the lead, doing 117 mph in a twenty-foot Raysoncraft boat. At that speed anything can happen. What happened to me was that the boat suddenly went airborne. Then it chined in—that is, it did a quarter roll and struck the water on its side. The impact blew in the fiberglass hull, and water sucked in, exploding the boat. In a fraction of a second, the boat completely disintegrated. Debris flew fifty feet in the air.

Somewhere in that plume of spray and fiberglass shrapnel was Michael Reagan, my body flopping around like a rag doll. A rescue boat fished me out of the water. They took me to the hospital and checked me over. Amazingly, I had no internal injuries or broken bones, but I had torn or stretched practically every muscle in my body. The doctors released me, and I went back to Offut's Bayou and watched the rest of the race.

The next morning I was awakened by the phone. When I tried to get out of bed, my body was so stiff and painful that I could barely move. I couldn't walk, so I crawled to the phone and answered it on the tenth ring. It was Dad.

"I heard about your crash," he said. "How are you doing?"

"Fine, just fine," I lied, gritting my teeth against the pain.

"Well," he said, "I still worry about you racing at such speeds. It's a dangerous business. There's no future in it."

"Dad," I said, "I know it's dangerous. Believe me, I know! But it's what I enjoy."

"I wish you'd find something safe to do," he said. "A steady job with a regular paycheck. Like selling boats."

But I didn't want a steady job. I wanted to be famous. I wanted to be loved. I wanted to blot out the fear and anxiety inside me that were put there when I was molested. Besides, I was having too much fun living the carefree life of the governor's son. People liked me, girls dated me, stores extended credit to me—all because I was the son of Governor Reagan. My debts were mounting, but what did I care? I was living the good life! What did I want with a steady job?

Six weeks after I blew up that boat in Texas, I had a new sponsor and a new boat. I was racing again—racing for something I could never reach, racing for something that always seemed to be just inches beyond my grasp: Love. Approval. Acceptance. Forgiveness.

## "WHO AM I?"

We are raising an entire generation of young people who look at the world the way I did when I was in my teens. They feel rootless and without a sense of belonging, just as I did. When I was growing up in the 1950s and 1960s, divorce was a departure from the norm across America. Kids overwhelmingly grew up in intact, two-parent families.

Today divorce and family chaos are the norm. Kids are growing up not knowing where they belong. They visit mom for a while; they visit dad for a while. Stepparents come into their lives, then disappear. They live most of the time with mom, but mom has a career, so most days are spent in day care. They are latchkey kids who grow up alone and raise themselves.

Kids today live under a cloud of impending doom. They were born under the threat of nuclear annihilation. Then came September 11, 2001, and they learned that the end of their world could come unexpectedly in a variety of ways—nuclear, biological, or chemical. They see a world that is on a fast track to hell, and they are just along for the ride. As I did at that age, they peer into the future and see only a brick wall. So they ask, "What's the point in living?"

Young people today are afraid of dying but even more afraid of living. So what do they do? They live for the moment. They live for thrills and highs and nothing more. If you want to know why the kids all around you are drinking too much, smoking dope, and risking AIDS and death through uncommitted and unprotected sex, this is why: They see no future. When you don't see any future, you just want to grab this moment and live it to the max—even if it kills you. Because it just might be the only moment you have.

Look at the youth culture: It's all about going to extremes. Today's young people listen to extreme music, seek extreme thrills, engage in extreme sports, and indulge in extreme sex. Why? Because their lives are so deadened and hopeless that every experience must be an extreme experience in order for them to feel anything. Believe me, I know. Life doesn't get much more extreme than racing a boat at over a hundred miles an hour.

Extreme thrills are a real high, but eventually you have to come down and look at yourself in the mirror. You have to remember your past and face the emptiness of your present and the blankness of your future.

What do kids today think about God? The same thing I thought of him. They rage at God, reject him, or simply ignore him. They feel like strangers in church because the language spoken there and the music sung there have no relevance to their lives. And yes, some of them curse God just as I did when I was pounding that Oldsmobile into a pile of junk.

Just as I was, today's young people are racing to nowhere. They are desperately chasing something they can't quite reach, something that is always just inches beyond their grasp: Love. Approval. Acceptance. Forgiveness.

What is the answer? If you tell them, "God is the answer," will they believe you? Why should they? What proof do we offer that God is the answer? They look at religious violence around the world, at people killing one another in the name of God. They see churches filled with hypocrisy and torn apart by factions and divisions. They see preachers caught with prostitutes and priests molesting children. They see a church picketing the funeral of a murdered homosexual, and the picket signs read, "God hates fags." How will we convince young people that God is the answer when all of these hateful, sinful, hypocritical people claim to speak for God?

But the biggest question of all is this: What do young people see when they look at your life and mine? Do they see the reality of God, the love of God, the redemptive grace of God? Or do they see just the same old religious hate and religious hypocrisy they see everywhere else?

If we want to reach the young people of this generation with the good news that God loves them and wants to build a relationship with them, then we need to give them a message that relates to their lives, and we need to talk to them in a language they understand. That means we must:

1. *Model healthy relationships.* In our homes, churches, and everyday lives, we should model healthy family relationships so that young people can see what a healthy relationship looks like. I grew up in a divorced family. I spent my school years in boarding school and my summers at summer camp. You don't learn healthy family relationships by watching the

example of priests and nuns. So I didn't always have healthy family role models to draw upon.

So where did I learn about healthy relationships? During my teen years I visited the homes of friends who lived in intact families, people like the Lobheres who lived down the street and the Tarnutzers who lived down the block. I would have holiday dinners in their homes, and they always made me feel welcome.

I had no concept of what a family unit was supposed to be. These families showed me. I saw how those moms, dads, and kids communicated with one another, loved one another, and did things together, and I wanted to grow up someday and have a family like they had. It's crucial that we provide healthy role models and show young people what healthy families look like.

2. *Become a mentor.* Be that person who will unlock the future for a kid who has no future. Give your time and give of yourself. Find a young person who is lagging behind in life, and become an inspirational and encouraging force in his or her life. Here are some things you can do:

Become a reading tutor at a local school. Help organize a neighborhood study site at a school or community center, and recruit volunteers to help kids with their homework. Become a mentor to kids through Scouting, Big Brother/Big Sisters, 4-H, or another mentoring program. Become a volunteer coach at a junior high or high school. Become a Sunday school teacher or youth group advisor. Volunteer as a counselor at a teen shelter or crisis pregnancy center. Open your home and become a foster parent. Adopt a child.

3. *Live a life that exemplifies hope and meaning.* We have to show the young people around us that we have a reason for hope within us. We have to demonstrate the joy that comes with a daily, continuous relationship with the living God. We have to show young people how knowing God has changed our lives, repaired our broken relationships, and restored our broken faith in the future.

That's what I'm doing in this book and on my radio show: I tell people every chance I get about what my life was like before I knew Christ and what my life is like today. Before Christ I had no hope, no future, no self-respect, no sense of being loved and accepted, no place of belonging. After I found Christ, I received all of these things and more!

You have a story of your own to tell, so go out and tell it! You don't have to write a book or go on the radio—although you're welcome to call my show. You can talk to the young people in your church, to the young people you meet in line at the theater, or to the young people you mentor as a volunteer in an after-school tutoring program or in scouting. Tell young people your story, and let them know that there is hope and meaning in your life because of your relationship with Christ.

As the apostle Peter told us, "Always be prepared to give an answer to everyone who asks you to give the reason for the hope that you have" (1 Pet. 3:15).

4. *Live a godly life.* Young people today are experience oriented. They are not persuaded by logical arguments or emotional appeals. They are persuaded by experience. In order for them to know that God is real, they have to experience the

reality of God in the way you interact with them. They have to experience his reality in the way you say what you mean and mean what you say. If your walk and your talk don't match, young people will turn and walk away from you and your faith.

The apostle Paul said, "Be imitators of God, therefore, as dearly loved children and live a life of love, just as Christ loved us and gave himself up for us as a fragrant offering and sacrifice to God. . . . For you were once darkness, but now you are light in the Lord. Live as children of light" (Eph. 5:1–2, 8).

5. *Be bold and clear about your identity in Christ.* One of the most troubling questions young people struggle with today is the question, Who am I? That was the question that haunted me throughout my early years. I didn't know where I came from or who I was. I didn't know where I belonged or where my home was. I couldn't even fill in the blanks of the hospital information form because I didn't know my own identity.

Young people today are feeling lost in the same way. They feel cast adrift in a meaningless universe. They don't know where they belong or where their home is. They don't know their own identity, and they can't fill in the blanks of their own existence. If you don't know your identity, you can never solve the riddle of life.

The only way we can understand who we are is through our relationships. The question, Who am I? really means, "Who am I related to? And who do I relate to?" The answer to the question of our identity tells us where we came from, where we are going, and how we are to live right now. The Christian answer to the Who am I? question is fourfold:

First, I am a person made in the image of God. Genesis 1:27 tells us, "So God created man in his own image, in the image of God he created him; male and female he created them." Whether you are a man or a woman, black or white, Gentile or Jew, Republican or Democrat, straight or gay or transgendered, you are made in the image of God. That perfect image in us has been broken by sin, but it is still in us. When we allow Jesus to become Lord of our lives, he starts restoring that broken image so that we can become whole again. The image of God within us is the basis of our self-worth and of our value to God.

Second, my primary relationship in life is my relationship with God. We were made to know God and to have a relationship with him. In John 17:3, in the prayer of Jesus just before he went to the cross, he said, "Now this is eternal life: that they may know you, the only true God, and Jesus Christ, whom you have sent." If you want to know what eternal life is, Jesus tells us in that verse: knowing God. How do we know God? By having a relationship with Christ, whom God sent.

Third, my purpose and meaning in life is to glorify God through the way I live my life. Let's take that religious-sounding word *glorify* and put it in everyday language. To glorify God simply means to live in such a way as to reflect his greatness and goodness to the world. If we call ourselves Christians and we reflect God's character by our love for one another, then we glorify God. But if we hate, slander, gossip, and mistreat other people, then we dishonor God. The Bible tells us that we should glorify God not only with our words but with every single thing we do. "So whether you eat or drink or whatever you do, do it all for the glory of God" (1 Cor. 10:31).

Fourth, my future is to enjoy God forever. What does it mean to enjoy God? It means that we find pleasure in being with God. We enjoy his company and find our deepest meaning and satisfaction in a relationship with him. The psalmist put it this way: "You have made known to me the path of life; you will fill me with joy in your presence, with eternal pleasures at your right hand" (Ps. 16:11).

Thrills are momentary. Only a relationship with God brings lasting satisfaction. Only a relationship with God brings us an accurate understanding of who we are, where we come from, and where we are going.

I spent my early life searching for my identity, racing for acceptance and love. Even when I won a football championship or a boat race, I came up empty. I couldn't find any peace or satisfaction because I didn't know who I was.

But all of that was about to change.

# 9

# MY REDEMPTION

*I* was twenty-eight years old and living the life of a playboy, dating eight girls at once. I dated strictly for fun. I wasn't looking for marriage, and I wasn't serious about any of those girls.

At the time I lived in the guest room of my boat-racing buddy, Bill Olson. I didn't own a car, so I would always borrow one of his for a date, either his 240Z or his mother's old Mercury. One day in late 1973, Bill's wife Barbara told me about a girl she wanted me to meet. "Her name is Colleen Sterns," Barbara said. "I know her from work, and I've told her all about you. I think you'd like her."

"Barbara," I said, "I'm already dating eight girls right now. I need another girl like I need a hole in the head."

"Just let me get you two together for one blind date," she said.

"Does it look like I need a blind date? I've got enough dates!"

"You've never met anyone like Colleen," Barbara persisted. "Look, if it doesn't work out, it's only one night out of your life, and you never have to see her again."

Just to get Barbara off my case, I finally agreed. On December 7, 1973, I met Colleen Sterns for the first time—a lovely brunette with big brown eyes. I was fascinated.

Barbara had fixed dinner for the four of us. Over dinner I became acquainted with the young lady who was about to change the course of my life.

Colleen's background and mine were as different as night and day. She was born and raised on a farm in Nebraska with her eleven brothers and sisters. She didn't have electricity in her home until she was twelve and no TV until she was fifteen. Most of her life the house she lived in had outdoor plumbing. She was born seventh in line and was the first to be born in a hospital. Clearly she came from a different life from my life in Beverly Hills!

And to top it off, she was a *Democrat!*

She told me that Barbara had said I was the governor's son, but she thought Barbara was putting her on. So she went to the library and looked up Ronald Reagan and found out that the governor really did have a son named Michael. She wanted to make sure I wasn't some sort of con man.

The thing that intrigued me most about Colleen was that she didn't seem the least bit impressed by the fact that I was the son of Ronald Reagan and Jane Wyman. It didn't seem to make a bit of difference to her at all. Looking back, I realize why I found that so attractive. It meant that she wasn't interested in my name or my celebrity parents or my connections.

She was interested in *me*.

We started going out week after week. The more I got to know her, the more intrigued I became.

## GOD'S GIFT TO ME

At the time Colleen came into my life, I was $25,000 in debt and had little hope of paying it off. I had discovered that when the banks found out I was Ronald Reagan's son, they would gladly lend me money. They figured that if I didn't pay it back my parents would, and I didn't tell them any different.

Most of that debt was boat-racing debt or debt I had racked up in clothing stores. Later Colleen made me pay it all back, every penny. In fact, she personally called all of my creditors to set up payment schedules. She was amazed to find that even with all that I owed them, many of those stores and companies would invite me to their next sale and were eager to extend me even *more* credit!

So that was my situation when Colleen entered the picture. I was deep in debt, and I had no money, no car, and no real job (I had just started in the boat-selling business but hadn't made many sales yet). In order to take her out on a date, I'd either have to borrow a car, or we'd take her car. I really can't imagine what she was thinking when she started dating me.

Colleen was exactly what I needed. She had incredible compassion and a sweet spirit combined with an amazing toughness. She needed to be tough if she was going to put up with my rough edges. In fact, if you were to ask her today why she put up with me, her answer would be, "He had potential."

I had no idea what God was doing when he brought Colleen into my life. But I later realized that she was the woman God had picked out for me to help me put the pieces of my life back together. She was God's gift to me. It was as if God were saying, "Michael, you've lived with this pain and anger for so many years. But now I am beginning the process of restoration in your life. And it begins with this woman, Colleen."

And that's exactly how my redemption began.

The change in my life didn't happen overnight. It wasn't easy for me or for Colleen. She saw me at my worst—the tantrums, the anger, the bitterness. I seemed confident and brash, but that was just camouflage to hide my lack of self-esteem. And when problems and frustrations would come up, whenever things went bad, I would still blame God. I was still filled with years and years of accumulated anger.

And you know what she did when I would fly into a rage? She would read the Bible! I thought, *How dare she do that? I'm mad at God, and she's reading the Bible!*

But my anger didn't intimidate her one bit. She was compassionate enough to put up with my pain yet tough enough to confront my deception and sin. She seemed to know that God had brought us together for a purpose.

On November 7, 1975, Colleen and I were married in a small chapel in Anaheim, across the street from Disneyland.

Most of Colleen's family flew in from Nebraska. Dad, Nancy, and Mom were all there too.

Before the wedding Dad gave me a letter that I have always treasured and tried to put into practice.

Dear Mike:

You've heard all the jokes that have been rousted around by all the "unhappy marrieds" and cynics. Now, in case no one has suggested it, there is another viewpoint. You have entered into the most meaningful relationship there is in all human life. It can be whatever you decide to make it.

Some men feel their masculinity can only be proven if they play out in their own life all the locker-room stories, smugly confident that what a wife doesn't know won't hurt her. The truth is, somehow, way down inside, without her ever finding lipstick on the collar or catching a man in the flimsy excuse of where he was till three a.m., a wife does know, and with that knowing, some of the magic of this relationship disappears. There are more men griping about marriage who kicked the whole thing away themselves than there can ever be wives deserving of blame.

There is an old law of physics that you can only get out of a thing as much as you put in it. The man who puts into the marriage only half of what he owns will get that out. Sure, there will be moments when you will see someone or think back on an earlier time and you will be challenged to see if you can still make the grade, but let me tell you how really great is the challenge of proving your masculinity and charm with one woman for the rest of your life.

Any man can find a twerp here and there who will go along with cheating, and it doesn't take all that much manhood. It does take quite a man to remain attractive and to be loved by a woman who has heard him snore, seen him unshaven, tended him while he was sick and washed his dirty underwear. Do that and keep her still feeling a warm glow and you will know some very beautiful music.

If you truly love a girl, you shouldn't ever want her to feel, when she sees you greet a secretary or a girl you both know, that humiliation of wondering if she was someone who caused you to be late coming home, nor should you want any other woman to be able to meet your wife and know she was smiling behind her eyes as she looked at her, the woman you love, remembering this was the woman you rejected even momentarily for her favors.

Mike, you know better than many what an unhappy home is and what it can do to others. Now you have a chance to make it come out the way it should. There is no greater happiness for a man than approaching a door at the end of a day knowing someone on the other side of that door is waiting for the sound of his footsteps.

Love, Dad.

P.S. You'll never get in trouble if you say "I love you" at least once a day.

Old-fashioned? Yeah, those words from Dad's heart are as old-fashioned as love itself. I'm not ashamed to say that I cried when I first read those words, and I have reread them many, many times since. And I have tried to put every word of that letter into practice throughout our marriage, including the P.S. I tell Colleen I love her every day, and I haven't missed a day in all the years we've been married.

Twelve days after the wedding, Dad went to the Press Club in Washington, D.C., and announced that he was going to run for president. I had known that Dad's announcement was coming, and I was all for it. I knew that, if elected, he would make a great president. But at the same time, the prospect of Dad's becoming president absolutely scared me to death! Why?

Those pictures.

What is true now was true then: We live in a world where everybody wants to know everything about everybody. Nothing is off-limits. If you run for political office, you can count on one thing: There will be people rummaging around in your closet and your trash cans, trying to find something they can use to destroy you.

So as I went around the country, campaigning for my dad, I couldn't help worrying and wondering about the man who had taken those pictures when I was a child. Did he still have them? Would he sell them to the *National Enquirer?* Would those pictures become public? I lived in a state of terror because of those picture.

And what about Colleen? I had never told her about the molestation or the pictures. What would those pictures do to my relationship with my wife if they ever came out?

## "Nyet" to the Soviets

In my entire life I only saw Dad defeated one time. That was in 1976, when he lost the Republican presidential nomination to Gerald Ford. After the Republican convention nominated Ford, our family was gathered in Dad's hotel suite. He looked at us and grinned in a wistful way.

"You know what hurts the most about not getting the nomination? It's that I was really looking forward to representing the American people at the SALT talks." The threat of nuclear war was Dad's greatest worry. He was especially concerned about the fact that the US had made too many concessions in its arms control agreements with the Soviet Union.

"I wanted to sit down at a big conference table with the Soviet Secretary General," he continued, "and I wanted him to tell me through his interpreter everything the United States would have to give up in order to get along with the Soviet Union. I was going to listen to him make his demands. Then I was going to get up from my chair, walk around that table, and whisper in his ear, 'Nyet.' I'm really sorry I won't get to say 'nyet' to the Soviets."

As I look back, I really believe that God was working in this country and across this globe to achieve his purposes through Ronald Reagan. God's timetable was better than Dad's. Had my father won the presidency in 1976, I think there's a good chance the Berlin Wall would *not* have come down and the Cold War would *not* have ended. Why? Because a number of key players were not yet in place.

One key player was Pope John Paul II, who would join with President Reagan in taking a stand against the "evil empire" of Soviet Communism; he was not elected by the College of Cardinals until 1978. Czech dissident Vaclav Havel did not publish his influential essay "The Power of the Powerless" until 1978. President Reagan's strongest European ally, Lady Margaret Thatcher, did not become prime minister of Great Britain until 1979. The occupation of the Gdansk shipyards in Poland, led by Solidarity leader Lech Walesa, did not take place until 1980. And Mikhail Gorbachev, who ushered in the era of *glasnost* (openness) and *perestroika* (reform), did not achieve office until 1985.

Though Dad was disappointed to lose the nomination in 1976, he was right on schedule, according to God's timing. Dad won the election in 1980, exactly when God had planned. The pieces of the global puzzle fell into place, a hunger for freedom swept Eastern Europe, the Soviet Union imploded, the Berlin Wall toppled, the Cold War ended, and the world is a better place to live in—all in God's good time.

## "RAINDROP HAS ARRIVED"

On May 30, 1978, Mom and Dad became grandparents when our son Cameron was born. In 1980, Dad ran for president again. This time he won the nomination and the election, becoming the fortieth president of the United States.

When Dad became president, Colleen and I knew that our whole world had changed, but we didn't realize how much.

One of the biggest changes was the constant presence of the Secret Service.

One of our favorite restaurants was the Casa Vega Restaurant on Ventura Boulevard in Sherman Oaks. The first time we went there with Secret Service agents, it was quite a production. The agents were in the front seat, and Colleen and I were in the back. As we pulled up, the parking lot attendant came up and said, "Park car." He spoke broken English with a Spanish accent.

The agent behind the wheel said, "We're United States Secret Service agents. We have the Reagans in the back. We'll park the car."

The attendant pointed to the "Valet Parking" sign and said, "No! Park car!" Meaning he, not us, was going to park the car.

The agent said, "No, we'll park the car. We have the Reagans."

The man insisted. "No! Park car!"

The agent turned to his partner and said, "He doesn't understand what I'm saying." So he reached into his coat pocket, pulled out his commission book, and flashed his Secret Service badge at the attendant.

The attendant's eyes bugged out and he shouted, "*¡Inmigración! ¡Inmigración!*" And he took off running down Ventura Boulevard, yelling "Immigration! Immigration!" in Spanish. The agent had to chase him down and tell him, "Hold it! We don't care where you're from. We just want to park the car ourselves."

The Secret Service had code names for everyone in the Reagan family. Dad was Rawhide, Nancy was Rainbow, I was Riddler, Cameron was Rhyme, Maureen was Radiant, and so forth. I don't know if the Rs were for Republicans or for Reagan. But I do know that the government paid somebody fifty thousand dollars a year just to come up with code names like those. Your tax dollars at work.

In 1983, Colleen was about to give birth to our second child, Ashley. Cameron was by natural childbirth; Ashley was by appointment. They gave Colleen an epidural anesthetic, so she was awake for the birth. After Ashley was born, the first thing Colleen heard was the crisp, professional voice of a Secret Service agent speaking into his walkie-talkie, "We have an arrival. Raindrop has arrived. Repeat—Raindrop has arrived."

Before she even heard our daughter cry or heard her name spoken, Colleen heard Ashley's Secret Service code name. Colleen couldn't see anything but the ceiling, so she looked at me and said, "Who's in the room?"

I looked around the crowded birthing room and said, "A better question would be, 'Who's *not* in the room?'"

Colleen groaned. "The Secret Service! Isn't *anything* private anymore?"

I said, "Not for us."

Both of our kids had Secret Service protection as they were growing-up. One thing's for sure—Cameron never lost a school-yard fight during the whole eight years of the Reagan Administration.

One day when Cameron was in preschool, the Secret Service agent was in the classroom, keeping a close watch on Cameron. As the agent stood against the wall, trying to do his job while remaining unobtrusive, a little boy came up to him and tugged at his trouser leg. "Mister, potty!" the little boy said, apparently assuming that all grown-ups in the classroom must be preschool teachers.

The agent brushed the boy's hand away and ignored him.

Again, the boy tugged on the agent's pant leg and said, "Mister, potty!"

The agent brushed the boy's hand away and, true to his training, kept his eyes focused on the president's grandson.

Finally, the little boy said, "Potty now!" The agent looked down and saw that the little boy had dropped his pants and was urinating right into the agent's tasseled loafers.

The next day the General Services Administration came out and installed a window in the classroom door so that the Secret Service agent could watch Cameron from *outside* the classroom.

Once again, your tax dollars at work.

## THE TURNING POINT

I started attending church in 1978, before Cameron was born. Colleen wanted us to attend church on a regular basis, so I agreed to go. Though she had been a committed Christian for years, I hadn't committed my life to Christ, and I didn't intend to. Fact is, I didn't believe I could. I still saw myself as condemned and beyond the reach of God's love and forgiveness. Still, to please Colleen, I agreed that we would go to church faithfully every Sunday.

So I went to church every Sunday, pretending to be something I wasn't, pretending to be a Christian. I smiled and shook hands and said hello to all the people I met on Sunday mornings, and they all assumed I was a Christian. I suppose they all figured that since my dad was a Christian and my wife was a Christian and I was in church every Sunday, then I must be a Christian too. But nobody ever asked, "Mike, how's your relationship with God?"

You know what people would ask me? They'd say, "Mike, how's your dad?" Everybody asked me about my dad, but nobody ever asked me how *I* was. It ticked me off that nobody even seemed curious about my relationship with God. I wasn't angry at the people in church; I was angry at Dad! He was so famous that he was all anybody talked about or asked about.

I wonder how many other people have felt the way I felt. How many times do people come to church and sit by themselves, and nobody reaches out to them, nobody really cares about them? How many times have we sat next to someone in church without even suspecting the turmoil and pain in that person's life?

People often come to church because they are dying inside; they are hurting and stretched to the breaking point. They just want someone to acknowledge that they exist and maybe pray with them. But nobody says anything, nobody demonstrates any caring, and that person leaves church feeling more empty and lonely than ever before. In fact, when you're perceived as rich, yes, even church people think you have no problems.

I remember the times I went to church and left feeling that nobody cared. I really needed somebody to go beyond the usual superficial pleasantries: "Hi, how are you?" "Doing fine, how are you?" I needed somebody to touch that raw, aching nerve deep inside my soul. I needed someone to reach out and ask me, "Mike, how are you doing? Don't just say, 'Fine,' Mike. Tell me how you're *really* doing because I want to be alongside you, praying for you, helping you any way I can."

But nobody said that to me.

I wished that I could know God and experience the peace and trusting faith that Colleen had. But the words of Deuteronomy 23:2 still echoed in my mind after all those years, telling me that a bastard could never enter into the congregation of the Lord. If I had gone to a pastor and asked what that verse really meant, I would have found out that I had agonized for decades over a misinterpretation. I was in my early thirties, yet I still looked at that verse through the frightened eyes of a seven-year-old boy.

The year 1985 was the turning point in my life. What was significant about that year? It was the year my son Cameron turned seven, the same age I was when I was molested.

For years I had hated myself. Now I had a seven-year-old son, and when I looked at Cameron, I didn't see Cameron. I saw the seven-year-old Michael Reagan. I didn't hate Cameron, but I hated Michael Reagan because I blamed

myself for being molested and for allowing those pictures to
be taken.

So I began to treat Cameron with all the anger and rage
that I felt for myself. I yelled at him, screamed at him, and
berated him. I told him he was bad. I didn't understand why
I did it. I truly didn't know.

During the year that Cameron turned seven, my rage came
to a full boil. The secret I hid was steadily building up pressure
inside me. I was angry all the time. I would yell at Colleen for
the smallest, stupidest things. Despite the way I behaved, she
kept praying for me and asking God to heal the anger inside
me. She didn't know what she was praying for; she didn't know
what she was dealing with. She could make no sense of my rage
because she was missing the biggest piece of the puzzle: the
molestation. Yet God honored and answered her prayers. Have
you ever prayed for someone and not know why?

I had never told Colleen what had happened to me when
I was seven. I was scared to death. I was convinced she would
leave me because I had been touched by a man, because I was
unclean. I was sure that if she knew the truth about me, she
would hate me as much as I hated myself.

Colleen was such a godly woman with such a strong
Christian faith. How could I tell her that her husband, the
father of her children, could never go to heaven? What would
she think if she found out that I was doomed to hell?

So that was the state of my emotions in 1985 as I started to
turn up the burner on my seven-year-old son. He had no way of
knowing why I was angry with him because I didn't even know.

One day I was in the master bedroom, and I absolutely flew off the handle with Cameron. I just started screaming at him. He backed away from me with fear in his eyes, but I couldn't stop myself. I kept verbally abusing him. Colleen heard me from the other end of the house, and she dashed in and placed herself between Cameron and me.

"Michael," she said, "what are you doing? What are you doing to our son?"

"I don't know!" I said.

"Michael," she said, "you can't keep doing this to him! You need to find God! You need to have Jesus take control of your life!"

She was right. I hadn't accepted Jesus into my life.

"You've been going *to* church, Michael," she said, "but you haven't been *in* church. You sit there and you listen, but you don't hear. None of it's real to you."

"What can I do?" I said.

And Colleen told me what I had to do, and I did it. I fell down on my knees beside my bed, and I prayed with tears streaming down my face: "God, forgive me for the way I've been hurting my son! Forgive me for the way I've been hurting Colleen. God, forgive me, make me clean, take over my life."

I was born illegitimate, I had been sexually abused, and my life was riddled with sin. The sin in my life was both real and imagined. The imagined sin was the molestation. I blamed myself for the sins against me. I thought that when I was molested and those pictures were taken of me, I had committed the ultimate sin, the unforgivable sin. I honestly didn't believe that Christ would come into a life like mine, but he did!

On Father's Day 1985, Colleen and I were baptized together at Faith Church in San Fernando Valley. She wanted to be baptized with me, even though she'd been a Christian for years and had been baptized as a girl.

So God began the rebuilding of Michael Reagan. He's still rebuilding me. I remain a work in progress.

When I received Christ as Lord of my life, I had a new life. But I still had a lot of residue left over from my old life. I still had a lot to learn and a lot of work to do. Even though I had Jesus in my life, I still hadn't told anyone about the molestation and those photos. I had Jesus, but I still had anger, shame, and horrible memories. I had Jesus, but I still saw everything through the eyes of a child. I had Jesus, but I still blamed Mom and Dad—and their fame—for my problems.

It was easier to blame Mom for putting me in boarding school, even though that was the best she could do as a single mother. I should have been grateful to Mom; instead I was resentful.

I blamed Nancy and Dad for making me sleep on the couch in Pacific Palisades. I should have been grateful that they took me in and put a roof over my head when they really didn't have room for me. But instead of being grateful, I was resentful.

I had a long way to go, but God had begun the process inside of me. He had opened my eyes so I could see his love, and I began learning how to put him at the center of my life. As Jesus became not only my Savior but also my Friend and my Lord, I stopped taking out my anger and self-hatred on my family. It took years, not minutes, but I gradually began to open up those dark and hidden areas of my life so that God could pour the light of his love into me.

But there was one area of my life that was still hidden. I kept it hidden from Colleen. I kept it hidden from my fellow Christians. I had never told anyone that I had been touched by a man as a child, and I intended to take that secret to my grave.

But God had other plans.

## "HONEY, WE'VE GOTTA TALK."

In 1987, there was talk of a two-million-dollar offer to write a book about my family. There was one big condition: It had to be a revealing tell-all book, one of those books in which Hollywood children tell the world what terrible parents they had. *Mommie Dearest,* Christina Crawford's 1978 tell-all about her mother, Joan Crawford, had been a runaway best seller; and Gary Crosby's sensational 1983 book about his father Bing, *Going My Own Way,* had also made a huge splash.

Now there was talk of a two-million-dollar advance if I would write a scathing tell-all book about my dad, an enormously popular sitting president, and my mom, an Academy Award-winning actress. That's a lot of money, a huge temptation. I thought, *Maybe this would be the easiest way out. I can*

*tell my story and blame all my problems on my parents.*
*I don't have to mention the molestation. I'll just blame it all*
*on them.* To top it off, I figured that I could put that money in
the bank and never have to work again.

I had been blaming Mom and Dad all my life. I had been
blaming everything that ever happened to me on my parents.
When one of my business ventures failed, I blamed it all on
Ronald Reagan and Jane Wyman because I thought they didn't
love me enough or support me enough. So I figured, since
I'm blaming them anyway, why not get *paid* to blame them in
a book?

I had accepted Christ as my Lord and Savior, yet I was
willing to sell out my parents. Why? Because even though
I had come to Christ, even though I had been baptized, I was
still dealing with all of those demons of the past. I was still
scared to death that someone might find out what happened
to me when I was a child and reveal it to the world.

I wanted people to love me the way they loved my dad
and mom, and I was convinced that if anyone ever knew that
I had been molested, people would shun me and shut me out.

I got together with my writer, Joe Hyams—who had written a number of major biographies, including *Bogart and*
*Bacall*—and we started working together on a book proposal,
a thirty-page treatment to show the publisher. But while Joe
and I were working together, God spoke to me and said,
"Michael, what are you doing? The story you want to tell isn't
true, and you know it. You've accepted my Son, Jesus. Now
start living like it. Tell the truth." I didn't hear an audible

voice, but I had a clear sense that God was speaking directly to me through my heart.

At that moment I just broke down and started crying uncontrollably. Well, you can imagine how Joe Hyams reacted. He backed away from me and said, "What is wrong with you?"

I said, "I can't do it, Joe."

Joe was to get half of the advance and royalties from this book, so as I broke down before his eyes, he was thinking, *There goes a million bucks, right out the window.* He said, "What do you mean, you can't do it?"

"I can't do this to my parents," I said, "because it's not their fault. They're not to blame for what happened to me. They never knew what really happened to me."

Joe said, "What happened to you?"

And I told Joe about the molestation. I told him briefly and without going into detail.

"So, you see," I concluded, "if I write a book blaming Dad and Mom for all my problems, the book would be a lie. I can't do that—not even for two million dollars."

I left Joe's house and went home to Colleen. I had kept this secret hidden from her throughout the twelve years we had been married. I was finally resolved to tell her the truth about my past, and if I didn't do it right away, I didn't know if I'd have the nerve to tell her later. She was in the kitchen when I got home. I said, "Honey, we need to talk." We went into the living room and sat on the couch. I grabbed her hand. I said, "I've got to tell you something about my life that you don't know. And I'm going to write a book about it."

I told her how Don Havlik molested me, took pictures of me, and had me develop one of the photos that had haunted me all those years. She was the first person ever to hear the details. I was scared to death the whole time I was telling her because she literally held my life in her hands. Everything depended on what she would say and do next.

I pictured her saying, "Michael, that's disgusting! After what you told me, I can't stay in this marriage." I expected her to say that, and I wouldn't have blamed her. Because right up to that moment, I believed that the molestation was my fault.

But she didn't say that.

Instead, she put her arms around me, she cradled my head as I cried, and she told me that she loved me. For the first time in my life, I truly felt loved. She told me over and over again, "I love you, Michael. You didn't do anything wrong."

I couldn't believe it. Colleen knew the story! And she still loved me!

All my life, until that moment, I thought I was hated by God. I thought God would never accept me into heaven. I thought that if I ever told my secret to any other human being—to my wife, my parents, the people in my church— then I would be rejected. I expected people to hate me.

Finally the secret wasn't a secret anymore. Now the healing could begin.

## SEEING THE WORLD IN COLOR

On Sunday, April 12, 1987, Colleen and I took the kids up to Dad's Santa Barbara ranch to celebrate Ashley's fourth birthday. While Colleen took the kids over to look at the horses in the corral, I walked with Dad and Nancy over to the edge of Lake Lucky, the pond where Dad took Nancy for canoe rides. They knew I was writing a book, and I knew they wanted to talk to me about it.

We stood there by the water, Dad in front of me, Nancy on my left. I was looking at Dad's belt buckle. I just couldn't bear to look him in the eye. Nancy said, "Michael, what's in the book that we don't know about?"

Still keeping my eye on that belt buckle, I began to tell Dad and Nancy my story. It wasn't a matter of simply saying, "I was molested when I was a kid." They needed to know exactly what Don Havlik did to me, so I didn't spare any details.

At one point Dad knotted his fists and said, "Where is that guy? I'll kick his butt!"

"Just let Mike talk," Nancy said. "He needs to get this out of his system."

As I told them the story, it was as though I went back in time. I was that little boy again, and I was crying my eyes out. I couldn't look at Dad. I just had to keep talking, or I'd never get through it. As the story spilled out of me, Nancy did a wonderful thing; she reached out to me and rubbed the back of my neck, just as she had when I was a little boy, sitting on her lap in the car on the drive to Malibu.

At one point I had to stop, as something inside me just exploded. I was weeping, my eyes and nose were running, and I was throwing up. I must have looked just like Linda Blair in

*The Exorcist* when all of the stored-up evil spewed out of her because that's what happened to me. All of that toxic emotion I had stored up for years suddenly came spewing out of me.

I told them that the man had taken nude photos of me, then he made me develop them, and I had lived in fear that those photos would come out and hurt my family.

Finally I looked up at Dad and met his eye. This was the worst part of all. "Dad," I said, "he took me in his mouth. He orally copulated me." Then I looked at the ground and waited for Dad to get mad at me.

But instead of getting mad, he put his arm around me. "Why didn't you tell me before?" he said. "If you had told me when it happened, I would have done something."

"I was afraid you wouldn't like me anymore," I said.

"Oh, Michael," he said softly, "you should have known better."

But I didn't.

Dad and I embraced. He had spent thirty-five years trying to understand why I acted the way I did and why I was so angry all the time. Now, for the first time, our relationship as father and son made sense.

From then on, all of my most important relationships began to rebuild and become stronger because they were no longer distorted by my secrets. They were based on the truth.

When the publishing industry found out that my book was not going to be a "Daddy Dearest" about Ronald Reagan, the two-million-dollar offer came off the table. That was OK with me. I just wanted to do the right thing and write an honest book. My publisher, Walter Zacharias of Kensington Publishing, supported me in that goal and was great to work with.

I sat down with Joe Hyams, and we hammered out a book that was as candid as I could make it. I talked openly in the book about the molestation and the pictures. The book was called *On the Outside Looking In,* and it quickly became a *New York Times* best seller. The book got a lot of media attention when it first came out. The press combed it for anything juicy and nasty they could use to put my dad in a bad light. But they quickly lost interest in the book when they discovered that it wasn't like Christina Crawford's or Gary Crosby's book.

The thing that amazed me most when I started to tell my story was how liberated I felt. For thirty-five years I had kept this secret buried inside me because I was afraid people would hate me if they knew the truth. Yet once I let go of this secret, once I told Colleen, Dad and Nancy, Mom, and the whole world, the secret lost its power over me. I was truly free.

The most important person I told my story to was God. That's right, I had to tell my story to God! Soon after I began working on the book with Joe Hyams in 1987, I sat down and had a talk with God. I said, "God, here's my burden. I've been carrying it around for thirty-five years, but now I'm going to put it all on your shoulders and let you carry it instead of me." And once I did that, God opened my eyes to some amazing discoveries.

I began to recognize that Dad had a strong Christian faith that I had never seen before. He had an abiding friendship and trust relationship with Christ that was as strong as any I've ever known.

I also began to realize that Mom had a softness, a depth of compassion and love that I had somehow missed during those years I was growing up. I hadn't realized how hard it must have been for her to send me and Maureen away to boarding schools. I hadn't realized all the great things and small things she had done over the years that demonstrated her sweet, motherly love for me. It was there all along, but I had been so wrapped up in guilt, shame, and self-hate that I was blind to it.

For the first time in my life, I truly saw that Mom and Dad loved me all along! I doubted their love when I was in boarding school and when I had to sleep on the living room couch in Pacific Palisades. But they loved me more than I ever realized, more than I ever imagined.

And you know what else I discovered? I loved them too! And I hadn't been showing it. Instead, I had been blaming them for everything that had gone wrong in my life. I played the role of victim better than anybody.

Whenever I failed at something, whenever I gave up on myself, I said, "It's because I'm illegitimate. It's because I was abused. It's because of those pictures that are out there." But when I said, "God, here's my burden; you take it," everything changed. Suddenly I was able to take responsibility for my own life. I quit blaming other people, and I no longer felt controlled by circumstances or memories of the past or poisonous emotions.

On my radio show I hear people playing the victim role all the time. They never take responsibility for their own success or failure. They just blame other people for their lot in life. As long as people refuse to accept responsibility for their own lives, they are doomed to feel powerless and helpless. But the moment they quit making excuses for their failure, they empower themselves to succeed.

I've had African-American callers who said, "I can't succeed because my ancestors were slaves, and I am a victim of the white slave-owning society." When I hear that, my response is, "What would your ancestors think if they heard you using their slavery as an excuse to fail? They'd say, 'We didn't go through all of this suffering and injustice just so you would have an excuse to fail!' They'd say, 'You have opportunities we couldn't even dream of. How dare you sit there in that land of opportunity and make excuses to fail?'"

Everybody goes through trials and traumas. But it's a waste of our God-given life to use those trials and traumas as an excuse to fail. Only when we give up our excuses are we finally able to succeed and achieve our dreams. While I was making excuses for myself, I remained a failure. I never finished anything, I never made a commitment, and I never experienced success.

But then Colleen taught me how to love, how to forgive, and how to stop blaming other people for all the problems in my life. Until Colleen taught me how to love, I couldn't love Mom and Dad, and I couldn't get past the trauma of the molestation. Once I learned how to love, I began to have a real relationship and real communication with Mom and Dad.

When I put away my excuses and took responsibility for my life, I was finally able to become a success in life. Instead of sleeping in guest rooms and borrowing other people's cars, I could buy my own house and my own car. I could hold down a job. I could support a family.

Another change took place in my life when I stopped blaming others and turned my burden over to God: Colors came back into my life. Before, my life was gray and dismal. I couldn't see the goodness in Mom and Dad, in my circumstances, in life itself, or even in God. I saw everything that happened in life as some form of attack on me. I couldn't sense Mom and Dad's love for me. There was no color, no joy, and nothing good or beautiful in my life.

When I stopped blaming others, I could see that I was loved all along, and that Colleen was God's gift to me. Where I once thought no one cared about me, I discovered that people have been praying for me all along. Suddenly my eyes were open to see the positive things in life. It was as if my black-and-white world was suddenly drenched in color.

To my amazement I found that God was even able to take something as painful and horrible as sexual molestation and use it to produce something positive in my life. What could that possibly be? I discovered that I owe my personality—and possibly even my success in radio and speaking—to the hurt that was inflicted on me by the molester. As a child, I developed an affable, class-clown personality to hide the hurt, shame, and anger that raged inside me. My outgoing, fun-loving personality began as a disguise; today it is simply who I am. By the grace of God, I have been able to find a shiny jewel in the manure of my childhood.

My entire world changed when I let God take the burden of the past off my shoulders. No more hiding, no more secrets, no more excuses. That's the story of my redemption.

The story began when God brought a wonderful woman into my life. Colleen was his gift to me. Without her I never would have found a relationship with Christ. Without her I never would have found recovery from my shame, guilt, and self-hate. Without her I never would have found redemption, and you wouldn't be reading this book right now.

## REDEEMING RELATIONSHIPS

What does *redemption* mean? Redemption is the recovery of an object that has been pawned or sold. Redemption is the liberation of a person who has been enslaved or held for ransom. Redemption is the salvation we receive from sin as a result of the sacrifice of Christ upon the cross.

When I married Colleen, I discovered something I never even knew existed: *redeeming love.* It's something we can all experience in our relationships if we choose to. Unfortunately, too few of us choose to love with a redeeming love.

What is redeeming love?

In his book *The Four Loves,* C. S. Lewis examined four forms of love that are found in classical Greek literature: affection (in Greek, *storge*), friendship (*phileo*), romantic love (*eros*), and charity (*agape*). Affection is the love parents have for children and children for parents. Friendship is a love in which there is a sharing of common values, common interests, and a common desire for fellowship; there is no jealousy or possessiveness in friendship. Romantic love desires to possess and join with the beloved; it's a beautiful love though it is an exclusive and jealous love.

What Lewis calls charity, and what the Greeks called *agape,* is the love I call "redeeming love." The other three loves are all emotions. *Agape* love, redeeming love, is a *choice* we make. If we love someone with redeeming love, then we can love that person even when he or she is not very lovable or lovely. It's the greatest love of all because it mixes with the other three loves and elevates them to the highest possible degree.

We have affection for our children when they are nice and well behaved; but when they are rebellious and hateful, full of rage and anger (as I was when I was young), then affection isn't enough. We must *choose* to love our children with a redeeming love.

We experience romantic love when we desire someone and want to have an exclusive, special, passionate relationship with him or her. We marry our mate while we are in the throes of romantic love, but to keep that marriage going for ten, twenty, forty years or more, we must *choose* to love our mate with a redeeming *agape* love.

How do we know what redeeming love looks like? By looking at the example of Christ. He is the ultimate example of God's redeeming love. God reached down into our lives with redeeming love, and he rescued us from our guilt and shame, from the horrors of our past. Through Christ, God recovered our souls from the debt of sin. He liberated us from our slavery to shame and guilt. Through Christ, God paid the ransom we couldn't pay and liberated us from the fear of death and hell. We have been redeemed from a horrible fate by the loving sacrifice of Christ upon the cross.

In John 3:16, Jesus describes God's redeeming love for us in these words: "For God so loved the world that he gave his one and only Son, that whoever believes in him shall not perish but have eternal life." And in John 15:12–13, he goes on to tell us that we should love one another—our husbands, wives, parents, kids, neighbors, fellow church members, friends, enemies, everyone—with the same kind of redeeming love that God showed us: "My command," Jesus said, "is this: Love each other as I have loved you. Greater love has no one than this, that he lay down his life for his friends."

In the original Greek language, the word used for "love" in these verses is *agape,* redeeming love—love that is not just an emotion but a decision, a deliberate choice we make to do good to people even when they do not deserve anything good, even when they are lost in the grip of sin.

How far does love go in seeking to redeem someone from sin? Well, how far did Jesus go? He went as far as anyone could go. He went to the cross. And he is our example. The cross of Christ defines what love is. With the cross as our definition, we can see that redeeming love is not a warm-fuzzy emotion. Jesus didn't feel warm and fuzzy as the people flogged him and spit on him and as they drove eight-inch nails into his hands and feet. Yet he hung on that cross and prayed, "Father, forgive them!"

I know that Colleen didn't feel warm and fuzzy toward me during all the times that I vented my rage, when I was filled with unreasonable anger and she couldn't understand why. She didn't feel warm and fuzzy when she found me screaming at Cameron and pouring out my self-hatred against an innocent little boy. She didn't feel warm and fuzzy when I finally told her the sickening details of what a child molester did to me and about the pictures he took of me.

But she loved me with a redeeming love. She pointed the way so that I could find Jesus so that I could be forgiven for my sins, which were so many and so great. And she held me and told me that when I was molested, I didn't do anything wrong. She reached inside my soul and cradled that seven-year-old Michael Reagan who had waited thirty-five years to find out that it was the molester who was to blame, not him.

Redeeming love! This is what we need to show one another in our marriages, in our families, in our churches, in our world. Redeeming *agape* love is the only thing that takes away guilt, shame, and self-hate. It's the only thing that heals corrosive memories that eat away at our insides. And redeeming love is the only reason I'm able to have a life today. It's the only reason people can listen to me on the radio or see me on television or read this book. Without the redeeming love of Christ and of Colleen Sterns Reagan, Michael Reagan would have been destroyed.

There was a time in 1987, as I sat next to Colleen on my living room couch, when my entire life—my past, present, and future—was compressed down to a matter of seconds. I held Colleen's hand and she held mine. I had just told her the deepest, darkest secret of my entire existence; and it was an ugly, disgusting secret. I had told her things I had never told another human being. And after I told her, I sat there with tears rolling down my face, holding my breath, wondering what she would do, what she would say.

Colleen literally held my life in her hands. Would she take her hand out of mine? Would she pull away? Would she take the children and leave me? I had every reason to believe she would.

But no, she loved me. She told me I didn't do anything wrong. In that moment she redeemed my entire life and took away my self-hate and my shame. She knew my story, she knew my secret, and she loved me!

May God fill your heart and mine with the desire to love others with his redeeming love.

# 10

# TWICE ADOPTED

*I* answered the phone. It was Cameron's third-grade teacher. "Mr. Reagan," she said, "did Cameron talk to you about a problem he's been having at school?"

"No," I said. "What problem is that?"

"I haven't been able to get the whole story from him. I was hoping you'd know what's troubling him."

"Where is he now?"

"On the front steps of the school—crying."

"I'll be right there."

I hurried over to the school and found Cameron on the steps, crying his eyes out. I sat down beside him and said, "Son, what's wrong?"

"Daddy," he said, "is Grandpa really my grandpa?"

"Of course he is," I said. "Why do you ask?"

He looked down at this shoes. "Because one of the kids told me that you're adopted. And if you're adopted, you're not really Grandpa's son. And if you're not really his son, then Grandpa's not really my grandpa."

Those words went through me like a spear, hitting me in one of my most vulnerable places: my adoption. Some school-yard bully had figured out that he could make himself bigger by taking away a piece of Cameron's identity from him—and a piece of mine.

It was the same message that had hurt me so many times over the years: "You're the *adopted* son of Ronald Reagan and Jane Wyman, not the *real* son. Adopted means second-class, not as good, not quite a full-fledged member of the family. Remember, Mike, it's DNA that really counts—not relationship, not love."

"Cameron," I said, "I was adopted into the Reagan family, and the Reagan family is my family. President Reagan is my father, and he's your Grandpa. You are the grandson of the President and part of his family just like I am." I pointed toward a man wearing a dark suit and sunglasses. "If you weren't the grandson of the President, you wouldn't have Secret Service agents around you all the time, would you?"

He looked at the agent, then grinned at me. "I guess not."

"Now go back to your class," I said, "and if anyone tells you that Grandpa's not your grandpa, you just laugh. Because anyone who would say a thing like that doesn't know what he's talking about."

"Thank you, Daddy," Cameron said, and he was off like a shot.

Cameron was always so proud that his Grandpa was the President of the United States. But over the years he has taken a lot of teasing and taunting. Out of spite or envy, some kids have tried to diminish a relationship that is very special— being the grandson of a president. Cameron is in his twenties now, and if you meet him on the street and ask him who his grandfather was, he won't tell you. People can cause a lifetime of damage with a few hurtful words.

Most people don't realize how that word *adopted* is often used to invalidate the connection between parent and child. In half the news articles about me, I'm still called "the adopted son of Ronald Reagan." Well, I *am* the adopted son of Ronald Reagan, so it's an accurate statement.

But being adopted doesn't make me any less related, so why do people use a qualifier like "adopted" to describe the relationship between me and my father? It's because, in the mind of the person who uses that qualifier, being adopted *does* make a difference. It's a way of saying that I'm "sort of" the son or "almost" the son of Ronald Reagan. That's why every time an adoptee hears the word *adopted* used that way, it reopens old wounds.

## DELUGED WITH FAMILY

I started searching for my birth mother in 1987. With help from Dad and California Governor Deukmejian's office, I was able to get a six-page, single-spaced report from the Department of Social Services in Sacramento. The report included an interview a social worker conducted with my birth mother a few weeks after I was born.

The report didn't include my birth mother's name, but it told me she was born in Kentucky and raised in Ohio. She was one of ten children—she had seven brothers and two sisters—and was raised in a Protestant Christian home. The social worker said she was 5' 3" and 115 pounds and attractive. At the time I was born, she was twenty-eight and working as a waitress and actress in Hollywood.

My birth mother also told the social worker about my birth father. He was Catholic, German-American, born in Kentucky or Ohio, and a corporal in the Army. She described him as 6' 1", athletic, and handsome, with green eyes and light brown hair.

The one page that riveted my attention was titled "Circumstances of Placement." It told me what I had been hoping to hear all my life: *My birth mother loved me.* This, in part, is what that page told me:

> Your birth mother told the social worker that she wanted to keep you. However, she stated that it would have been impossible to raise you out of wedlock in her hometown. Therefore, she made the decision to place you in an adoptive home. According to your birth mother, the members of her family had no knowledge of her pregnancy or your birth. The social worker noted that your birth mother had a genuine attachment for you.

*My birth mother loved me!* She wanted to keep me, but she couldn't make a home for me, so she gave me to a prominent Hollywood family. It broke her heart to give me up, but she was comforted to know that I wouldn't lack for anything as I grew up.

When I finished reading that report for the first time, I felt a powerful wave of peace wash over me. One of the biggest questions of my existence had been answered. From the day Maureen told me I was adopted until the day I read that social worker's report, I thought my birth mother didn't want me. I had been angry with myself because I thought there was something wrong with me. I had been angry with her for conceiving me out of wedlock and for sending me out of her life. No matter how much love I received from my adoptive parents, I couldn't feel complete as long as I believed that my birth mother had rejected me.

I read that report several times, until I had memorized the most important passages. All of my old anger toward my birth mother evaporated. Now my heart went out to her. More than that, I *missed* her. I wanted nothing more than a chance to meet her and thank her for loving me enough to give me life and give me a home.

Receiving that report was just the beginning. Only a week later I received another huge break that would reveal to me an entire family I never knew I had. That break came completely out of the blue, from a source that many people would call "coincidence" but which I call a miracle of God.

I was in a hotel room in Vancouver, B.C., and I couldn't sleep. So I decided to call my answering machine in LA and pick up my messages. One of the messages was from a woman named Margie. I had only met her a few times, one of those times in Hawaii, and I had no idea where she had gotten my phone number. She said, "Mike, if you want some information about your birth family, call me back," and she left me a number in the LA area.

My mind churned with questions, and I wasn't able to sleep all night. At nine in the morning, I returned Margie's call. I said, "What information do you have about my birth family?"

"It was the oddest coincidence," she said. "I was on a business trip in Ohio, and I met with a man who runs a furniture business. We were in his car, driving down the street, and a commercial came on the radio about Hawaii vacations. Just to make conversation, I mentioned that I had met President Reagan's son, Michael, in Hawaii. He said, 'You know Michael Reagan? Have I got a story for you!' And he told me that he's your half-brother. His mother is your birth mother."

I was shaken. "What's his name?"

"Barry Lange," Margie said. "He said his mother told him all about you before she died a year and a half ago."

I gasped when she told me my birth mother was dead.

"Michael," Margie said, "are you OK?"

"Yeah," I said. "What else did he say?"

Margie related some other things Barry had said. His mother had kept a scrapbook on the Reagan family, and Barry had thought at first that his mom was a Ronald Reagan fan. Then, in 1980, when Dad ran for president, his mother started dropping hints that there was something about Ronald Reagan she wanted Barry to know. Barry knew that his mom had briefly been an actress in Hollywood during the 1940s, and his first thought was, *Ohmigosh! Mom had a fling with Ronald Reagan!*

Finally, in 1980 or 1981, Barry and his mother were in his car, driving to a Cincinnati Reds game. After months of hinting around, Barry's mom finally told him her secret: She'd had a baby out of wedlock, a little boy, which meant he had a brother. She was afraid Barry would hate her, but Barry assured her that he didn't. "Actually," he told her, "I think it's great. I've always been an only child, and now I have a brother. Where is he now?"

"Your brother," Irene said, "is the son of the President of the United States."

Barry nearly drove off the road.

After that, whenever my birth mother saw me on TV—campaigning for Dad or appearing at a convention or the inauguration—she would call Barry and tell him that his brother was on TV. She died on December 26, 1985, and Barry inherited the scrapbook and a box full of pictures clipped from magazines.

Barry told his story to a few close friends, and they all said, "Call him up!" But he would say, "Oh, I don't want to just knock on his door and say, 'Hi, I'm your brother!' Someday our paths will cross, and if he's interested, fine. If not, that's fine too."

Well, that day had come. Our paths had finally crossed.

Margie agreed to carry messages between me and Barry. Relying on the information in the adoption report that I had received only a week earlier, I came up with a series of questions to relay to the man who claimed to be my half brother: What color were his mother's eyes? How many brothers and sisters did she have? How old was she when I was born?

I gave those questions to Margie, and she told me she'd call me back. I went to a gym to work off some anxious energy.

Margie called back soon after I returned to my room. She went through the questions and Barry's answers. Some answers tallied, some were different from the information I had. Halfway through the list, the results were looking inconclusive.

When Margie got to the question about my birth mother's name, she said, "Barry says her name was Betty Arnold."

The name meant nothing to me. Nancy had told me my birth name was John L. Flaugher. I said, "Are you sure that was her maiden name?"

Margie checked again. "Oh, no. That was her acting name in Hollywood. Her maiden name was Irene Flaugher." She pronounce it "flower," though I later learned it is pronounced "FLAW-er." Margie spelled it for me: F-L-A-U-G-H-E-R.

"Irene Flaugher," I said, turning the name of my birth mother over in my mind. A pretty name.

There was one more question on the list. Barry would only know the answer if my birth mother had told him. "Margie," I said, "does Barry know my birth name?"

"John," she replied. "Barry said your birth name was John."

I said, "Tell Barry he has found his brother."

A short time later Barry flew to LA, and we met at the home of my writer, Joe Hyams. (Joe and I were nearing completion of *On the Outside Looking In,* and we were able to include the story of my meeting with Barry in the epilogue of the book.) I arrived at Joe's house first and paced the floor until the doorbell rang. I opened the door and was stunned to see a guy standing there who looked a lot like me!

We hugged, then I stood back and looked at him. We were the same height and build, and we even had the same slouching shoulders! We were facially similar as well. He was seven years younger than me, and the family resemblance was strong. Barry told me I looked just like his Uncle Jim, and I can't tell you how happy I was to learn that I looked like my mother's side of the family—or that I looked like *anybody,* for that matter! Until that moment I didn't resemble anybody I knew!

Instantly, we were talking like long-lost friends. The bond between us was amazing. We kept noticing similar mannerisms. Barry and I are both animated talkers, we gesture with our hands when we talk, and we stand alike. Barry and I both have "the Flaugher forehead," a receding hairline.

Barry had brought several scrapbooks and photo albums with him, including the scrapbook that Irene had kept of me. There, clipped from newspapers and movie magazines, was my whole history in the Reagan family. I could imagine Irene cutting those clippings and pasting them onto pages. Each page in that scrapbook told me of her love for me.

"She was so proud of you," Barry told me. "She was thrilled that you became the son of the President. If she had known that you wanted to meet her, she would have flown to California in a heartbeat."

Barry told me the story of my birth, as Irene had told it to him. "She was an actress and very pretty," he said. "It was near the end of the Second World War. She found herself pregnant and went to a home for unwed mothers. She was befriended by the woman who ran the home. When Ronald

Reagan and Jane Wyman came to the home, looking to adopt, this woman said, 'I know a young woman you should meet.'

"After you were born, Mom kept you for three days before Jane Wyman came to take you home. Mom actually took you and placed you in Jane Wyman's arms. It must have almost killed her to do that, but she wanted to do the best thing for her baby.

"She felt that by giving you to a family like the Reagans, she'd be giving you a great start in life. And every time she saw your picture in a magazine or on TV, it reassured her that she had done the best thing for you. That made it easier for her to live with the sorrow and guilt. She'd tell herself, 'At least he's having a great life.'"

Barry told me that Irene had shared the story of my birth with a few family members, including her older sister Margaret, who then lived in Florida. He suggested I call Aunt Margaret. So I dialed the number, and a woman answered. I said, "Do you know who this is?"

She said, "Michael?"

She recognized my voice! I was stunned. I later asked Barry if he had told Aunt Margaret to expect my call. He hadn't. I guess she knew a "Flaugher voice" when she heard it. I talked to Margaret for a while, and she told me that Irene would have been hurt to learn that I had been molested. At least she was spared that hurt.

I took Barry for a drive and showed him the house where I was raised on Beverly Glen Boulevard. I pointed out the tree by my bedroom window where I used to climb down and run to the neighbors when Mom sent me to my room. I indicated the various houses in the neighborhood and told them who all of our neighbors were in those days. I pointed to the house behind ours where the Freibergs had lived (Connie Freiberg, you may remember, was the little girl I used to kiss).

Barry said, "The Freibergs? Was that Fred Freiberg, who used to run the Bullocks store in the Valley?"

I said, "Yeah. Why?"

"I used to work for him," Barry said. As we talked, we were astonished to find that we had lived less than a mile from each other in Sherman Oaks for several years.

Barry had come to California from Ohio in 1972 and started working as a TV writer for *Happy Days* and *Laverne and Shirley*. (He actually brought together the famous comedy writing team of Lowell Ganz and Mark "Babaloo" Mandel.) Barry eventually grew tired of the corrosive Hollywood values, so he went to work for Bullock's Department Store for a few years, then moved back to Ohio.

Before Barry and I parted company that night, I told him I wanted to come to Ohio and see Irene's grave. "I'd like it if you and I could visit the grave site together," I said, "so she can finally be with both of her boys."

A few months later we did just that.

In 1990, I attended a Flaugher family reunion in Newcastle, Pennsylvania, and got to meet dozens of cousins, aunts, and uncles I never knew before. After years of wondering about my birth family history, I was suddenly deluged with family. God had a plan to unlock the mystery of my birth family, and he accomplished his plan in his own good and perfect timing.

## SHUT UP AND KEEP DRIVING

I got my start in talk radio completely by accident in July 1983, and it all began because my wife was late for lunch.

Colleen and I were supposed to have lunch with Kitty, a longtime friend from Omaha. Kitty and Colleen had moved to California together, and Kitty was working at Radio KABC in LA. I arrived before Colleen did, and the receptionist said that Kitty was in with the station's president and general manager, George Green. The receptionist sent me in, Kitty introduced me to George, and the three of us talked for a few minutes.

"Gee, Michael," George said, "you've got a nice personality. Ever think of doing talk radio? We need a guest host for Michael Jackson on Monday." (This was, by the way, Michael Jackson the liberal talk-show host, not Michael Jackson the moonwalking pop star and alleged pedophile.) I agreed to take the gig and had a lot of fun, and I've been doing talk radio ever since.

My first full-time radio job was hosting a local show in San Diego. The show first aired on January 16, 1989, and my first caller was President Ronald Reagan, who was just four days from leaving office.

On September 7, 1992, I debuted my nationally syndicated talk show. I was on five stations, four of them tape delayed. Only one of my five stations carried the show live, and it was preempted every Monday night for football. On those nights when I was preempted, I was trying to do a live call-in show without a live listening audience, and that meant no callers.

So my syndicator and I got, shall we say, "creative." That is, we created callers out of thin air. My syndicator would call me from another office line and say, "Hi, this is Bob from Atlanta—longtime listener, first-time caller," and I'd say, "Hi, Bob, how are you? What do you want to talk about tonight?" Then the syndicator's wife would call from a pay phone outside the door (so the phone would have different background noises), and she'd say, "Hello, Michael, this is Linda from St. Louis. I love your show!" We'd get callers from all over the country, but if you listened closely, you might notice that Bob from Atlanta sounded a lot like John from Providence who sounded a lot like Larry from Seattle.

I was living in LA and driving 262 miles round trip to my studio in San Diego, every night, five nights a week. We needed a certain number of stations before the program would start to make money, so there were days I came home from the studio almost in tears because there was no money. I couldn't pay my bills or buy groceries. Our house, which had been one of the nicest houses on the block, was becoming one of the worst-looking houses on the block. The roof was shot and the paint was peeling.

My first year as a syndicated talk-show host, I worried that Colleen wouldn't be able to stand by me through this trial. I wondered how long before she finally had enough and decided to leave me. I needn't have worried. She was committed to the Lord, and she was committed to me—for richer, for poorer.

Every night I'd get home at around ten-thirty or eleven, and I would find Colleen sitting in bed with her reading glasses on, her red-leather Bible open on her lap, reading as she waited for me to get home. I'd see her there and say, "What are you doing?"

She'd smile and say, "I've just been praying for you, Michael."

Then I knew I was home, and everything was OK—at least until the next day when I had to go out and do it all again.

During that trying first year in radio, I called Mom on the phone and said, "Mom, I don't know what to do anymore. I need to quit and find a regular job. What do you suggest?"

Mom knew that I was just feeling sorry for myself, so she said, "Shut up and keep driving."

So I shut up and kept driving.

Was Mom being too harsh? Not at all! She gave me good advice, loving advice. She knew what it took to build a successful career in the entertainment business because she had done it. She knew that you can't succeed without focus, patience, hard work, courage, and perseverance. And she also knew that you can't accomplish anything while you're feeling sorry for yourself. So she told me, "Shut up and keep driving."

It's the same lesson she tried to teach me when I was a ten-year-old rich kid in Beverly Hills and I wanted her to buy me a new ten-speed bike. I tried to play the same game that so many kids of divorced parents play: "Buy me what I want, and I'll love you forever."

But Mom wouldn't play that game. She said, "I'll get you the bike, but you have to earn the money to pay me back. I build men, not boys." She was teaching me the same lesson in 1993 that she tried to teach me in 1955: If you really want something, then go out and earn it, work for it, sacrifice for it, focus, and persevere. Shut up and keep driving.

I told Mom, "We tried it your way for over forty years, and I'm still struggling. Could we try it my way now? Could you give me the money?"

"Just keep working," she said. "You'll make it."

And she was right.

Since then the show has grown tremendously, and we have changed syndicators. We are nearing two hundred stations coast-to-coast and we are carried over the Internet by Radio America of Washington, D.C. (www.radioamerica.org). I also appear as a contributor on the Fox News Channel, where you might have seen me on *Hannity and Colmes*.

People kept predicting that my show would fail, and there were times when it looked like they were right. Dad even went to bat for me in the last year of his presidency. He called Rush Limbaugh's syndicator and said, "My son is doing a talk show on radio, and I think it would be a good compliment to Rush Limbaugh's show. You could have Rush in the morning and Michael Reagan in the evening."

Rush Limbaugh's people called me and said, "Let's talk." We met at the National Association of Broadcasters convention in Dallas, and I gave them some tapes and told them my vision for the show. It was a pleasant meeting. Two weeks later they got back to me. "We've given your show a lot of thought," they said, "but we don't believe it can be successful."

They said no to me—and to Ronald Reagan.

While I was hosting my local show in San Diego, my producer, Marna McClure, once said something to me that puzzled me and stuck with me. She said, "Michael, I don't know what's going to happen to you, but if you can unlock all the locked safes inside you, all the different areas of your mind, no one will be able to touch you."

I didn't understand what that meant at the time. Now I think I do. She was telling me I needed to bring the person I am and the life I've lived into my show. Scores of radio personalities talk about political issues. But I've lived experiences that few of them have ever lived.

I don't have to read a book about child molestation because I know about it—I was molested. I don't have to research the effects of child pornography on children because I lived with the memory of those pictures. I don't have to do research on adoption, illegitimacy, divorce, or the effect of broken homes on children because I have been there. Over the past few years, I have tried to unlock those safes, take out those experiences, and lay them out for my listeners.

As I have opened the newspaper and seen heartbreaking stories of children molested by priests, or the story of an angry, fatherless boy shooting innocent people in Washington, D.C., I have sensed God telling me, "Mike, look at these people who are going through what you've gone through. Look at all the people who don't understand what these news stories mean or why they are happening. You know why these things are happening because you've been there. Mike, this is why I've given you this story to tell. People need to hear it. So tell your story."

Sometimes I look at everything I went through, and I sit back and say, "God, are you sure I'm supposed to handle all of this? You know, God, there are people in this world who have been born illegitimate. There are people who have been molested, people who have been abused by child pornography, people who come from broken homes, people who had to deal with one or two of these things. But for some reason, God, you said, 'Michael, I'm going to load you up with all of these things.'"

And I just have to sit back and laugh! And I think, *Now I'm on a radio show. Now I'm writing a book, and I'm able to share these stories. I'm able to tell other people that you can survive what I survived. But you only survive them by giving them up to God. That's what I did, and that's what saved me.*

## My birth father

In 1988, soon after *On the Outside Looking In* was published, a woman in northern California wrote me and said, "I read your book and saw you on *The Phil Donohue Show*. I once dated a man who bragged that his son had been adopted by Ronald Reagan and Jane Wyman. I didn't believe him at the time, but after hearing your story, I thought you should know about this man in case you wanted to contact him."

She had enclosed a photo with the man's name and phone number on the back. The name on the photo was John Bourgholtzer. I decided not to follow up on it.

At the same time, my birth father, John Bourgholtzer, was living in Florida and reading a copy of *On the Outside Looking In*. Irene Flaugher had told him that I had been adopted by the Reagan family, and he had followed my life for years. After reading my book, he looked up my brother Barry Lange and asked him to get a message to me.

As it happened, Barry and I were scheduled to do an appearance together on Arsenio Hall's late-night TV show. So Barry flew to California, and before the show he told me about the call from my birth father. Later Barry and I called John together and talked to him.

A year or two later, when I was still doing my show from San Diego, John Bourgholtzer came out to California and we met. We sat down together, and, to be candid, the meeting was awkward for both of us. He was defensive, and while I was certainly curious, I didn't feel a connection with this man like I felt with my brother Barry.

The fact is, most adoptees don't really care that much about meeting their birth dad. They usually have lots of questions for the birth mother—especially, "Why did you send me away?" But adoptees rarely show much interest in their birth father. I was no exception.

But there was one wonderful thing John Bourgholtzer did for me: He introduced me to a brother and a sister I didn't know I had, Rick and Terry. I only had one conversation with my half brother Rick Bourgholtzer, and he passed away a few years ago.

However, John's daughter, Terry Dougela, has become close and dear to me. John gave me Terry's phone number when we met in San Diego, and I called her at work. She and her husband were going to Las Vegas for a convention (Terry's husband worked for Chevrolet), so we agreed to meet there. Terry picked me up at the airport, and we spent the day together, getting acquainted.

Terry has a strong Christian faith, and she prays for me all the time. She lives in Georgia, and I talk to her by phone on a regular basis. She has told me more about my birth father than he was able to tell me himself.

What kind of man was John Bourgholtzer? For most of his life, John was an outdoorsman—a tall, athletic, rugged, handsome man. He was a boxer in the army, as well as a hunter, a fisherman, and a boater. He was also a charmer and a womanizer. Irene Flaugher was apparently one of many women who succumbed to his charm, though Terry tells me that John truly loved Irene and might have married her if they had not been kept apart by the war.

At the age of sixty, John was in the hospital, diagnosed with kidney failure. Terry once told me, "Daddy hasn't lived a very good life, but he made a pact with the Lord: If God would heal him, he would stop running around with women, and he would live for God. He recovered and lived for seventeen more years as a Christian. He went to the First Baptist Church in Jacksonville, and he kept his promise to the Lord.

"Daddy did a lot of wrong things, Michael, but he did love you. He told me about you when I was eleven years old, and he told no one else. He followed your life all those years. Whenever he saw you on TV, he'd call me and tell me to turn on the TV. He had regrets about giving you up for adoption, but he felt it was best to let you live your life and not intrude. He was probably afraid that you wouldn't accept him and forgive him."

When Terry and I met in Las Vegas, she showed me a box of pictures John saved—pictures of Irene and newspaper clippings of me. "He was very proud of you," Terry told me, "though he was a different kind of man and had a hard time saying what he felt."

On September 22, 1993, after a series of strokes, my birth father died in the Veterans Hospital in Lake City, Florida. Terry called me later and told me that she had scattered his ashes in the St. John's River which flows into the ocean at Jacksonville.

## FACING OUR LOSSES

In 1991, Colleen and I began attending the Church on the Way in Van Nuys, California. I immediately found myself in a prayer circle. Prayer circles are part of every Sunday morning worship service at the Church on the Way. For three to five minutes, the congregation divides into small groups. People share needs, join hands, and pray for one another.

When I took part in my first prayer circle at church, I had never seen anything like it before, and I felt a little threatened. I wasn't about to tell *my* story to these people! I wasn't about to let anyone else see *my* pain! After all, they thought I had a perfect life. Why ruin it?

I had already told my story to the entire world three years earlier when I wrote *On the Outside Looking In,* yet I still couldn't share my story face-to-face in a prayer circle. I feared what people would think of me after reading the story of my molestation. I feared being branded "homosexual" by people at church. Though I had accepted Christ by this time, I still lacked trust in my fellow Christians, and I feared that they would judge me and reject me.

Week by week Colleen and I kept coming back and praying together in the prayer circles. I heard Christians saying, "I need help in this area," and, "Please hold me accountable in that area," and, "Please pray for me as I face this crisis in my life." I began to see how healthy it is for Christian brothers and sisters to come together, share their real problems and hurts with one another, pray for one another, and find healing together.

Today I'm stronger. I have learned to trust my brothers and sisters in the church, and I'm able to share my story—not only in prayer circles but with the entire congregation. In November 2003, I told my story to the church at a Sunday evening service. I arrived at the church with an overpowering feeling of God's presence. It was such an awesome feeling that I couldn't even sit with other people. I had to go off and be alone with God until the service began.

When I spoke, I told the story that I've told in this book. At the end I did something I've never done before: I gave an altar call. I invited people to come forward so that the pastors could pray with them, and they could commit their lives to Christ. A dozen people responded.

When I saw the Holy Spirit draw twelve people to Christ through the story that God has given me, I suddenly realized what a miracle of transformation God had done in my life. I once hated and blamed God for all of those experiences. Today I praise and thank God for those same experiences because he is using the story of my life to draw people to himself.

Pastor Jack Hayford, the founding pastor of the Church on the Way, has been a great Christian mentor to me. He and I have had many breakfast meetings together, and his influence has accelerated my Christian growth in the years since I accepted Jesus Christ as Lord of my life.

Pastor Jack's son-in-law, Scott Bauer, also became a great friend to me. The hours I've spent talking, praying, and golfing with Pastor Scott have contributed so much to my emotional healing and my spiritual growth. He was a good listener and a trusted advisor whenever I faced a major decision in my life. Scott served alongside Pastor Jack for fifteen years and succeeded him as senior pastor in 1999. It came as a terrible shock when Scott, who was only forty-nine, died of an aneurysm on October 24, 2003.

Scott and I felt a real kinship while he was on this earth. We understood each other well. Scott was the son-in-law of a man who is an icon in the Christian world. His wife, Rebecca, is the daughter of Pastor Jack Hayford. Pastor Jack had been training and mentoring Scott to take over the roles that he himself had filled in the pulpit and on the radio. Because Scott was Pastor Jack's son-in-law, people would look at him and say, "He's only on the radio or in the pulpit because he married Pastor Jack's daughter." Some people couldn't see Scott's own unique giftedness, even after the church had grown from ten thousand to twelve thousand members under his leadership.

I understood Scott's dilemma because of who my own father was. So I would uplift Scott and call him and give him a hug after the worship service. I would tell him how God had spoken to my heart through his message. And when I would appear on *Hannity and Colmes,* Scott would call me and lift me up We both understood that when your father or father-in-law is an icon, it is hard for some people to look past the icon and see who you really are. So when Scott left our presence and moved into the presence of God, I lost a dear friend and a kindred spirit.

As Scott's family and our church family have been going through this loss, I have thought a lot about the unique way Christians grieve. We all have been sorrowing over Scott, but not as people who have no hope. Along with our sadness is a gladness that Scott loved Jesus, and he is now home with his Lord. As Christians, we all need to experience what it means to grieve with sadness and rejoicing, because we all face losses.

It has been a challenge and an encouragement to me, as I'm now going through losses in my own life, to watch how Scott's family—his wife Rebecca, daughter Lindsey, and sons Kyle and Brian—have accepted this sudden and unexpected loss in their lives with courage and faith.

I believe Scott made it easier for his family to accept his loss because he gave his family a wonderful gift. It's the same gift that I have received from my own Mom and Dad. It's the gift of a lifetime of faith, the gift of a Christian testimony.

Looking back, I can see that Mom and Dad gave me a lot of great gifts over my lifetime. Mom gave me the gift of her work ethic, her values, and above all, her love. She could have indulged me and spoiled me, but she chose to raise me to be a man, and that is a great gift. Dad gave me the gift of Saturdays at the ranch, his wonderful role model, and the legacy of his great name.

But there is one gift that my parents have given me that outshines all the rest. Now, as my dad's ninety-year journey through life has been completed, and as my mother approaches ninety, quick as a whip but ailing due to advancing age, I'm more grateful than ever for the gift they've given me. I know where Dad is now. I know where Mom is going. And I'll know that I will see them again one day in eternity.

It was incredibly painful to watch my father slip into the shadow of Alzheimer's disease. People often said, "How can you stand it? Why are you smiling? How can you be happy when your dad is suffering with this disease?"

And I would tell them, "Because I know where Dad is going. I know that this illness won't last forever. When it's over, Dad will be at home with God." Now that he's finally home at last, those words are more true than ever. When you know that a loved one is safe in the arms of God, how can that be sad?

## GOD'S CHILDREN ARE ALL ADOPTED

Another healing experience I have had at the Church on the Way is the discovery that God truly designed his church to be a redemptive and adoptive family. It's a place where people who feel lost and unloved, shamed and guilt ridden, can come to find forgiveness, a new beginning, and a place of belonging.

At the Church on the Way I discovered that the Bible has a special view of adoption and adoptees. I learned how God has used adoptees in important ways to accomplish his purpose. For example, in Exodus 2:1–10, Moses was born to a Hebrew woman, but the mother of Moses had to give him up in order to save his life. So Moses was placed where he would be found by Pharaoh's daughter, and he was adopted as a son in Pharaoh's household. Only by being adopted into Pharaoh's household could he become the liberator of the Hebrew people.

And in Esther 2, Esther was an orphan who was adopted and raised by her uncle Mordecai. She eventually became the queen of Persia, and God used her to save the lives of the Hebrew people when they were in captivity.

Did you know that, according to the New Testament, *all* Christians are adopted? That's right. You can't be a Christian unless you are adopted. Nobody has ever been born into God's family. The only way you can get in is the same way I got into the Reagan family—by adoption.

The apostle Paul explained it this way: "For you have not received a spirit of slavery leading to fear again, but you have received a spirit of adoption as sons by which we cry out, 'Abba! Father!' . . . We ourselves groan within ourselves, waiting eagerly for our adoption as sons, the redemption of our body" (Rom. 8:15, 23b NASB).

Notice how Paul intertwines the concept of redemption with the concept of adoption. He is telling us that when we are adopted, we are redeemed; when we are redeemed, we are adopted. Redemption, as I said in the previous chapter, is the recovery of something that has been pawned or sold or the liberation of a person who has been enslaved or held for ransom.

I can relate to this biblical concept in a personal way. I was born into a situation where I had no hope. I was the child of an unwed mother who was unable to keep me and care for me. So what did my birth mother do? She put me up for adoption.

Along came Ronald Reagan and Jane Wyman. They *redeemed* me from my hopeless situation by *adopting* me. As an act of supreme love and supreme sacrifice, my birth mother placed me in the arms of a redeemer—my mother, Jane Wyman. You see? Redemption and adoption go hand in hand.

The apostle Paul tells us that, apart from a relationship with Jesus Christ, we are sold into slavery, but when we receive him into our lives as Lord and Savior, we are redeemed from slavery and adopted as God's own children.

Paul explains it this way: "So also, when we were children, we were in slavery under the basic principles of the world. But when the time had fully come, God sent his Son, born of a woman, born under law, to redeem those under law, that we might receive the full rights of sons. Because you are sons, God sent the Spirit of his Son into our hearts, the Spirit who calls out, 'Abba, Father.' So you are no longer a slave, but a son; and since you are a son, God has made you also an heir" (Gal. 4:3–7).

As an adoptee, that is a powerful statement to me. It hits me right where I live. It tells me that God sent Jesus to redeem me so that I am no longer a slave to guilt, shame, rage, and self-hate. God has adopted me as his own son, and I have the full rights of a son of God, including the right to be God's own heir.

How was this accomplished? Not by anything I did. An adoptee doesn't choose his parents; his parents choose him. That's why Paul writes that God "predestined us to be adopted as his sons through Jesus Christ, in accordance with his pleasure and will" (Eph. 1:5). In other words, God chose us, he made a decision about us ahead of time—to bring us into his family because having us in his family brings him pleasure. He has redeemed us from slavery and adopted us as his children because he loves us and he delights in us.

Because God has redeemed and adopted us, we now have an intimate relationship with him. Paul describes that intimate relationship by telling us that we have "received a spirit of adoption as sons by which we cry out, 'Abba! Father!'" That word *abba* is an Aramaic word that was used by little children to address their fathers; the closest equivalent in English would be *daddy* or even *da-da*. It's an intimate and childlike word.

In Mark 14:36, Jesus calls God the Father "Abba" when he prays in the garden of Gethsemane and begs his heavenly Daddy not to send him to the cross. Now that you and I have been adopted as God's children, we have been given this same kind of intimacy with God the Father, so that we can go to him and call him "Abba, Daddy," and ask of him anything we want.

When I was little, my "abba" was Ronald Reagan. He was my daddy. That was the only name I had for him. For eight years during the 1980s, almost everyone else in the world was required to call him "Mr. President"—but not me. If I called him on the phone, I called him Dad. Being a son gives you an intimacy with your father that the rest of the world can't have. To me, Ronald Reagan was always my "abba."

As Christians, we have that same relationship with God. As his adopted kids, we have been brought close to the heart of God. We don't take a backseat to God's "birth kids" because he doesn't have birth kids. His entire family is an adoptive family. You can't get into God's family any other way. We start life as slaves, and we are adopted as God's sons and heirs. God gives us the right to crawl up into his lap and whisper in his ear because he has redeemed us and adopted us as his children.

Unfortunately, we live in a society which has long viewed adoption as an abnormal or second-best family arrangement. Even in the church, we have accepted this notion that adoption is a deviation from the norm. Even in Christian families, siblings sometimes tease each other, joking, "Oh, didn't Mom and Dad ever tell you that you were adopted?" Behind this teasing is the assumption that an adopted kid is different and inferior—a misfit.

As Christians, as God's own adoptees, we need to elevate our view of adoption. We need to see every adopted child as a gift of God's grace to the family and the family as the gift of God's grace to the adopted child.

## FINALLY HOME

Adoptive relationships aren't easy, of course. Over the years I've had strained relations with my adoptive parents. I would get mad at my father because I saw in him a man who could go out and talk to the world, and audiences loved him, and he loved them. Yet, when I was growing up as his son, I often wondered if he loved me.

One of the reasons I doubted Dad's love for me was that the never told me that he loved me. Here he was, the male role model in my life, yet it seemed that there were so many things I wanted him to do for me that he wouldn't do. I wondered, *Why doesn't Dad take me to football games and baseball games? Why doesn't he take me to Disneyland?*

Here's something you may not know about Ronald Reagan: He helped Walt Disney open Disneyland. The first

Disney theme park opened in July 1955, when I was ten years old. Walt Disney asked three people to host the live television broadcast of Disneyland's opening day: Art Linkletter, Bob Cummings, and Ronald Reagan.

So Dad hosted the whole world at Disneyland, but he never took me. And the fact that he never took me to Disneyland or to football and baseball games caused me to doubt his love for me. When I was growing up, I wondered, *Why doesn't Dad do those things with me that other fathers do with their kids?* And I used to get angry with Dad because of that.

Today, however, I understand why he didn't do those things. Today I know that Dad didn't go to public places because he didn't want to be mobbed by fans and autograph seekers. The moment one fan recognizes him, it's all over. Soon, he's surrounded, and he becomes a bigger attraction than the attraction he came to see.

As I matured, I also began to see that Dad was a godly man and a devoted Christian. One of the most revealing moments came during Easter weekend 1988, when I flew with Dad from Washington, D.C., to California, less than a year before he left office. I had been in Washington to appear on *Larry King Live* to talk about my first book and had spent the night at the White House. As Air Force One descended toward the airbase at Point Mugu, not far from Dad's Santa Barbara ranch, I noticed he was counting to nine on his fingers.

I said, "What are you doing, Dad?"

He said, "I'm counting the months until I can go to church again. Just nine more months."

"What do you mean?"

"Ever since I was shot and they threw me in that car," he said, recalling the March 1981 assassination attempt, "I have felt I shouldn't go to church. I remember looking out the car window and seeing people lying on the ground and bleeding because of me."

When Dad said that, I recalled how painful it was for him that three men, including his close friend Jim Brady, were wounded by the same gunman who had shot him.

"I didn't want that scene repeated in a church," he added. "So I haven't attended church on a regular basis since that day. I didn't want some guy with a gun coming into church and hurting other people to get to me. When I finally leave Washington in January, I can start going to church again because I really want to spend that time with our Lord."

I said, "Why don't you go this Sunday? I think you should."

"Well," he said, "I'll think about that."

As it turned out, Dad did go to church that Easter Sunday. And as soon as he was out of office, he never missed a Sunday service until the Alzheimer's disease progressed to a point where he simply could no longer attend. In this, as in every other aspect of his life, Dad was true to his word.

The assassination attempt, which occurred just two months and ten days into his first term, profoundly affected Dad's faith and his view of himself as president. When I visited him at

George Washington University Medical Center immediately after the assassination attempt, he told me, "Michael, I've thought a lot about how close I came to losing my life. Not only would my earthly life have been over, but everything I wanted to do for the American people would have ended right then and there. I believe God spared me for a purpose. Michael, I want you to know that I've decided to commit the rest of my life, and the rest of my presidency, to God."

My sister Patti tells another story about Dad in the days right after the assassination attempt. When Maureen, Patti, Ron, and I went to see Dad in his hospital room, he told us about being wheeled into the operating room. He described the room to a T. He told us about the nurses and doctors in the room and said that they were all dressed in white. He said he could actually see them operating on him and taking the bullet from his chest, just underneath his heart. Dad was describing things he shouldn't have been able to see; he was having a near-death experience.

Years later Patti decided to write a book on angels (*Angels Don't Die: My Father's Gift of Faith,* HarperCollins, 1995), so she went back to Washington and interviewed the doctors and nurses who operated on Dad that day at George Washington University. They showed Patti the room where Dad lay close to death, and it was exactly as he had described it. She told the doctors and nurses the story Dad had told us. The hospital staff looked at each other in awe.

Then one of the doctors said, "Let me show you something." And he showed Patti some doctors and nurses who were scrubbed and dressed for surgery. They were dressed in green, not white.

Who were the white-gowned figures Dad saw when he was so close to death? I know who they were: *angels*. There were angels with Dad that day and throughout his presidency. Angels kept him alive in the operating room. Angels guided him through eight years in the White House. Angels have been with him for a long time. They were with him right up to the last moment of his life.

I look back at the things I have gone through in my life, and as painful as it has all been, I know that angels have been with me too. God is going to take all the hurt I've gone through, even the molestation itself, and he's going to redeem it, transform it, and use it to heal other people. I can't see white-robed figures, but I believe they're around me.

In gratitude to God for what he is doing in my life, I have to say, "I can't blame God, I can't blame Dad, I can't blame Mom, I can't blame Irene Flaugher or John Bourgholtzer for the things that have hurt me. I'm through blaming my birth parents and my adoptive parents and my heavenly Father for everything that's gone wrong in my life."

I used to play the blame game all the time. Every time I failed, I had a built-in excuse. Every time I got angry, I blamed my parents and I blamed God. My father never told me he loved me, so why should I say "I love you" to anyone else?

Sometime in 1991, while I was in prayer, I felt God speaking to me within my spirit. He said to me, "Michael, you've been angry because your dad hasn't hugged you, but when was the last time you hugged your dad? You've been angry because your dad hasn't said, 'I love you,' but when was the last time you told your dad, 'I love you'?"

I told God, "You're right. I've never hugged him. I've never told him 'I love you.' It's time for me to start." God was working on my heart, ridding me of the last vestiges of my blaming and excuse-making. And I decided right then and there that the next time I saw my dad, I was going to tell him, "I love you."

That opportunity arrived when Dad made a special trip to San Diego to be a guest on my KSDO radio show and talk about his new book, *An American Life*. He arrived at the radio station along with several Secret Service agents. I walked out to meet him in the reception area. As soon as I saw him, I wrapped my arms around him and said, "Dad, I love you."

And you know what he said? "Well," he replied, "I love you too."

Wow! At that moment, the thought hit me, *Michael! All your life, you've been blaming your dad for not hugging you and saying, "I love you," when all you ever had to do was to make the first move!*

Thank God, I listened to his voice within me, and I did what he was prodding me to do! That hug and those words began a tradition between Dad and me. From then on, whenever I saw my dad, I would hug him and say, "I love you," and he would hug me back and say those same words to me. Thank God, I didn't wait, because three years later, in 1994, Dad told the world that he had been stricken with Alzheimer's disease.

As time passed, and the disease progressed, the day eventually came when Dad could no longer say my name, let alone "I love you." But he did recognize me. Whenever I walked into a room and Dad was there, he would open his arms, waiting for me to give him a hug and tell him, "I love you, Dad." I could see the recognition in his eyes, even though he couldn't say my name.

One time, after the disease had progressed to the point where Dad could no longer speak, Colleen and I went to visit him. He sat in a chair in the den, and we sat with him, sometimes holding his hand, mostly conversing with Nancy. Finally, it was time to go, so Colleen and I said good-bye to Nancy, and we got up and left. I had neglected to do what I always did. I had neglected to give Dad a hug.

Colleen and I walk out of the den and out the front door, toward the driveway. Meanwhile, there was Dad in his chair, and he counted on that hug every time I visited. Only this time, I didn't hug him! Dad couldn't say my name, but he knew who I was: I'm the guy who hugs him.

So he got up out of his chair and followed me. He couldn't call out my name. He couldn't walk very fast, and his footsteps can't match mine. But he followed as best he could.

I had almost reached my car as Dad got to the front door, where he had to stop. Colleen turned and saw him, and she said, "Michael, you forgot something."

I said, "What did I forget?"

"Turn around," she said.

I turned and there was my dad. He was standing at the door with his arms outstretched. He was waiting for his hug.

I ran back and hugged him, and I told him, "I love you, Dad."

None of this would have happened if God hadn't begun the process of redemption in my life. That process began when God sent a wonderful, godly woman into my life—my wife, Colleen. Unbeknownst to me, God had been preparing her, building her character and strengthening her faith, so that she would be able to persevere through my anger and my self-hatred until I was able to unlock my deepest secret. She prayed for me every day until I found Jesus Christ and was adopted for the second time, this time by God.

When I was only *once* adopted, I was full of rage, shame, guilt, and self-hatred. I didn't know who I was or where I belonged.

My search ended when I was *twice* adopted.

God is my Father, and I am his child. I'm finally home.

# EPILOGUE

It's been fifty years since I was molested. Fifty years is a long time. So I'm surely over it by now, right?

Wrong.

I'll never be over it. I think about it every day—every single day.

One time about five years ago, I appeared on a television talk show as one of a number of child sex abuse survivors. The taping had begun and there was a family out on the set with the host, telling their story to the studio audience. I was back in the green room, watching the show on the monitor, waiting for my turn to go out. There was a young woman in the green room with me, and she was also a survivor of sex abuse.

As I listened to the family describe the pain their children went through, I started to get teary eyed, and then I just broke down and cried. And the young woman looked at me with alarm and asked, "How long ago were you molested?"

I said, "Forty-five years."

"And it still affects you this deeply?" she said.

"Yeah," I said, wiping my eyes. "It still does."

Perhaps she was hoping that a day would come in her own life when the memories wouldn't hurt anymore. I don't think

**319**

that day ever will come for me—not this side of eternity. Few people understand the depth of that kind of trauma.

But you can't live your life in a traumatized state. You have to go on. As Colleen has told me many times, "Never let another person determine your attitude—unless that person is God." I know now that I allowed my molester to determine my attitude toward people, toward God, and toward myself from the time I was seven years old. If you hate yourself, you're no good to anybody. In order to live a happy, productive life, you must be able to wake up every morning knowing that someone loves you—and most of all, that God loves you.

Whenever I go out and speak, I'm conscious of the statistics that one-third of all girls and one-fifth of all boys will be sexually molested during their lifetime. So if I'm speaking to a group of two hundred people, it's probably a safe bet that fifty or more have been molested. Add in all the ones who have been adopted or had divorced parents or were raised by single parents, and I figure that most of the people in that room can personally identify with some part of my life story.

How about you? Are you using some experience from your past as an excuse to fail in life? "I'm a failure because I was molested, because I was adopted, because I came from a broken home, because I never had a good role model for healthy relationships, because I felt God hated me." It's time to put away the excuses. It's time to stop allowing other people to determine your attitude and the course of your life.

Ever since I put away my excuses, I have had a great life. I have given my burden and trauma to God. I enjoy my family, my career, and my church. I have a strong relationship with my Lord and Friend, Jesus Christ. So in one very real sense, I am healed.

But in another real sense, I am still broken. There are moments when it doesn't take much to open the floodgates of memories, emotions, and pain. How do I deal with the pain, problems, and obstacles in my life?

I reach into my pocket and take out my stone of David.

## NO MATCH FOR GOD

A few years ago Pastor Jack Hayford spoke to a men's group at our church and told us the story of David and Goliath. You remember the story from Samuel 17.

Two armies faced each other across a battlefield—the godless army of the Philistines and the army of God's people, Israel. Goliath, the champion of the Philistines' came out—nine feet tall, powerfully built, wearing two hundred pounds of bronze armor, and carrying a spear as long as a telephone pole. The soldiers of Israel took one look at Goliath and started quaking in their boots.

Then, from among the Israelites, stepped David. He was a mere teenager, yet he was the only person in Israel who dared to stand up to the Philistine giant. David walked out onto the battlefield and started dissing Goliath: "Today, the Lord is going to hand you over to me. I'm going to knock you down and cut off your head. When I do, the whole world will know that there is a God in Israel, and everyone here will know that this battle is not a battle of swords or spears; this battle is the Lord's!"

Goliath charged at David, and David charged at Goliath. As David ran, he reached into his bag and took out a stone—one of five smooth stones he had taken from a stream. He put the stone in his sling, then he flung it at the Philistine. The stone struck deep into Goliath's forehead, felling him instantly. And just as he promised, David took Goliath's head home with him as a trophy.

The point of the story for your life and mine? Pastor Jack explained it this way: Every battle is the Lord's. We can't fight our battles with swords or spears; our enemy is too great. Throughout our lives you and I keep coming up against Goliaths—enemies that are nine feet tall, carrying spears as long as telephone poles. We're no match for the Goliaths we face, but there's good news:

Goliath is no match for God!

After Pastor Jack told us that story, he passed out smooth stones to all the men. I took a stone and I keep it with me every day, wherever I go, because I never know when I'm going to face another Goliath.

What are my Goliaths?

I have many Goliaths in my life. I still deal with the memories of being sexually abused. I still deal with feelings of shame and guilt. I am still tempted to become angry. I'm still tempted to blame others. The residue of the molestation is still a big Goliath in my life after all these years. Even with Jesus Christ as my Lord and Savior, even with all the progress I've made, even with so many people praying for me, I face Goliaths in my life all the time.

# EPILOGUE

Apart from the issue of being a child sex abuse survivor, I have the normal temptations that are common to every human being. You face them too. Here are some of the most common temptations, and I'm sure you'll find your own vices on this list: anger, gossip, pornography, flirting, sexual sin, drinking to excess, smoking, drug abuse, laziness, gambling, coveting, lying, stealing, overspending, overeating, wasting time on the Internet, cursing, and on and on.

We all face Goliaths. Whether you're a man or woman, young or old, in the workplace or in your home, you face enemies that are bigger and more powerful than you are. Every day there's a Goliath-size challenge to overcome: a temptation you can't handle, a problem with your kids, a conflict in your marriage, a crisis at the office, a collision at the intersection, an audit notice from the IRS, bad news at the doctor's office, a death in the family, a bout with depression, a rumor that's destroying your reputation. Whatever that enemy may be, that's your Goliath.

Every issue I've talked about in this book is a Goliath: anger toward God, fear that your secrets will be exposed, shame and guilt from past sins, distorted family relationships, feelings of worthlessness, feeling that God can never forgive you, feeling unloved, feeling violated, hatred toward God, feeling hated by God, fear of hell. These were the Goliaths that towered over me through most of my life.

What do you do when you face struggles, obstacles, pressures, emotions, fear, trials, sorrows, and temptations beyond human endurance? What do you do when Goliath is coming at you like a Mack truck, and you have nowhere to hide?

I'll tell you what I do. I reach in my pocket, and I wrap my fingers around that stone, and I pray, "God, take over and fight this battle! This Goliath is too big for me. It's your battle, not mine."

And with that stone in my hand and that prayer on my lips, I slay my Goliaths. That's the only way I can get through each and every day.

What are your Goliaths? I know you have them. We all do. Whatever your Goliath may be, give it over to God. He's got the broadest shoulders in the world. He can carry your burden. He's certainly carrying mine. If he wasn't, you wouldn't be reading this book, because my Goliaths would have destroyed me a long time ago.

## THANK YOU, MAUREEN

I owe my life to the women who had such a nurturing, strengthening influence on my life: My birth mother, Irene, made the crucial decision, even before I was born, to give me life and a future. My mother, Jane, loved me, provided for me, gave me my strength, and taught me never to give up.

My wife, Colleen stood by me, put up with me, prayed me into God's kingdom, and was the first to hear the details of my worst secret. She held my life in her hands, and she held it lovingly. She had the absolute power to destroy me with a word when I told her my secret, yet she gave me love, understanding, and compassion.

And then there was Maureen. My sister was my best friend in my early boyhood and my protector and nurturer at Chadwick School. She was my earliest encourager and counselor. She was my guardian angel.

In 1988, Maureen read my first book, *On the Outside Looking In,* which included the story of how my molester guided my hand in that green-tinged darkroom as I developed the photograph that destroyed my life. After reading that story, she told me, "Now I know why you always hated green."

Maureen was a completely selfless person who would totally throw herself into the causes she believed in. After Dad was diagnosed with Alzheimer's disease, Maureen was on fire for Alzheimer's. She raised funds, raised awareness, and testified before Congress on behalf of funding for research.

She was so involved with Alzheimer's, in the effort to do something for Dad and the thousands of other people suffering with that disease, that she neglected to take care of her own health. By the time she was diagnosed with melanoma, the cancer was advanced. Even after she knew that her illness was terminal, she was always thinking about Dad, about Mom, about her husband and daughter, about me—never about herself. She was the mother hen, watching over everyone.

In December 2000, Colleen and I visited Maureen at St. John's Hospital in Los Angeles where she was being treated. Her husband Dennis, daughter Rita, and Nancy were also there. At one point Maureen chased everyone out of the room except me. There was something weighing on her mind, and she needed to talk to me about it.

When it was just the two of us, she said, "Michael, I know you're busy with your radio show, writing, and speaking, but I want you to do something for me. I've been hoping and praying that I would beat this cancer, but if I don't make it through the chemo, I want you to promise me that you'll carry on the work I've been doing."

I promised her I would. So I joined The John Douglas French Alzheimer's Foundation, chaired by Art Linkletter, which is doing an outstanding job of funding Alzheimer's research that is truly getting results and making progress. I've been involved with the Memory Walks program, the Adopt-a-Scientist program, and other programs that are supporting the search for a cure for this terrible disease. In honor of Maureen, I added the Alzheimer's Foundation to my job description, alongside the work I do honoring Dad's legacy through support of the USS *Ronald Reagan* (CVN-76) aircraft carrier with the Santa Barbara Navy League.

Maureen also asked me to take care of Mom, and I promised to do that too.

While we were growing up together, my sister and I had the shared experience of Catholicism, yet in all of our years together as brother and sister, we had never really talked at all about our relationship with God. So when the two of us were in her hospital room, it was the first time in my life that I was able to share my faith with my sister. It was scary at first because I didn't know how she would take it.

I told her about Pastor Jack's message on the story of David and Goliath. Then I gave her a smooth stone that I had taken out of my own garden that morning and cleaned up—a stone of David that she could keep.

I said, "Right now, cancer is your Goliath. But God is bigger than anything the cancer can do to you." We hugged and cried and told each other, "I love you." After that, she always kept that stone by her bed.

We talked about her faith in Jesus Christ, which was very strong. Both her illness and the difficult adoption process with her daughter, Rita, had driven her deep into her Catholic roots and her dependence on God. She was happy in the Lord and very much at peace. I was glad that, for the first time in our lives, we had been able to talk about our faith with each other in a positive and spiritual way. I know I'll see Merm again in eternity, and I look forward to that day.

By July 2001, the cancer had metastasized to Maureen's brain. That month I went to visit her at the hospital in Sacramento where she was being treated in the last days of her life. The nurses told me I could have an hour with her, but Maureen wouldn't let them kick me out of the room, so I stayed much longer.

On August 4, our whole family drove up to Sacramento to say good-bye to Maureen. By this time she was back in her home. It was a good visit, despite the tears. Maureen said good-bye to Colleen, Cameron, Ashley, and me, and she was in good spirits—very up, very happy. It was a good day for her and for all of us.

Four days later, on August 8, 2001, my sister went to be with God.

Her funeral Mass was a beautiful Catholic service, which made Mom very happy. The priest who officiated was a long-time friend of the family. There were politicos from both sides of the aisle, people who had befriended Maureen over the years. Patti, Ron, and I were given responsive prayers to read, to which the congregation would answer with an "Amen."

However, being the radio talk show host that I am, I couldn't stick to a script; I had to go off page. For one thing, I heard a number of testimonials to Maureen in terms of her accomplishments and charitable and political activities. But I didn't hear any testimonials to the dear, sweet sisterly side of Maureen. That was the Maureen I knew and loved and missed.

As I thought about what Maureen meant to me, I realized that in all the years I had known her, I had never thanked Maureen for putting her ninety-seven cents on the counter to bring me into the Reagan family. Not even in the last few months of her life did I thank her. So I decided that it was high time I did. I used my time at the funeral to talk about my sister Maureen and all she meant to me and to thank her for bringing me into the family and helping to mold me into the person I am today. Then I read the responsive prayer and sat down.

There is a time in a Catholic service where the people turn and hug one another, and I went to Mom and hugged her, and she thanked me for what I said and for talking about the personal side of Maureen. It made Mom happy to see me expressing my love for my sister at such a time, and I knew that, even though I had gone off script, I had done the right thing.

Meanwhile, life goes on, and you and I must face our Goliaths one by one. That's the bad news.

The good news is that we have an awesome God who is able to lead us through all the tangled, painful circumstances of our lives—even illegitimacy, molestation, divorce, and cancer. He wraps his love around us, saves us, adopts us, and redeems us.

That is the message God has given me to share with you: God loves you more than you can imagine. He has always loved you. He has never stopped loving you. His love for you is infinite and unchanging, and it is deeper, higher, and wider than anything that has ever happened to you, or anything you have ever done.

Just as my father stood in that doorway, waiting for me to turn and run back to him and give him a hug, Christ stands in the doorway of your life with arms wide open, ready to receive you. Let him embrace you, redeem you, and adopt you into his family.

Say yes to his amazing love, for he is an awesome God.

# ENDNOTES

## Chapter 1, Once Adopted

1. Franklin B. Krohn, Zoe Bogan, "The Effects Absent Fathers Have on Female Development and College Attendance," *College Student Journal,* December 2001, electronically retrieved at http://www.findarticles.com.

## Chapter 2, A Broken World

1. Michael J. McManus, "Mutual Consent—Not No-Fault Divorce," 14 December 2002, electronically retrieved at http://www.marriagesavers.org/Columns/C1111.htm.

2. Judy Parejko, "Fox Steps on an Industry's Toes," *The Middletown Journal* (Middletown, Ohio), 30 July 2003, electronically retrieved at http://www.stolenvows.com/fox.htm.

3. Allen Parkman, cited by Michael J. McManus, "Mutual Consent."

## Chapter 3, In the Care of Strangers

1. Cathy Young, "Women Put Limits on Male Domesticity," *The Detroit News,* 23 March 2000, electronically retrieved at http://www.detnews.com/EDITPAGE/0003/23/young/young.htm.

2. Alysse Michelle Elhage, "Too Many Fatherless Children," North Carolina Family Policy Council, June 1999, electronically retrieved at http://www.ncfpc.org/PolicyPapers/Findings %209906%20Fatherless.pdf.

## Chapter 5, Slayers of the Soul

1. Denise Lavoie, "Attorney General Reilly Issues Scathing Report on Clergy Sex Abuse," *The Associated Press,* 24 July 2003, electronically retrieved at http://www.telegram.com/static/ crisisinthechurch/072403.html.

2. Sean P. Murphy, "Letter Says Druce Was Abused as Boy,"

*The Boston Globe,* 13 September 2003, electronically retrieved at http://www.boston.com/globe/spotlight/abuse/stories5/091303_druce.htm.

3. Richard Sipe, "Priests, Celibacy, and Sexuality: A Preliminary Expert Report," electronically retrieved at http://www.richardsipe.com/sipe_report.htm.

4. Richard Sipe, "Catholic Priest Scandal," USAToday.com Talk Today, 11 March 2002, electronically retrieved at http://www.usatoday.com/community/chat/2002-03-11-sipe.htm.

5. Richard Sipe, "Loss of Faith," 10 December 2002, electronically retrieved at http://www.richardsipe.com/Articles/Loss%20of%20Faith.htm.

6. Mary Cagney, "Sexual Abuse in Churches Not Limited to Clergy," 6 October 1997, electronically retrieved at http://www.ctlibrary.com/ct/1997/oct6/7tb090.html.

7. Toby Druin, "Churches urged to develop policies to prevent child abuse," *The Baptist Standard,* 30 September 2002, electronically retrieved at http://www.baptiststandard.com/2002/9_30/pages/childabuse.html.

## Chapter 6, The Age of Rage

1. Quoted by Gail Russell Chaddock, "Sharp Differences in Strategies for Dealing with Rage," *The Christian Science Monitor,* 21 December 1999, electronically retrieved at http://search.cs monitor.com/durable/1999/12/21/p16s1.htm.

2. Quoted by Clarence Page, "Columbine Killers' Parents Get Up-close and Personal," syndicated column for 4 September 2001, *Jewish World Review,* electronically retrieved at http://www.jewish worldreview.com/0901/page090401.asp.

## Chapter 7, Sex Education

1. Joseph Farah, "The Anything-But 'Super' Bowl," WorldNetDaily Exclusive Commentary, 3 February 2004, electronically retrieved at http://www.worldnetdaily.com/news/article.asp?ARTICLE_ID=36905.

2. Gary Gentile, "Hefner Burger Ads Upset Rev. Schuller," *Associated Press,* 12 December 2003, electronically retrieved at http://www.newsday.com/business/nationworld/wire/sns-ap-hefner-burger-ads,0,5979237.story?coll=sns-ap-business-headlines.

3. Reported by American Family Online, a filtered Internet service provider, electronically retrieved at http://www.afo.net/statistics.htm.

4. Charles R. Swindoll, "An Open Letter Concerning the Number One Secret Problem in Your Church," electronically retrieved at http://www.netaccountability.com/ver2/letter.cfm.

5. Reported by American Family Online, a filtered Internet service provider, electronically retrieved at http://www.afo.net/statistics.htm.

6. ABC News, "American Porn: Corporate America Is Profiting from Porn—Quietly," 28 January 2003, electronically retrieved at http://abcnews.go.com/sections/primetime/DailyNews/porn_business_030128.html.

7. ABC News, "A Profile of an Eighteen-Year-Old Porn Star," 23 January 2003, electronically retrieved at abcnews.go.com/sections/primetime/ DailyNews/porn_love_030123.html.

8. Gene Edward Veith, "Out of the Dungeon," *World Magazine,* 10 March 2001, electronically retrieved at http://www.worldmag.com/world/issue/03-10-01/cultural_1.asp.

9. Henry J. Rogers, *The Silent War* (Green Forest, Ark.: New Leaf Press, 1999), 63.

10. James Dobson, excerpt from *Complete Marriage and Family Home Reference Guide,* electronically retrieved at http://www.family.org/docstudy/solid/a0005855.html.

11. Quoted by Pat Williams and Jim Denney, *It Happens on Sunday* (Nashville, Tenn.: J. Countryman, 2001), 68.

12. Kitty Bean, "Group Seeks Ban of Adult Films from Hotels," *USA Today,* 23 September 2002, electronically retrieved at http://www.usatoday.com/news/nation/2002-09-23-porn-hotels_x.htm.